THE
ISLAMIC WORLD IN
DECLINE

THE
ISLAMIC WORLD IN
DECLINE

From the Treaty of Karlowitz to the Disintegration of the Ottoman Empire

Martin Sicker

Westport, Connecticut
London

Library of Congress Cataloging-in-Publication Data

Sicker, Martin.
    The Islamic world in decline : from the Treaty of Karlowitz to the disintegration of the
Ottoman Empire / Martin Sicker.
      p. cm.
    Includes bibliographical references and index.
    ISBN 0–275–96891–X (alk. paper)
    1. Turkey—History—1683–1829. 2. Turkey—History—1829–1878. 3.
Turkey—History—1878–1909. I. Title.
DR473.S53 2001
956.1'015—dc21   00–032386

British Library Cataloguing in Publication Data is available.

Library of Congress Catalog Card Number: 00–032386
ISBN: 0–275–96891–X

First published in 2001

Praeger Publishers, 88 Post Road West, Westport, CT 06881
An imprint of Greenwood Publishing Group, Inc.
www.praeger.com

Printed in the United States of America

The paper used in this book complies with the
Permanent Paper Standard issued by the National
Information Standards Organization (Z39.48–1984).

10 9 8 7 6 5 4 3 2 1

Contents

Introduction

The political ascendancy of Islam that began with its founding in the seventh century was predicated in no small part on its synthesis of geopolitics and religion, or theopolitics, which effectively transformed Islamic imperialism into a religious obligation. The conflation of geopolitics and religion in Islam is reflected in the traditional concept of *jihad* (struggle), a religious obligation imposed by their faith on all Muslims until the final victory of Islam. The *jihad* may be understood theopolitically as a *crescentade*, in the same sense as the later Christian crusade of the medieval period, which sought to achieve ostensibly religious goals by militant means.

As a practical matter, the concept of being in a state of perpetual war with the non-Muslim world often bore little relation to the political realities of the greater Middle East that as often as not saw Muslims and non-Muslims aligned against and at war with other Muslims. Nonetheless, the concept underlay Muslim geopolitical thinking throughout the long period of its political ascendancy and inspired the dramatic expansion of Muslim rule. It provided an extraordinary religious and ideological context for the naked imperialism that succeeded in creating an Islamic universe reaching, at its zenith, from Spain and North Africa to Southeast Asia, and from the Indian Ocean littoral to the steppes of Russia and the gates of Vienna.

The long era of Muslim political ascendancy that began in a small region of western Arabia reached its pinnacle some nine hundred years later with the siege of Vienna by Suleiman the Magnificent in 1529. Sitting outside the Hapsburg capital, with his army beset by seemingly insurmountable logistical problems, Suleiman was brought to conclude that the Ottoman Empire could expand no farther into Europe, that Muslim expansionism in Eurasia had reached, indeed, had probably extended, beyond its destined territorial limits. Undefeated, he withdrew from Vienna determined to concentrate his energies on preserving the gains already achieved.

Unfortunately, from an Ottoman perspective, maintaining the status quo in a volatile geopolitical environment exceeded the abilities of Suleiman's successors, and the empire came under continuing assault both from within as well as from without over the next four centuries until it almost literally came apart at the seams. The decline of Ottoman power also meant, in effect, the decline of political Islam, which had been so intimately bound to it for centuries. Islamic imperialism, the embodiment of the *jihad*, had run its course.

The problems faced by the Ottoman Empire were replicated with regard to the Persian Empire, which similarly underwent a period of political decline and territorial retrenchment. Competitors for dominance for centuries, both the Ottomans and Persians were ultimately forced to resolve their differences in the face of the imperialist pressures they were subjected to from Europe and Asia. Both empires were affected by the same geopolitical reality, namely, that empires that cease to expand are almost invariably compelled to contract. For both sultan and shah, maintaining the status quo became an unrealistic goal. They were confronted by the imperialist ambitions of the continually reconfiguring states of Central and Eastern Europe that challenged the Ottomans and by the new Russian tsarist imperialism that confronted both Ottomans and Persians along their northern frontiers from the Balkans to Central Asia.

But perhaps the greatest challenge to the world of political Islam came from Western Europe, especially France and Great Britain, states somewhat remote from the frontiers of the Ottoman and Persian Empires, but states with expansionist goals that went beyond the acquisition of contiguous territories. From the moment that Napoleon Bonaparte entered the Middle East by invading Egypt, the region and its constituent components were transformed into instruments of international geopolitics and grand strategy. Napoleon's initiative was part of a grandiose scheme that he concocted for using the region as a base for an assault on British interests in India. The fact that he failed to achieve his aims did not reverse the new role that was assigned to the Middle East. The Ottoman and Persian Empires assumed a global importance in the nineteenth century not because of anything in them of intrinsic economic value but because of their geopolitical and geostrategic significance. They became, in effect, a buffer zone separating Europe from the wealth of the East, much as ancient Palestine had served as a buffer zone between Africa (Egypt) and Asia (Mesopotamia), at a time when European imperialism was on the march in Asia.

It thus came about that the rivalries of the Great Powers, most especially those of Great Britain, France, and Russia, were played out in the Middle East. Napoleon wanted Egypt because it was a key to Asia; he wanted to build a canal that would connect the Mediterranean with the Red Sea and thereby eliminate the advantage held by Great Britain with its effective control of the maritime route from India around Africa to Europe. When the Suez Canal was ultimately built decades later, it was Britain that managed to gain and retain control of it for the next century. Similarly, it was long a fundamental of British policy to maintain the territorial integrity of the Ottoman Empire as well as that of Persia as a means of preventing overland access to South Asia from Europe. And, when Russian encroachment on Persian territories in Central Asia brought the tsar's frontiers perilously close to British India, Britain fostered the emergence of an independent Afghanistan as an additional buffer with which to block the Russian advance toward India.

As a result of their conflicting imperialist ambitions, especially from the outset of the nineteenth century, the Great Powers represented the principal agents of change in the broader region for at least the next century and a half. In the course of the period of time examined in this work, the world of political Islam was under virtual continual attack. The Ottoman Empire was driven almost entirely out of Europe and truncated into its present form of contemporary Turkey, and the Persian Empire was reduced by more than half to the dimensions of contemporary Iran. While the Middle East remained overwhelmingly Muslim in religion, the linkage between politics and Islam grew tenuous in much of the region as it became subject to non-Muslim domination and influence. The connection was severed completely in the extreme case of primarily Muslim Turkey. After the collapse of the Ottoman Empire, a separation of state and religion was instituted as a deliberate policy of its secular government. A similar approach was subsequently followed to one degree or another by several of the states that were carved out of the Ottoman Empire.

This book examines the geopolitical forces and other relevant factors that brought about the political decline of the Islamic world from its zenith in the early part of the sixteenth century to its nadir at the beginning of the twentieth. It will also explore in some detail the role of the European powers in creating the geopolitical circumstances that have contributed mightily to the chronic instability of the Middle East in the twentieth century.

Like the proverbial bull in a china shop, the major powers, Great Britain, France, and Russia, wreaked political havoc in the historically volatile region. They arbitrarily created artificial states and boundaries in the Middle East and applied the principle of national self-determination selectively to some, in the context of what best served their own special interests, and denied it to others, such as the Armenians and Kurds, who did not satisfy that criterion. The eventual withdrawal of the European powers from direct control of the region after World War II therefore fostered a variety of irredentisms and neonationalisms that have plagued the Middle East ever since. But that latter aspect of the story goes beyond the scope of the present book, which ends with the Treaty of Lausanne that finalized the disintegration of the Ottoman Empire in the wake of its defeat in World War I.

In dealing with the long period of history covered in this book, it has been necessary to introduce the names of a large number of political leaders, as well as place names, many of which may not be familiar to the nonspecialist. Wherever possible, their dates of office have been provided to assist the reader in maintaining a grasp of the time frame in which the events that they are concerned with took place. It should also be noted that the literature on the region reflects wide variances in the transliteration of Arabic, Persian, and Turkish names. As a result, some inconsistencies in the spelling of such names may be reflected in the pages that follow.

1

The Ottoman-Safavid Conflict

For forty years, since he first succeeded in centralizing power in the Safavid throne, Shah Tahmasp managed to maintain a balance of power and influence between the Turkic *qizilbash* and the Persian (Tajik) elements within the realm. However, his death on May 14, 1576, ushered in a period of internal disarray in Persia that once again made it a tempting target for Ottoman expansion.

The *qizilbash* saw an opportunity to reassert their position of dominance in the Safavid state, although they were themselves divided into contending factions. At the same time, a new force composed of Armenians, Circassians, and Georgians had emerged within the state, further complicating the internal struggle for power and making it far more difficult to resolve. Nonetheless, the *qizilbash* managed to place Ismail II (1576–1577), who had been imprisoned by Tahmasp for twenty years on suspicion of treason, on the throne. It proved to be a serious mistake. Ismail turned out to be a somewhat deranged if not maniacal drug addict, and his reign of about a year engendered a bloodbath that wiped out a substantial portion of Persia's leadership class. He was succeeded in November 1577 by Sultan Muhammad Shah (1577–1588), who also turned out to be an ineffective ruler and was popularly perceived as being under the influence of, if not virtual control of, his harem.

These changes in the Safavid regime helped precipitate a new instability along the relatively quiescent Ottoman frontier. Local Kurdish chiefs, who had earlier aligned themselves with the Safavids, now offered their allegiance to Khusraw Pasha, the Ottoman governor of Van, thereby presenting a new opportunity for the extension of Ottoman hegemony to Kurdistan. Of course, doing so would require the unilateral abrogation by the sultan of the 1555 Treaty of Amasya, which would surely trigger a new war with the Safavids. At the Sublime Porte, the grand vizir Sokullu Mehmed argued strenuously against another Persian war but was overridden by the sultan. The latter was inclined to take the advice of the prowar activists who saw the chaos in Persia as affording a unique opportunity to reconquer those areas of the Caucasus and Azerbaijan that Suleiman had once seized but not retained. The sentiment for war was reinforced by an appeal from the Uzbeks for a coordinated attack on both of Persia's flanks and pressure from the orthodox clergy, who wanted to lend support to the Sunnis who lived under Safavid rule. The latter pleaded that the sultan should seize the moment of Safavid weakness to bring about a complete end to Shiism in Persia.

As the Uzbeks swept into Khorasan, ravaging the province, the Ottomans advanced into the Caucasus through Ardahan, taking Akhiska in August 1576 and Tiflis in August 1578. The Safavids, clearly unable to conduct effective campaigns simultaneously on their western and eastern flanks, met with repeated setbacks that forced them to withdraw into the Persian heartland. The seizure of the Caucasus by the Ottomans gave them a direct land connection from the east to the khanate of the Crimean Tatars for the first time. Many of the princes of Georgia soon capitulated to the sultan in return for appointments as Ottoman governors of their respective lands.

Shirvan fell before the end of the summer of 1578, giving the Ottomans control of most of the western Caspian coast and opened the way to both Armenia and Azerbaijan, which were attacked in 1579 by a force containing a large contingent of Crimean Tatars. However, the tide of battle soon began to turn against the Ottomans as the Safavid forces, under the leadership of Hamza Mirza and Mirza Salman, successfully counterattacked in Shirvan and Qarabagh and captured the Tatar chief, Adil Giray Khan. In the meanwhile, pressure from the Uzbeks in the east abated as their ruler, Abdallah Khan (1560–1598), was distracted from the Persian campaign. His own position in Transoxiana was under threat from incursions by the Kirghiz-Kazakh tribes of Central Asia, and he urgently needed to conduct a simultaneous campaign against them in Kashgaria. Then, as soon as the Ottoman pressure on them was reduced as a result of the Safavid offensive, the Georgian princes repudiated their allegiance to the sultan and shifted their support back to the Safavids, which they demonstrated by massacring large numbers of Sunnis. Nonetheless, and despite these reversals, the Ottomans remained determined to persevere, and the struggle continued for another decade, with the tide of battle ultimately shifting in favor of the Ottomans once again.

The Safavids suffered a decisive reversal in the Caucasus on May 7–11, 1583, during the Battle of the Torches so named because the fighting went on day and night throughout the period. Ottoman control was reestablished as far as the Caspian, with Shirvan and Daghestan coming under direct Turkish rule. The sultan's suzerainty was imposed once again on Georgia, and Erivan and most of Armenia were occupied by Ottoman troops. The reverses that the Safavids suffered on the battlefield only seemed to intensify the internal factional power struggles in Persia. It was not long before both Mirza Salman and Hamza Mirza were assassinated. This left a leadership vacuum in the Safavid regime that permitted the military situation to deteriorate even further. In 1585 a large Ottoman army under Osman Pasha invaded Azerbaijan and broke through to Tabriz, which was to remain in Ottoman hands for the next two decades. In 1587 a separate Ottoman force operating out of Iraq succeeded in occupying the provinces of Luristan and Hamadan on Persia's western frontiers. That same year, the Uzbeks returned to the offensive on Persia's eastern front with a massive invasion of Khorasan in December. Herat, which was soon put under siege, fell in February 1589 after holding out for nine months. The Uzbeks then struck at Mashad and Sarakhs. It appeared that the very existence of the Safavid state was now in question.

In the face of these difficulties—exacerbated by the revolt of Murshid Quli Khan, the powerful leader of the Ustajlu tribal faction that controlled Khorasan, who staged a coup in the capital at Qazvin—Sultan Muhammad Shah abdicated and turned over the throne to his son Abbas I (1588–1629). The political situation at the time that Abbas took the reins of power was extremely precarious. Almost all the provinces bordering the Ottoman Empire were under enemy occupation, while in the east the Uzbeks were in full control of half of Khorasan. Internally, the Persian imperium seemed to be unraveling.

Abbas moved decisively to impress his personal stamp on the Safavid state. He began by establishing a set of priorities that reflected a realistic appraisal of the resources at his disposal. His first overall priority was internal consolidation, that is, the restoration and restructuring of the army and the reform of the country's financial system. His highest external policy priority was the reversal of the prevailing situation in Khorasan. Abbas evidently concluded that the Uzbeks posed a more immediate threat to the viability of the Safavid state than did the Ottomans, and he therefore deferred reconquest of the territories seized by the sultan until the Uzbeks were driven out of Khorasan and back across the Oxus. However, to do this, he first had to make sure that the Ottomans would not undertake an offensive against him while he was fully engaged in the east. He therefore took the painful step of signing a humiliating peace treaty with the Ottomans on March 21, 1590, that ceded to them the territories of Azerbaijan, Ganja, parts of Georgia, Qarabagh, Qarajadagh, Kurdistan, and Luristan.[1] He also agreed to cease Shiite propaganda in Ottoman territory and to end the persecution of Sunni Muslims in areas under Safavid control. The sultan was quite willing to call an end to the war on these terms since he was becoming distracted once again by problems with the Hapsburgs along the Hungarian frontier. As in the past, he did not relish the prospect of having to pursue hostilities simultaneously on distant fronts in Asia and Europe.

Actually, neither the Ottomans nor the Hapsburgs were anxious for another war, although neither seemed capable of preventing provocative cross-border incidents from occurring. Particularly nettlesome were a series raids into Ottoman territory by Christian Uskoks, refugees from Albania, Croatia, Dalmatia, and Serbia, who ostensibly were being employed by the local Hapsburg governors to retaliate for similar incursions from Ottoman territory. It appears that the Venetians also became involved in encouraging and assisting Uskok raids along the Adriatic coast, although they managed to shift the entire blame onto the Hapsburgs through the lavish use of bribery in Istanbul.

Notwithstanding the fourth renewal of the Ottoman-Hapsburg treaty of 1547 on November 29, 1590, it seemed clear that war would break out once again in the near future. The growing intensity of the Uskok raids precipitated a major retaliatory strike by Hasan Pasha, the Ottoman governor of Bosnia, which resulted in the capture of a number of Hapsburg strongholds in Croatia, along with the seizure of large amounts of booty. The Hapsburg emperor renounced the treaty in November 1592 and launched a major assault against the Bosnian forces at Sisak in June 1593 that resulted in heavy Ottoman losses. In the meanwhile, confident that the Ottomans would quickly prevail in a new conflict, the grand vizir Sinan Pasha, along with other persons of influence at the Porte, had been urging the sultan to make war on Austria. The news of the military disaster at Sisak settled the matter, and war was declared on July 4, 1593.

Contrary to Sinan Pasha's expectations, however, the war dragged on indecisively for thirteen arduous years. During much of this period the Ottomans were also faced by a serious deterioration of their position along the lower Danube, where Moldavia, Wallachia, and Transylvania had revolted against Turkish domination in 1594, and had made common cause with the Hapsburgs. The defection of these provinces raised a serious threat to the security of the Ottoman lines of communication between Istanbul and Belgrade, Buda, and Gran since the Danube constituted a primary route for the transport of munitions and supplies to the Hungarian front. Accordingly, the Ottomans were compelled to commit a large part of their forces to the defense of the river line, something that had not been anticipated by their war planners. It was only after the collapse of the troubled alliance between Austria and the Danubian principalities, particularly the reversal of alliances by Transylvania in 1605, that the war entered a decisive stage. The alignment of Transylvania on the side of the sultan shifted the military balance in the region in favor of the Ottomans.

At this point, the Hapsburgs were ready for peace as were the Ottomans, whose military capabilities had been severely drained by the prolonged struggle. The Austrians had nothing to gain from a continuation of the conflict and ran the risk of incurring significant but unwarranted losses. On his part, the sultan was anxious to become free to deal decisively with the rebellions that had been raging in Anatolia since 1596, as well as to put an end to the campaign of reconquest that had been undertaken by the Safavids in 1603. The war with the Hapsburgs was formally concluded with the Treaty of Zsitva-Torok (November 11, 1606) on terms that were only slightly advantageous to the Ottomans.

The Ottoman preoccupation with Europe for such a long period left Shah Abbas free to focus his energies on the reconstitution of Safavid power. He spent the first decade of his reign in securing control over the Safavid state and in building a new standing army that was loyal to him. As the chronicler of his reign put it:

Because the rivalries of the *qezelbash* tribes had led them to commit all sorts of enormities, and because their devotion to the Safavid royal house had been weakened by dissension, Shah Abbas decided (as the result of divine inspiration, which is vouchsafed to kings but not to ordinary mortals), to admit into the armed forces large numbers of Georgian, Circassian, and other *gholams* . . . which had not previously existed under the Safavid regime . . . . Without question, they were an essential element in Abbas's conquests, and their employment had many advantages.[2]

Abbas also moved the capital from Qazvin to more centrally located Isfahan, which placed him in a better position to shift forces to either the eastern or western frontiers as needed.

This was also a period that saw the Uzbeks move south from Khorasan to overrun Sistan. Further east, Qandahar had been lost to the Moghuls of India as early as 1590. The eastern frontiers of the Safavid state seemed to be under continuing and successful assault. It was only with the death of the Uzbek leader Abdallah II (1583–1598) that a critical window of opportunity to turn the tide emerged. An internal struggle among the Uzbek chiefs over who was to succeed Abdallah as paramount chief left them momentarily vulnerable, and Abbas took full advantage of the situation. He launched his campaign of reconquest from Isfahan in April 1598 and drove into Khorasan, taking Mashad by the end of July. From there he marched on Herat and managed to snare the Uzbeks under Din Muhammad Khan into a pitched battle, something that they previously tried to avoid if at all possible, preferring hit-and-run tactics. Abbas succeeded in emerging victorious from the confrontation after a costly but decisive struggle that effectively smashed the Uzbeks as a coherent force. He was soon able to stabilize his northeastern frontiers through a series of alliances with individual Uzbek chiefs.

Upon his return to Isfahan, Abbas was confronted by the need to reach a fundamental decision regarding the future course of the Safavid state. There were substantial disagreements among his advisors in this regard.

The newly arrived English adventurers, Sir Anthony and Sir Robert Sherley, urged him to consider a renewal of the war against the Ottomans, taking advantage of the sultan's preoccupation with the Hapsburgs in Hungary. Such a move would in effect have made Persia an ally of Austria. His vizirs, on the other hand, urged that he maintain the peace with the sultan for as long as possible. They argued that a war with the Ottomans at that time would be too costly in both men and materiel. Moreover, they were concerned that the Safavid treasury simply could not bear the financial burden of such a war. They also expressed concern that there was no assurance that the Hapsburgs and their allies would continue the war in Hungary and that, if they concluded a truce with the sultan, the shah might be left to face the Ottomans alone. They therefore reasoned that if the Ottoman-Safavid peace were to be broken, it should be the sultan and not the shah who bore the responsibility.

The vizirs suggested that, instead of precipitating another conflict with the Ottomans, Abbas should direct his attention southward and attempt to dislodge the Portuguese from Hormuz. Were he able to do this, the shah would have gained effective control of the Persian Gulf and the lucrative proceeds from its commerce. If Anthony Sherley's contemporary account of the discussion is reliable, it provides a fascinating insight into the political and strategic implications of the alternate views presented to Abbas for consideration. Sherley countered the proposal of the vizirs, in part, with the following argument:

Lastly, how strange a conclusion you have made, I will desire you to behold with better consideration. You will not have the King to make warre with the Turke, to avoid expence of money and munition, where the best parts and most plentifull of both countries are confining, which would give abundance, and cheaper living to an Armie; but you will have him go to Larre, to Ormus, sterile countries farre removed, where the charges only of supplying victuals to an Armie, would be of more cost then all other munition and expence of the Armie besides. And besides; there is no danger of the King of Spain, who hath ever held a fashion of maintaining himselfe rather then encreasing. Besides the nature of his force is of a contrarie qualitie to give us feare of his too great inlargement, having neither abundance of horse nor men, but only gallies which assure his forts, with which also he is sufficiently contented. And how wearying out a warre to his Majesties treasure, and men, that must be where he must fight but at the enemies pleasure and advantage, the strength of his enemie standing upon the Sea, in which the King hath no sort of shew of power . . . besides the infinite danger by the nature of the lying of the state of the Turkes and the King of Spaines, and the essentiall of their potenties were of such a condition, that whatsoever was diminished from his Majesties, or the King of Spaines, was an absolute addition to the Turke; who by that advantage of the weakening each others forces, should have a more facile entrie upon any one or both of them.[3]

Although there does not appear to be any evidence that Abbas was swayed by Sherley's argument, by 1602 the shah concluded that the prevailing situation was most favorable for taking on the sultan. The Ottomans were not only still engaged with the Austrians, but were also occupied with the Hapsburg-backed uprisings in Moldavia, Wallachia, and Transylvania, in addition to being faced by a series of internal indigenous (*Jelali*) rebellions in Anatolia. Abbas sought to create an offensive alliance against the sultan with one or more European states, but the effort came to nothing and he decided to proceed unilaterally.

The Ottoman deployment of forces in the Caucasus region was designed primarily to exercise control of the main lines of communication and the principal points of strategic importance, not for repelling a major invasion from the south. Accordingly, the Turkish positions were maintained by thin garrisons, with little support from the indigenous populations of the region, which were generally far more inclined toward the Safavids than the Ottomans.

Abbas's campaign against the relatively poorly prepared Ottomans began in September 1603 with an assault on Tabriz, which fell rather easily. From Tabriz, Abbas marched on Nakhichevan, effectively forcing all the Ottoman forces south of the Aras River to withdraw to Erivan, where they hoped to regroup. Erivan came under siege that winter and was compelled to surrender in June 1604. The systematic and carefully constructed campaign began to take its toll of the Ottoman forward positions as the shah's commander-in-chief, Allahverdi Khan, registered a series of significant victories. The decisive battle of the campaign came on November 6, 1605, at Sufiyan, near Tabriz, where the Safavid forces once again emerged from the struggle victorious, placing Abbas in a position to launch an offensive into eastern Anatolia.

The Ottoman defeat at Sufiyan also resulted in the defection of a number of local Turkish and Kurdish chiefs, as well as a new series of *Jelali* revolts in Anatolia that spread as far as Cilicia, insurrections that were not quelled until the summer of 1608. Notwithstanding the end of the war with the Hapsburgs, these uprisings made it virtually impossible for the Ottomans to take effective measures against the Safavids. They were forced to move their main lines of defense back to Van and Diyarbekir, abandoning control of Kars, as well as the cities of Baku, Derbent, and Tiflis to the enemy. By 1607 the borders between the Safavid and Ottoman Empires were approximately the same as originally set by the Treaty of Amasya in 1555. As noted by the Turkish chronicler Naima: "The frontier lines were to remain as they were in the reign of Sultan Selim Khan . . . . When once the Turkish fortresses or redoubts, which had been erected for the purpose of preventing unfortunate Russians from passing and repassing [presumably on pilgrimages to Jerusalem], were relinquished, the shah was, under no pretext whatever, to place garrisons in them."[4]

With the quelling of the indigenous rebellions in Anatolia, the Ottomans were able to organize an offensive under the leadership of Murad Pasha that was designed to force Abbas to withdraw from the positions he had recently recovered. The campaign was disrupted, however, when the ninety-year-old general died in August 1610. For reasons that are not entirely clear, Sultan Ahmed I (1603–1617) suddenly became resigned to making peace with the shah on the basis of the old treaty between the empires. That is, the sultan acknowledged Safavid control of Azerbaijan and parts of the Caucasus, and a new agreement to that effect was concluded on November 20, 1612. In return, Abbas agreed to cooperate with the sultan in joint efforts to stem the Russian advance into the Caucasus.

Because both the Safavids and Ottomans had occupied pockets of territory on opposite sides of the old border for some time, it seemed unnecessarily cumbersome if not impracticable to seek to transfer the populations of these enclaves to align with the new border. It was decided instead to allow each party to retain these enclaves and to demarcate the new boundaries accordingly in both Azerbaijan and northern Iraq. However, Georgian and Kurdish insurgents repeatedly interrupted the process of border demarcation, provoking a number of border incidents that soon led to a general resumption of hostilities between the Ottomans and Safavids in 1615. A large Ottoman force laid siege to Erivan in 1616 but failed to take the city. The Ottoman commander of the expedition, Muhammad Pasha, eventually agreed to a preliminary peace agreement that essentially restored the previous territorial arrangements. But the sultan subsequently repudiated this preliminary agreement. He dismissed Muhammad Pasha from his command and replaced him with Khalil Pasha, who was instructed to prepare for another invasion of Persia that was to be carried out in conjunction with the Crimean Tatars.

Abbas responded to this new threat by once again adopting the now-traditional scorched-earth policy, originally introduced by Tahmasp, to impede the Ottoman advance and to force the Turks to conduct a sustained campaign without being able to live off the land. This would make Ottoman continuation of the campaign critically dependent on the timely delivery of supplies over long distances, something the Ottomans were evidently not very good at doing. Accordingly, the shah ordered his commander-in-chief to lay to waste the entire region between Erivan and Van through which the Ottoman army had to pass. As it turned out, this delaying tactic proved particularly successful because it coincided with political events taking place in the Ottoman capital that worked in the shah's favor. By the time that Khalil Pasha was ready to bring up the main body of the Ottoman army for the invasion of Persia, Sultan Ahmed died and a struggle over the succession ensued. He was succeeded briefly by Mustafa I (1617–1618, first reign), and then by Osman II (1618–1622), who was far more inclined to reach a peace agreement with Abbas than to continue the war.

Osman's desire for peace with Persia was motivated primarily by his wish to be free to confront Sigismund III (1587–1632) of Poland. He considered the latter to have violated his commitments to the Ottomans by supporting the Hapsburgs in the Thirty Years' War (1618–1648) and by doing nothing to prevent Cossack raids into the northern Principalities. Accordingly, the Ottoman-Safavid agreement of 1612 was reconfirmed in a new peace pact on September 26, 1618. Except for some minor incidents, the Ottoman-Safavid peace held for another half dozen years as Osman redirected his attention to Europe, where he fought an inconclusive war with Poland that was terminated by a new peace agreement on October 6, 1621.

The Ottoman-Safavid peace left Abbas free to deal with the Portuguese on his southern flank in the Gulf. Lacking the naval power to directly challenge the Portuguese, Abbas hoped to compensate for this deficiency by involving the English on his side. Perceiving a threat to their dominant trade position in the Gulf from the new English interest in the region, the Portuguese demonstrated overt hostility to English traders and merchantmen. Abbas sought to reap advantage from this agressiveness by welcoming the East India Company to Persia as early as 1613. As John Chardin, perhaps the best informed of the Europeans who visited Persia during the period, observed:

The Portuguese, who were sole masters of the Commerce throughout all the Indies, not being willing to share any thereof to these new Comers, but on the contrary, being resolv'd to oppose their Undertaking as much as they could; they thwarted them on all Occasions, and amongst other Hardships, they made them pay at Ormus, (where lay the main traffick of the Gulph of Persia) more Duties, than all the other Nations. Abas the great, the then King of Persia, who was very well inform'd of what pass'd among the Europeans in those Parts, caus'd an Offer to be made to the English, of the trade in his Ports of the Continent. He sent them Presents: He allure'd some of them to his Court, where he caress'd 'em very much; and in fine, in the year 1620, he engag'd them in a League with him, to drive the Portuguese out of the Gulph of Persia.[5]

With English help, the Portuguese were forced out of Hormuz in 1622. In return for its services, the East India Company was granted control of the fort on the island, free use of the port, and half of the customs collected at Hormuz. However, they soon found the shah to be an unreliable partner. The Portuguese, although pushed out of Hormuz, were still in control of some other footholds on the Persian mainland as well as Muscat, which they now developed as their major port in the Gulf region and which they retained until 1649. It was not, however, an adequate substitute for Hormuz. Muscat was itself vulnerable to attack in its rear from the Arab tribes of Oman. As a result, the Portuguese became desperate to find a means of maintaining a viable trade position in the Gulf. Accordingly, in 1625 they finally reached an acceptable accommodation with Abbas. In exchange for the surrender of their enclaves along the Persian coastline, the Portuguese were granted rights to the pearl fisheries at Bahrain and half the customs duties from the port at Bandar-Kongo.

This agreement with the Portuguese reflected a solid grasp by Abbas of the subtleties of the international politics of the period. The Dutch East India Company had been founded in 1602 and immediately became a major competitor for control of the spice trade from the East Indies. At first the Dutch cooperated with the English to dislodge the Portuguese, and then became themselves England's foremost European competitor for worldwide commercial preeminence, a rivalry that could not but be manifested in the Indian Ocean and the Persian Gulf. Thus, as Chardin observed: "The Persians, in granting such advantageous Conditions to the Portuguese, managed them Politickly, that they might draw Succors from them when Need should require, against the English and Dutch, if they should chance to fall out among themselves."[6]

The Ottoman-Safavid peace, followed by the end of the Polish war, permitted Osman to concentrate on the abysmal state of Ottoman internal affairs. However, no sooner did the sultan attempt to introduce administrative reforms within the empire than he was rewarded with a *coup d'etat* by the Janissaries on May 19, 1622. He was assassinated soon thereafter, and Mustafa I (1622–1623) was restored to the Ottoman throne. But Mustafa's notorious incompetence quickly precipitated a series of revolts that shook the regime and created political and financial anarchy in the empire. As a result, he was deposed on September 10, 1623, in favor of Murad IV (1623–1640).

The new sultan was immediately confronted by a new and serious threat on his eastern frontiers from the Safavids. The threat arose primarily as a consequence of the prevailing turmoil within the Ottoman Empire, particularly the revolts in Anatolia that cut off Istanbul from the rest of the empire in Asia. Abbas found himself in an especially advantageous position in Iraq because of the internal disarray caused by a Janissary revolt in Baghdad in 1623. The city fell to the Persians on January 14, 1624, after having been in Ottoman hands for ninety years. All the Sunni inhabitants who did not manage to escape were slaughtered as were the Janissaries who had cooperated with the Safavids in the conquest of the city. Abbas evidently reasoned that if they betrayed the sultan, they would certainly betray him when it served their purpose, and he was disinclined to wait for that to happen. The fall of Baghdad had a devastating effect on the morale of the Ottoman garrisons at Kirkuk, Mosul, and Shahrazur, whose troops started to desert. This exodus soon contributed to the loss of these important fortified towns as well as the Safavids pushed westward as far as Mardin.

The loss of Baghdad was completely unacceptable to the Ottomans for symbolic as well as practical reasons. It was not only the former seat of the Sunni caliphate, but was also critical to Ottoman control of the important Persian Gulf-Aleppo trade route. Murad appointed Hafiz Ahmad Pasha as commander-in-chief of the Persian front with orders to retake Baghdad. In response, Abbas once again razed the entire Erivan-Van region to slow the Ottoman advance and moved south to reinforce Baghdad with the main body of his forces. By the time Abbas arrived at Baghdad with his army, the siege, which was begun by Hafiz Ahmad Pasha in November 1625, had been under way for more than six months. Rather than risk a frontal assault on the Ottoman forces, Abbas elected to attempt to break the siege by cutting the Ottoman lines of communication, causing them to run out of supplies. While doing this he also would break through the Ottoman blockade of the city to bring critically needed supplies to the Persian garrison in the citadel.

Abbas dispatched troops in all directions to interdict the Ottoman supply lines. One task force was sent to intercept supplies that came down the Tigris by boat from Diyarbekir and Mosul; another intercepted supplies coming north from Basra; still another blocked the Ottoman main supply route from Aleppo. By mid-1626, these steps began to take their toll on the Turkish forces, and a Persian supply convoy succeeded in breaking through to Baghdad. Hafiz Ahmad Pasha became convinced that he had no choice but to attempt a risky frontal assault on the Persian relief forces under Abbas. The gamble failed and the Ottomans were repelled, suffering heavy losses. On July 4, 1626, the Ottomans abandoned the siege of Baghdad.

The perceived weakness of Murad's regime that resulted from the loss of Baghdad helped trigger a new series of revolts in Anatolia that kept the Ottomans busy for the next several years. The new grand vizir, Khusraw Pasha, tried to take Baghdad again in the fall of 1630, but the Ottomans were once more compelled to break off the siege and withdraw, this time primarily because of the poor organization and direction of the campaign.

The Safavid successes in Iraq also had repercussions throughout the Arab lands where revolts against Ottoman authority began to break out, especially in some of the more remote and less accessible territories of the empire. In Egypt, the mamluk slaves of the Ottoman officials wrested political power and began to siphon off the tax revenues that were supposed to be remitted to Istanbul and the Holy Cities. In the Yemen, the Zeydis reasserted their power, emerging from the mountainous interior of the country to take Sana once again in 1631. In Mount Lebanon, the Druze chief Fakhr ad-Din II of the House of Man had begun to extend his control over most of the vicinity as early as 1590. He gained command of the land routes between Syria and the Hejaz and posed a threat to the Ottoman position in Damascus. In 1613 his local opponents aligned themselves with Hafiz

Ahmed Pasha, the governor of Damascus, and together forced Fakhr ad-Din to flee to Europe, where he came under the protection of Cosimo II, grand duke of Tuscany, and later that of Philip III of Spain. He obtained permission to return to Lebanon in 1618 and soon reestablished his dominant position there, extending his influence as far south as Nablus and Safed in Palestine, again threatening to seize control of the pilgrimage routes to the Hejaz. He defeated the Ottoman governor of Damascus in 1625 and ruled Lebanon as a virtually independent state for another decade.

The relative decline of Ottoman power was soon to be matched and then exceeded by that of the Safavids. The Safavid Empire had reached its zenith under Abbas I, and with his death at the beginning of 1629, the dynasty entered a period of unrelenting decline. As Chardin remarked of Abbas some forty years after the event:

> He was a Just and Equitable Prince, and all his Endeavours had this one Tendency, to render his Kingdom flourishing, and his People happy. He found his Empire all torn to Pieces and Usurp'd, and the greatest part of it Impoverish'd and Pillag'd. But it is scarce to be believ'd, what Effect his good Government had, throughout his Dominions . . . . As soon as that Great Prince ended this Life, the Prosperity of Persia ended likewise.[7]

Nonetheless, it seems clear that the subsequent decline of Safavid power, in no small measure, was a consequence of policies adopted by Abbas himself.

One of the major internal problems that beset Abbas when he first came to power was the influence of the *qizilbash* chiefs who had placed him on the throne. He soon became determined to free himself of their dominance. However, since they constituted the core of the Safavid army, he considered it necessary to build a new independent military force that was loyal to him personally rather than to the *qizilbash* commanders. Thus, Abbas undertook the innovative step of building a standing army rather than relying on tribal levies. Having proceeded to do this, Abbas was next faced by the problem of how to pay for it. Traditionally, the Safavid state had operated on a feudal basis, with the governorships of the various imperial or "state" provinces assigned to *qizilbash* chiefs who were permitted to keep most of the provincial revenues in return for providing levies for the army when called upon by the shah. Since only a small part of the provincial revenues was returned to the central government, and only a small part of even that remittance was in cash, Abbas was hard-pressed to come up with the funds needed to pay a standing army from that source.

The principal source of income for the shah was from "crown" lands, whose revenues were collected directly by the royal stewards. Under these circumstances, Abbas began the process of obtaining the needed revenues and weakening the power of the *qizilbash* at the same time, by incrementally converting "state" provinces, principally in the relatively secure interior of the country, into "crown" provinces. The provinces along the volatile eastern and western frontiers were left for the most part in the hands of the *qizilbash*, who could be expected to fight hard to protect their lands. This process of provincial status conversion enabled Abbas to build and support a core standing army. However, it also began to diminish the stake of the *qizilbash* chiefs in the perseverance of the Safavid state, and dealing with the Ottoman threat clearly required the draft of major levies from the provinces to augment the standing army.

The process of converting state lands to crown lands continued under Abbas's successor Safi I (1629–1642) and reached a dangerous point under Abbas II (1642–1666). For the first time, the latter brought the important provinces of Azerbaijan, Gilan, Khorasan, Kirman, Mazanderan, Qazvin, and Yazd directly under the administration of the central government, although the *qizilbash* chiefs were reappointed as governors of these provinces in times of war, a not very satisfactory arrangement from their standpoint. Moreover, the conversion of the key strategic provinces of Azerbaijan and Khorasan, the eastern and western gateways to the heart of Persia, was a particularly risky move.

The Ottomans, plagued by internal revolts and recurrent problems on their European frontiers, were in a poor position to take immediate advantage of the change of regime in Persia on the death of Abbas. Although Murad began to gain a firm grasp on the reins of power in the early 1630s, he was still preoccupied with Europe, particularly with the Polish frontier that became destabilized once again after the death of Sigismund III in 1632. The following year, largely in response to the pleas of the Russian tsar, Michael Romanov (1613–1645), who was trying to drive the Poles out of western Russia, Murad authorized a new campaign against Poland. He soon came to have second thoughts about the wisdom of his decision as it became apparent that the war could not be brought to a rapid conclusion. Murad did not wish to become bogged down in a long and difficult campaign for uncertain ends, particularly since he wanted to be free to take advantage of the situation in Persia to settle accounts with the Safavids. He therefore was quite receptive to the truce terms offered by the new Polish ruler, Vladislav IV (1632–48), and the conflict was brought to an end.

Murad was now free to direct his attention to dealing with the Safavids but decided first to settle matters in southern Syria and Lebanon; he was reluctant to leave his right flank exposed to a strong and hostile regime in Lebanon as he moved on Persia. In 1634, bolstered by large reinforcements, the Ottoman governor of Damascus, Kuchuk Ahmed Pasha, was able to defeat Fakhr ad-Din and restore unquestioned Ottoman control over the region. The sultan then marched into the Caucasus and Azerbaijan in the summer of 1635 and easily took Erivan in August and Tabriz in September. However, once again, the Ottomans were not prepared to sit out the winter in the field, and no sooner did they return to Istanbul to await the spring than the Safavids reoccupied both provinces.

Recurrent problems in Europe, in both the Crimea and Transylvania, kept Murad preoccupied until 1638. At that time he launched a determined campaign to retake Baghdad. The city fell toward the end of December after a forty-day struggle. Murad spent the rest of that winter in Mosul preparing an invasion of Azerbaijan in the spring. It was probably a delightful surprise for him when Shah Safi, plagued by Moghul expansionism on his eastern flank that had just cost him the important city of Qandahar, offered to make peace, resolve all outstanding territorial issues, and demilitarize his western frontiers with the Ottoman empire. The sultan readily accepted these terms. He was pleased to be able to bring an end to the Ottoman-Safavid struggle that had gone on intermittently and inconclusively for more than a century and a half. A peace treaty was signed on May 17, 1639, on the plain of Zuhab, near Qasir-i Shirin, which set the boundaries between the two states that have remained in effect, with little change, until modern times. The Safavids gave up their claims to Iraq, Erivan, and parts of the Caucasus, and further agreed to cease all Shiite propaganda activities in Ottoman domains.

With his eastern front neutralized and stabilized, Murad, as well as his successors, were left free to deal with the mounting internal problems of the empire as well as with the deteriorating geopolitical situation along the Ottoman frontiers in Europe.

NOTES

1. As Roger Savory observed: "Abbas signed away large areas of Iranian territory in order not to have to fight on two fronts, and in order to have his hands free to deal with urgent problems at home" (*Iran under the Safavids*, p. 85).

2. Eskandar Beg Monshi, *History of Shah Abbas the Great*, vol. 1, p. 527.

3. Anthony Sherley, *Relations of Travels into Persia*, p. 91.

4. Mustafa Naima, *Annals of the Turkish Empire*, p. 416.

5. John Chardin, *Travels in Persia*, p. 101.

6. Ibid., p. 65.

7. Ibid., p. 139.

2

Turbulence on Persia's Frontiers

The stabilization of the Ottoman-Safavid frontier not only enabled the sultan to focus on arresting the decline of his position in Europe, it also freed the shah to give greater attention to the problems on Persia's other frontiers. In 1648, in what was to prove to be the only bright spot in the otherwise dismal record of Safavid decline in the east, Abbas II recovered Qandahar from the Moghuls. The latter attempted to retake it without success in 1649 and again in 1652. The province long remained a bone of contention between the Persian and Moghul Empires, although not one of sufficient weight to precipitate a major war over it. Toward the end of the century, Shah Alam, the governor of Kabul and a son of the Moghul emperor, attempted to induce the Ghalzai Afghans, the powerful tribe that populated much of Qandahar, to revolt against Persia, thereby opening the way for the Moghuls to retake the province. Nothing came of the effort at the time. However, when the Ghalzais finally revolted in 1709, for reasons unrelated to Moghul ambitions, they chose independence rather than subordination to the Moghuls.

In the north, following the consolidation of power in Russia by Michael Romanov (1613–1645), the Safavid position in the Caucasus soon began to erode in the face of Russian advances in the region. As early as 1639, Teimuraz, king of Kakhetia, repudiated the suzerainty of the shah and took an oath of fealty to the Romanov tsar. In 1664, Tsar Alexis (1645–1676) dispatched a diplomatic mission consisting of two ambassadors and a retinue of some eight hundred others to Isfahan with letters and gifts for Abbas II. The real purpose of this rather large "embassy" evidently was to exploit its diplomatic status to avoid paying customs duties on the large quantities of goods they brought into the country for sale. When the Persians discovered the ruse, Abbas reacted strongly and the Russian ambassadors received some ill treatment that resulted in the death of one of them. The tsar was unwilling to go to war over the affair, but was also unwilling to allow the shah to go unpunished for the offense. Accordingly, Alexis instigated a punitive raid into Persia by the notorious bandit chief Stenka Razin and a band of some five hundred Don Cossacks. Stenka Razin ravaged Mazanderan repeatedly and for a time took direct control of the Ashurada peninsula in the southeastern corner of the Caspian Sea.

However, it was not until the accession of Peter the Great (1682–1725) to the throne that a clear Russian policy with respect to Persia and the Caspian region began to take shape. Peter wanted to link the Caspian to the Black and Baltic Seas through the Russian river system augmented by a series of canals. He placed great value on the Caspian as a means of providing access not only to Persia and the Persian Gulf, but also to the regions of Transcaspia and Central Asia, and perhaps India as well. Initially, Peter's aims were primarily commercial in nature. He hoped to obtain a share of the lucrative transit trade in silks and other commodities that reached Europe across Persia through connections at Aleppo and Smyrna. His ambitions in the Caspian region and beyond were further stimulated in 1700, when he received the allegiance of the khan of Khiva.

At the same time, relations between the Russians and Persians became increasingly testy. In 1697 a Russian ambassador delivered a note to the Persian government protesting that Lezgi, Circassian, and other Caucasian tribesmen, ostensibly Persian subjects, had rendered assistance to the Ottomans during their siege of Azov. The note also called for a Persian declaration of war against the Turks and the repayment of the sum of three hundred thousand tomans, which it asserted was owed to the tsar since the days of Shah Safi. As it turned out, the Russian envoy was thrown in prison and kept there until 1699 because of a dispute over diplomatic protocol in Isfahan; the tsar took no further action. The following year, a Russian naval squadron demanded free entry into the port of Baku, a demand that the Persian authorities rejected out of hand. Once again nothing happened. Although they kept probing for signs of weakness, the Russians were not ready to seriously consider starting a war with Persia.

In the mid-seventeenth century, significant developments also took place on Persia's southern flank. In January 1649, Imam Sultan ibn Saif of Oman succeeded in driving the Portuguese out of Muscat and began the construction and organization of a powerful Omani fleet. The Omanis soon began to attack Portugal's outposts along the Indian Ocean littoral in Africa and Asia, raiding both Mombasa and Bombay in 1661. With the accession of Saif ibn Sultan (1679–1711) to the imamate, the Omanis began to launch piratical attacks against ports on the Persian side of the Gulf as well as on European shipping in the Gulf and Indian Ocean. Since Persia had done very little to develop a naval capability of its own during the Safavid period, its only recourse was to increase its shore defenses, effectively conceding dominance of the Gulf to Oman and the Europeans. The menace from piracy to commerce in the region, mostly but not exclusively Omani in origin, caused the rival European states, England, France, and Holland, to coordinate their efforts in countering the common threat. About 1700 France was assigned the primary responsibility for the security of the Persian Gulf.

The growing impotence of the Safavids became increasingly evident after the accessions of Suleiman (1666–1694) and Sultan Husain (1694–1722) to the throne. Both father and son were given over almost completely to debauchery and drink, and showed little interest in state affairs, even when matters of vital importance were at stake. It was said of Suleiman by a contemporary: "He thought so little like a King, that when it was represented to him what Danger he was in from the Turks, who when they had made Peace with the Christians, would come and attack his finest Provinces, if he did not put himself in a Condition to repel them, he answer'd indifferently, that he did not care, provided they left him Isfahan."[1] Fortunately for Persia, the Turks were too preoccupied with Europe at the time to take advantage of the situation.

When ambassadors from Europe approached Suleiman, urging that he enter into an alliance with them against the Ottomans and thereby gain the opportunity of retaking Baghdad and other lost territories, he simply indicated that he preferred to maintain the peace with the sultan. As a resident Carmelite cleric observed in 1685: "Many ambassadors are coming here from the Christian princes to stir up the king to make war against the Turks, but in vain; for he rather shows displeasure at the defeats of the latter, besides which his object and world is nothing else than wine and women."[2] It is important to recognize that Suleiman's position on relations with the Ottomans was not a matter of deliberate policy, but rather the result of indifference. Had it been the former, it would likely have been accompanied by diplomatic initiatives to assure that the Ottoman-Safavid peace remained solid. As it was, the shah's attitude invited trouble, and trouble was not long in coming.

Persian complacency toward the Ottomans was characteristic of Suleiman's successor Sultan Husain as well, as amply demonstrated in the matter of the control of Basra in southern Iraq toward the end of the seventeenth century. Ottoman control of the relatively remote vilayet of Basra had become increasingly problematic during the 1690s as a result of three factors. First, the preoccupation of the sultan with affairs in Europe; second, a series of local insurrections that took place in southern Iraq during the period; and finally, the outbreak of a plague in 1690 that decimated the Ottoman garrison in the city. Taking advantage of the severely weakened Ottoman grip on the province, Mani ibn Mughamis, sheik of the powerful Muntafiq tribe, seized Basra for a brief period in 1694, and again the following year, the second time holding it for a period of eighteeen months. Mani, however, also chose to intervene in a domestic quarrel in the Persian province of Khuzistan (Arabistan) that involved the governor of the province, Sayyid Farajullah, and his brother, with Mani taking the side of the latter. As a consequence of this interference, Sayyid Farajullah, acting under the authority of the shah, obtained permission from the Ottoman governor of Baghdad to drive Mani and the Muntafiq out of Basra, which he succeeded in doing in March 1697. Sayyid Farajullah subsequently sent the keys of the city to the shah, who in turn transmitted them to the Ottoman sultan. However, even though the shah had thereby effectively acknowledged Ottoman sovereignty over Basra, the Persians remained in control there until 1701, when the Ottomans became determined to reassert their effective authority in the city. When a strong Ottoman force arrived at Basra in March of that year, the Persian governor, Daud Khan, abandoned the city without a struggle.

As a result of the shah's basic disinterest in strategic affairs, Persian military capabilities declined dramatically and the external as well as internal security of the state became highly problematic. This was amply demonstrated within a few months after Sultan Husain ascended the throne, when trouble broke out in Georgia. Georgi XI (Shah Nawaz Khan III), the king of Kartli and governor of Georgia, had been deposed by Suleiman in 1688 but was reinstated in 1691. As a result of an intrigue in which he was involved, Georgi was deposed once again in 1695, this time by Sultan Husain. However, the shah soon relented in his displeasure and brought Georgi to his court, although he did not restore him to his former position in Georgia. Then, in 1698–89, a powerful force of Baluchi tribesmen under Mir Khusraw Shah struck into Persia, overrunning and ravaging the province of Kirman. One wing penetrated almost as far as Yazd, while another headed southwest and threatened Bandar Abbas. Sultan Husain turned to Georgi for assistance in repelling the invaders. Georgi, who was anxious to be able to return to Kartlia, refused. To induce his cooperation, the shah offered him the governorship of Kirman, and Georgi accepted. In November 1699, Georgi dispatched a force of Georgians under his brother Levan and followed himself with another contingent of Georgian troops in May 1700. The Baluchis were engaged and defeated, suffering heavy losses. The most significant outcome of the whole affair was its political implications. As one commentator observed:

This story speaks for itself; that a Safavid king should have to turn for help to a visiting Georgian prince was humiliating enough, but the inferences one may draw from this are alarming: either Shah Sultan Husayn did not know where else he could find a body of troops to deal with an emergency, or he had the troops but did not trust them.[3]

NOTES

1. Judasz Tadeusz Krusinski, *The History of the Late Revolutions of Persia*, vol. 1, p. 58.

2. *A Chronicle of the Carmelites in Persia and the Papal Mission of the Seventeenth and Eighteenth Centuries*, vol. 1, p. 421.

3. Roger Savory, *Iran under the Safavids*, pp. 241–243.

3

Balance of Power in Southeastern Europe

The brief revitalization of the Ottoman Empire under Murad came to an end with his death on February 8, 1640. Under his completely dissolute successor Ibrahim (1640–1648), it went into sharp decline once again, partly as a consequence of the execution in 1644 of the competent grand vizir Kemankesh Qara Mustafa Pasha, a holdover from the regime of Murad.

Under the late vizir's leadership, provincial revolts were suppressed and, in cooperation with the Crimean Tatars, the Cossacks were driven out of Azov, again preventing the Russians from gaining a foothold on the Black Sea. Relations with Venice were restored and the truce with Poland was reaffirmed. However, the corruption of the Ottoman court, particularly under the growing influence of the harem on affairs of state, was pervasive and brought the grand vizir down. Then, and notwithstanding the fact that the imperial treasury was nearly depleted by the sultan's debauchery, the queen mother and her coterie convinced the sultan to seize Crete from the Venetians. The rationale for the move was that the island was serving as a base for pirates that attacked Ottoman ships, including those transporting pilgrims to and from Mecca and Medina. It was also used as a base for raiding coastal settlements in the eastern Mediterranean. Although Venice was formally opposed to and discouraged such acts of piracy, it found it politically impossible to deal with the problem effectively. It was unable to close its harbors in Crete and elsewhere in the eastern Mediterranean to the ships of the militant Christian orders of the Knights of Saint Stephen and the Knights of Saint John at Malta. The fact that their piratical depredations were poisoning relations between the Ottoman Empire and the Christian states of Europe was outweighed by other considerations.

War with Venice broke out in September 1644, when ships carrying pilgrims to Mecca were attacked and captured by a Maltese squadron and taken to the island of Karpatos, northeast of Crete. Ibrahim brought together a flotilla of some four hundred ships and more than one hundred thousand men and landed in Crete on June 24, 1645. To his surprise, the Turkish forces met with a friendly welcome from the local Greek population, which had long been kept under a tight rein by the Venetians, who also suppressed the Greek Orthodox clergy on the island. The major port of Canea was captured within a few weeks along with vast supplies of Venetian cannon and other military equipment. However, the Ottomans failed to follow up immediately on their initial advantage and withdrew to return home for the winter, leaving a small garrison to hold the port until the following spring. Ironically, and probably because the amount of booty brought back was not large enough to satisfy the harem, most of the commanders of the successful expedition were executed and replaced by incompetents.

In the meanwhile, with the assistance of the pope, the Venetians assembled a new and powerful fleet with which to confront the Ottomans. When the latter returned to Crete in July 1646, almost a whole year was frittered away with the search for booty on the island. It was not until July 7, 1647, that a blockade of the capital at Candia, on which Venice concentrated its defenses, was undertaken. As long as the Venetians held Candia, the Ottomans could not claim the conquest of Crete, and by 1648 the Venetians were sufficiently reinforced to seem to be able to hold out there indefinitely. At the same time, the Venetians mounted their own maritime offensive against the Ottoman lines of communications and positions in the Adriatic littoral.

The Venetians sought to cut off the supply of men and munitions to the Ottoman forces on Crete by either defeating the Ottoman fleet in a major naval action or by bottling it up in Istanbul through a blockade of the Dardanelles. The Venetian plan failed because they did not have sufficient ships to blockade both the Dardanelles and the channel between Chios and the Anatolian mainland that provided an alternate line of communications to Crete. Nonetheless, the blockade of the Dardanelles from April 1648 to May 1649, and the threat of a breakthrough into the Sea of Marmara, threw Istanbul into a panic and helped precipitate the overthrow of Ibrahim in 1648, in favor of Mehmed IV (1648–1687). The threat to Istanbul was renewed on June 26, 1656, when a Venetian fleet severely mauled the Ottoman navy near the Dardanelles, and reinstituted the blockade. This time the Venetians not only cut the Ottoman lines of communication to Crete, but also those linking Istanbul with Egypt, a critical source of food supplies for the capital.

The ensuing crisis forced the sultan to install a new grand vizir, Mehmed Koprulu, and to give him the authority to do whatever was necessary to preserve the empire. Koprulu decided that the problem with Venice could only be resolved by the final conquest of Crete, and he proceeded to build a new fleet and to assemble the required expeditionary force. The first task for the new fleet was to break the Venetian blockade of the Dardanelles. An attempt to do this was made on July 17, 1657, but it was initially unsuccessful. Then, an accidental explosion of the arms magazine on the Venetian flagship created chaos in the Venetian line and provided an opportunity for the Ottoman fleet to break out into the Aegean. With the blockade broken, the Venetians were forced to withdraw. However, the Ottomans were unable to take advantage of their new naval superiority because of developments in Europe, complicated further by the outbreak of a major revolt in Anatolia.

Sensing the growing weakness of the Ottoman state, George Rakoczi II (1648–60), the powerful prince of Transylvania, decided to make a bid for independence from the sultan. In December 1656, he joined an alliance of the king of Sweden and the princes of Moldavia and Wallachia that had been formed for the specific purpose of conquering and subsequently partitioning Hungary and Poland, in conjunction with Russia, Brandenburg, and the Cossacks. The Ottomans considered it necessary for them to intervene in order to prevent Rackozi from becoming strong enough to overrun all of southeastern Europe and subsequently defeated him at the Vistula in the summer of 1657. When Rackozi still refused to submit to the sultan, an Ottoman army consisting mostly of Crimean Tatars invaded and ravaged Transylvania in June 1658. Rackozi managed to flee to refuge in Hapsburg territory, while the Ottomans garrisoned a number of fortresses in Transylvania to prevent any resurgence of the movement for independence in the province.

After Rackozi's death in 1660, the leadership of the Transylvanian independence movement was taken over by one of his generals, Janos Kemeny, who obtained substantial support from the Hapsburgs. Indeed, for the next eighty years the Hapsburg foreign policy agenda was determined primarily by the state of the festering conflict with the Ottomans. Kemeny was elected king of Transylvania by a diet of nobles and managed to seize control of most of the province by the beginning of 1661. However, he too was soon forced to seek refuge in Hapsburg territory after his defeat by Ottoman forces from Bosnia and was replaced in September 1661 by Michael Apafy, who agreed to accept Ottoman suzerainty and to cooperate in the suppression of any further rebellions.

While these events were transpiring in Europe, Abaza Hasan, an Ottoman official, led an insurrection in the summer of 1658 that threatened the secession of all of Anatolia from the sultan's realm. The threat did not end until February 16, 1659, when Mehmed Koprulu contrived to have Abaza Hasan and his chief followers murdered during a truce banquet in Aleppo. Although the revolt was smashed, the situation in Anatolia remained volatile because nothing was done to deal with the fundamental grievances that underlay it, and repeated stirrings in the Ottoman heartland served as a constant source of distraction for the Porte.

It was not long before Ottoman attention was drawn to Europe once again as a result of renewed attempts by the Hapsburgs to intervene politically in Transylvania in 1663. When subsequent Ottoman demands for an increase in the annual tribute payments from the Austrians were rejected, Tatar raiders crossed Transylvania into Moravia and Silesia, provoking a general movement in Europe to lend support to the Hapsburgs, who were seen as the front line of defense for Christendom. The mood in Europe at the time was such that even France, the primary opponent of Hapsburg ambitions for primacy in the continent, felt the need to send some six thousand troops to join the imperial army. A new Holy League was formed under the patronage of Pope Alexander VII that rendered enough support to the Hapsburgs to allow Austria to take the offensive against the Ottomans in the spring of 1664.

The Turkish-Austrian War was brought to a conclusion soon thereafter at Saint Gotthard, a monastery near the village of Morgersdorff, where a decisive battle took place on August 1, 1664. The Ottomans made the tactical blunder of engaging the Austrians before they had brought their entire army across the Raab River. As it happened, even though the Austrian forces were outnumbered, the Ottoman advance column was fought to a standstill, and the rest of the army was prevented from crossing the river and advancing on Graz and Vienna. At this point the sultan offered to make peace, and to the astonishment of the Austrian generals, who saw the battle as a victory that turned the tide in their favor, the emperor Leopold I (1640–1705) readily agreed. It seems that Leopold was wary of becoming further entangled with the Ottomans at a time when he saw a much greater danger emerging on his own western flank from the French, whom he believed might turn on him while he was preoccupied with the Ottoman threat to Europe. As a biographer of the emperor noted:

Leopold himself wrote to his cousin archduke Sigmund Franz of the Tyrol on 1 October 1664 that he had been forced to make "a virtue of necessity" in view of the general danger to Europe and to the house of Austria represented by France, which could be expected to seize quickly any advantage offered by Austrian distraction in the east.[1]

Indeed, the French would have loved to see the Hapsburgs caught between themselves and the Ottomans in a two-front war, and this was something that Leopold was determined to prevent, if at all possible. The peace agreement that was concluded at Eisenburg (Vasvar) on August 10, 1664, which was to last until 1682, effectively restored the prewar situation. The Austrians agreed to evacuate Transylvania and to pay an annual "gift" of two hundred thousand gulden to the sultan, in exchange for an Ottoman commitment to nonbelligerence that was made contingent upon a cessation of cross-border raids from Hapsburg territory.

It was only after the conclusion of the Austro-Turkish war that the Ottoman vizir Fazil Ahmed finally undertook the conquest of Crete, placing Candia under siege once again in early 1667. In the meanwhile, the Venetians had been reinforced with troops and materiel from France, Malta, and the papacy. However, disagreements within the alliance caused the latter to abandon Venice and withdraw from the conflict in August 1669. At that point the Venetians despaired of holding out alone any longer. On September 5, 1669, after a siege of some two and a quarter years, and more than two decades after the first blockade of Candia, the Venetians accepted the highly favorable peace terms offered by the Ottomans. The latter were equally tired of the war and wished to bring it to an end as quickly as possible.

Under the terms of the peace agreement, Crete became part of the Ottoman Empire, but Venice was permitted to retain the three ports of Suda, Spinalunga, and Carabusa, as well as a strip of land on the Dalmatian coast. Furthermore, no indemnities were imposed and, perhaps most important from Venice's standpoint, its trade privileges within the Ottoman Empire were restored.

The Ottomans had barely recovered from the war with Venice when they were forced to deal with a host of new problems in Europe that were to set the stage for dramatic changes in the balance of power there by the end of the seventeenth century. A crisis with Poland had been brewing since 1660, when it concluded a peace agreement with Sweden. This left the Polish king, John Casimir (1648–1668), free to compete with Russia for control of the Ukraine and the Cossacks of the Dnieper. In 1665 the new hetman of the Cossacks, Peter Doroszenko, sought to gain Cossack independence of both powers by attempting to create an alliance with the Crimean Tatars, who were vassals of the sultan. Doroszenko promised to acknowledge Ottoman suzerainty if the sultan lent his support to the enterprise. Although Russia and Poland agreed in 1667 to partition the Ukraine between them at the Dnieper River, the Poles took advantage of Russian weakness at the time, coupled with divisiveness among the Cossacks, to defeat Doroszenko in October 1671 and occupy most of the Ukraine by themselves. This move precipitated an Ottoman intervention in 1672 that went on for the next five years and brought a number of new territories under the sultan's control.

The most significant of the new Ottoman acquisitions was the strategically important province of Podolia, which was surrendered to the sultan by the new Polish king, Michael Wisniowiecki (1669–1673), under the terms of the Peace of Buczacz on October 18, 1672. Located between the Dnieper and Dniester Rivers, Podolia gave the Ottomans virtually total control of the Black Sea littoral for the first time. However, following the death of Michael on November 10, 1673, his successor, Jan Sobieski

(1674–1696), violated the treaty by invading the Ukraine. This brought Ottoman expeditions into the territory in 1675 and 1676, but they were unable to dislodge the Poles. Nonetheless, the outbreak of a new war between Poland and Sweden forced Sobieski to seek an accommodation with the sultan to defuse the volatile situation on his southern frontier. The resulting Treaty of Zoravno (October 27, 1676) confirmed Ottoman control of Podolia and its suzerainty over the remainder of the Ukraine. The treaty represented a milestone in that the Ottomans had never before penetrated Eastern Europe so deeply.

At this point, however, Doroszenko and his Cossacks switched allegiance from the sultan to Tsar Alexis (1645–1676), and they joined the Russians in a broad attack on the Ottomans from the north. The ensuing conflict with Russia over control of the region between the Dnieper and the Bug Rivers produced no results. The Ottomans, now pressed by new difficulties in Hungary and concerned about being stretched too thinly along a front extending across all of eastern and much of central Europe, ultimately agreed to a peace accord at Bahchesaray on January 8, 1681. The treaty confirmed the abandonment by the sultan of his claims on the region and his recognition of the Dnieper as the northern limit of the Ottoman Empire.

With the 1664 Austro-Turkish Treaty of Vasvar coming to its scheduled termination in August 1682, the Hapsburgs were anxious to get the sultan to commit to an extension of the peace. At stake was the future of the Hapsburg position in Hungary. Magyar resentment at Austrian domination, backed by a Protestant fear of Hapsburg Catholicism, helped trigger a strongly anti-Hapsburg indigenous nationalist movement, supported with French money, that called for national independence in Hungary. The principal leaders of the movement, Nicholas Zrinyi and Count Imre Thokoly, turned to the Porte for help and committed themselves to a recognition of Ottoman suzerainty in return for the sultan's support. The latter, in turn, saw this as an opportunity to consolidate his position in east central Europe, and he recognized Thokoly as "Prince of Middle Hungary."

In Istanbul, the French had been busy behind the scenes, encouraging and orchestrating this new Ottoman-Hapsburg war. They were interested in enlisting the sultan's involvement in support of their own conflict with the Hapsburgs by getting him to open a second front in the east. The French representative at the Porte let it be known that Louis XIV was amassing an army on the Alsatian frontier, and the thought of mounting a two-front war against the Hapsburgs was very appealing to the Ottomans. The grand vizir, Kara Mustafa Pasha, was convinced that the opportunity was at hand to take Vienna, a feat that had escaped the great sultans of the past, although this was not to emerge as the Ottoman objective in the conflict for some time. A decision for war was made on August 6, 1682, and Ottoman forces invaded and conquered all of upper Hungary that same summer.

For their part, the Hapsburgs sought to organize an alliance of European states to offset the Turkish threat, an effort that was strenuously opposed with some success by France. Indeed, in March 1683, an imperial communique put the matter quite bluntly: "The Turkish war is essential to the King of France for the accomplishment of his designs."[2] It was at this point that Pope Innocent XI, in addition to appealing to Savoy, Tuscany, and Venice for a new Christian crusade against the Ottomans, went so far as to attempt, unsuccessfully, to enlist the aid of the Safavids against the common enemy. He hoped to entice them to join with the Russians in an attack on the Turkish rear.

In the meantime, despite efforts by the French to derail it, an Austro-Polish alliance was concluded on March 31, 1683, that was directed specifically against the Ottomans. The agreement called for mutual military assistance and operations according to a common plan. Leopold of Austria was to launch diversionary attacks in Hungary while the Poles were to advance into Podolia and the Ukraine. Furthermore, no separate peace with the Ottomans was to be sought by either party and the alliance was to be left open for additional states to join. Of particular importance, in light of what was soon to take place, was the provision of the accord which stipulated that if either Vienna or Kracow were to be threatened, the ally whose capital was not in immediate danger was to come expeditiously to the aid of the other.

The sultan went to Edirne, where the mobilization of a massive Ottoman force for the forthcoming conflict was begun, and then to Belgrade in early May 1683, the jumping-off point for the Ottoman offensive. Kara Mustafa was named commander-in-chief and soon led the large Ottoman army across the frontier. However, Kara Mustafa was so beguiled with the thought of conquering Vienna that he disregarded the well-founded advice of his commanders not to attack Vienna before first reducing the fortresses of Gyor and Komarom. Indeed, when it became evident that the Ottoman objective was taking Vienna, the sultan is reported to have been dumbfounded: "But the goal was the fortresses of Gyor and Komarno! There was no talk of Vienna. The Pasha has committed a serious impropriety in seizing upon this idea. Very well and good, may Ever Magnificent Allah grant him success! Nevertheless, if he had said this before, We should not have given Our consent."[3] To make matters worse, it was Kara Mustafa's dream to seize the purported great wealth of Vienna, and for this purpose it was desirable to force the city to surrender rather than have it destroyed in battle. In the latter case, it would be very difficult to prevent the Turkish troops from looting the city for their own benefit.

Vienna was placed under siege in July 1683, with little attention given to the relief forces that were being mobilized and dispatched to the city. Thus, while the Austrian forces under General von Starhemberg stalled the Turks at the walls of the city, a Polish relief column under Jan Sobieski and a German force under Charles of Lorraine attacked them in the rear, creating chaos in the Ottoman camp. For a second time, the Ottomans failed to take Vienna, largely because of the successful intervention in its defense by Sobieski and his Polish troops. The Turks were compelled to abandon the siege in September 1683. While in retreat, the Ottoman army came under heavy attack and sustained a major defeat at Gran on November 1. Although Kara Mustafa attempted to regroup his forces to prevent an all-out assault on the Ottoman position in Eastern Europe, it was already too late for him. His opponents at the Ottoman court managed to cast the entire blame for the debacle at Vienna at his feet. The sultan had him arrested and executed at Belgrade on December 15, 1683. With his demise, the Turkish forward defense system became a shambles, and the Europeans were poised to mount a major offensive that might have driven the Ottomans out of much of southeastern Europe.

Fortunately for the Ottomans, the Hapsburgs were prevented from pursuing their immediate military advantage by the actions of the French. Louis XIV had exploited the distraction provided by the Ottoman attack on Vienna to invade the Spanish Netherlands, forcing Leopold to hold off from actively pursuing the war with the Turks until the situation in the West was clarified. It was not long, however, before the French reached a separate accommodation with the Hapsburgs, reflected in the twenty-year Truce of Ratisbon, and Leopold was again free to act in the East. Although the Austrians and Poles were now able to direct their full attention to the war with the Turks, they were incapable of moving decisively by themselves because of their lack of naval forces with which to attack the Ottoman rear. For this they needed Venice, which had been at peace with Turkey since 1670. After some coaxing, Venice was prevailed upon to break the peace and join a new anti-Ottoman alliance of powers, the Holy League, which had been formed under the patronage of Pope Innocent XI. As noted by a French observer at the time: "In the present circumstances, nothing could have been more disturbing to the Turks than to have the Venetians for enemies. The coasts were badly guarded, the maritime towns unfortified, and the galleys were in very bad condition. They could not hope to equip a fleet for a long time because their armies absorbed all their money."[4]

The Porte feverishly attempted to reach an agreement with both France and Russia that would alleviate the pressure it was feeling from the Holy League, but its efforts went unrewarded. While Louis XIV was prepared to exploit the Turks in his own interest, he was not ready to permit the situation to be reversed. Furthermore, the conventional wisdom at Versailles was that the Christian armies would become bogged down in Hungary, unable to inflict a decisive defeat on the Ottomans. Consequently, there was no need for France to openly support the enemy of Christendom. At the same time, the Russians were being courted assiduously by the Holy League, and Freiherr von Blumberg was dispatched to Moscow in April

1684 in an effort to recruit the tsar. Blumberg suggested that in addition to the tsar's responsibility to join with the rest of Christendom in a crusade against the "Christ-hating enemy," the enterprise also entailed expansionist opportunities that exceeded even the dreams of Peter the Great. He declared: "Now is the opportunity for Russia . . . . The way is opened to the Black Sea . . . . The Red Sea longs for you with outstretched arms . . . . All Greece and Asia wait upon you. You could easily conquer the Crimea."[5]

The Russians, who were uncertain as to whether the Holy League was sufficiently powerful to defeat the Ottomans, decided to play a duplicitous game. By threatening to join the alliance, they were able to extract a number of valuable concessions from the Porte, benefits they would forfeit if they joined the league. Moreover, it was necessary for the Russians to reach a prior agreement with Poland that would transform the existing truce between them into a peace treaty, to avoid the risk of a two-front war of their own. Under pressure from Leopold, Poland met the Russian terms at Lemberg on April 26, 1686, and the tsar joined the Holy League.

The sultan was now forced to fight on an extended front in Europe that stretched across the entire length of the Ottoman frontiers. He was faced by Venice in Albania, Dalmatia, and the Morea; by the Hapsburgs in Hungary, Bosnia, and Serbia; by Poland in the Ukraine; and possibly by Russia in the Crimea and the Principalities. By the end of the spring of 1687, all of Hungary north of the Danube was under Austrian control, while Transylvania and the southern part of the country were left virtually defenseless. The sultan's forces fared better on the Polish front where Sobieski's attempts to take Podolia and Moldavia were defeated. This loss was due in part to the refusal of the Hapsburg emperor to lend his support to the Polish campaign (he had his own plans for those territories) and partly because of the substantial assistance given to the Ottoman forces by the Crimean Tatars. Repeated Polish attempts to drive across the Dniester into Moldavia between 1684 and 1687 were repulsed. Similarly on the Venetian front, the Ottomans were able to hold on everywhere except in the Morea, where they were defeated primarily by an indigenous revolt that was instigated by papal and Venetian agents. However, by 1687 the Venetians were able to move north from the Morea into mainland Greece, where they took Athens on September 25. Back in Istanbul, the dissatisfaction with the overall incompetence of the sultan's regime, and its conduct of the war, reached the point where Mehmed IV was soon deposed in favor of Suleiman II (1687–1691).

Matters improved somewhat during Suleiman's brief reign, not so much because of his attempts to restructure the Ottoman regime as from the fact that the Venetians and Poles became preoccupied with internal problems that diverted them from continuing the war with the sultan. However, this was not the case on the Austrian front where the Hapsburgs crossed the Danube and took Belgrade on September 8, 1688. The penetration of the Ottoman Danube defense line opened the way to an invasion of the Balkans and soon led to a series of insurrections against Ottoman rule in the region. Recognizing the seriousness of this development, the sultan concluded that it was essential to bring the conflict with the Hapsburgs to an end so that he might be free to deal with the emerging internal threat to the integrity of the empire.

Suleiman put out feelers to the Hapsburgs for a peace on the basis of the existing situation on the ground, offering to acknowledge the loss of those Ottoman territories already conquered by the Austrians in return for an end to the war. The Hapsburgs were quite prepared to negotiate on this basis since they were anxious to redirect their attention to the west where the French, with one eye on developments in the east, decided to go to war once again in the Rhine-Moselle region. As noted by a biographer of Louis XIV, the French

were convinced that a show of force would keep the Turks in the war and thus prevent the emperor from disengaging his forces in the Danube basin. . . . Louis did not wish to become an ally of the Ottoman Empire, but he needed its support as a deterrent upon the German Hapsburgs. Thus the crumbling Turkish armies were undoubtedly a major consideration in the decision to go to war.[6]

However, while Leopold was willing to concede the territories south of the Danube to Suleiman as the price of peace, the emperor's allies, who were not as concerned with the French actions as he was, were less amenable, and the negotiations broke down on June 11, 1689. One Hapsburg army now drove into Bosnia, while another crossed into Transylvania and Wallachia. Then, no less surprising to the Ottomans themselves than to the Hapsburgs, the sultan's armies were able to regroup during that winter and mount a major counteroffensive that soon drove the Hapsburgs, who had already withdrawn some forces that were sent to the Rhine, back across the Danube.

Before long, the Orthodox populations of Serbia, Transylvania, and Wallachia became quite disenchanted with the imposition of Roman Catholic rule by the priests of the Hapsburg armies. They began to appeal to the sultan for assistance in restoring their religious freedom, which was greater under Ottoman rule than under that of their fellow Christians. Imre Thokoly launched an insurrection against the Hapsburgs in Transylvania, while the latter, again preoccupied with the French in western Europe were unable to deal with the challenge effectively. The Hapsburg front in Hungary collapsed and the Ottomans retook Belgrade on October 14, 1690, restoring the Danube as the Ottoman forward defense line. By 1691, faced with the problems of conducting a two-front war, Leopold was now anxious for a peace based on the existing situation on the ground. However, the French successfully blocked such an agreement by managing to convince the Ottomans that it was in their interest to continue the war. Nonetheless, the Ottoman counteroffensive soon ground to a halt. Suleiman died on June 22, 1691, and was succeeded by Ahmed II (1691–1695), just as the grand vizir, Fazil Mustafa, crossed the Danube near Karlowitz. Then, at nearby Slankamen, Fazil Mustafa and his army were ambushed and severely mauled on August 20. The Turks withdrew south of the Danube, which once again became the effective boundary between the Ottoman and Hapsburg Empires.

The opposing forces had reached a stalemate, but could not find a way to make peace. As a result, the frontier war continued inconclusively for several more years. Ahmed II was succeeded by Mustafa II (1695–1703), who led three major campaigns against the Hapsburgs between 1695 and 1697, ultimately meeting with military disaster at Zenta on September 11, 1697, at the hands of Prince Eugene of Savoy. The Ottoman offensive ground to a halt and, with the army in a severe state of disarray, the sultan's territories in Europe were left virtually defenseless.

At the same time, Peter the Great made a serious bid to break through the Ottoman wall to connect Russia to the Black Sea. From a Russian strategic and economic perspective, this was essential. Much of the internal commerce within the vast country took place along and between its major river systems. The Don emptied into the Sea of Azov, which in turn fed into the Black Sea. Further west, the Dnieper, Bug, and Dniester Rivers all emptied into the Black Sea within a short distance of each other. Thus, whoever controlled the northern littoral of the Black Sea was also in a position to dominate much of the commerce of Russia. This accounted in part for the repeated Russian attempts to seize the Crimea between 1676 and 1687. In the latter year, Basil Golitsyn, on behalf of the regent Sophia, twice attempted to attack the Crimea directly, but to no avail. These efforts failed primarily because the Russian forces were operating far from their home bases and were unable to maintain control over their overstretched lines of communication, which were continually harassed by the sultan's Crimean Tatar allies. In 1696, however, Peter managed to reverse the situation. He cut the Ottoman lines of communication and broke through to the Sea of Azov, where he quickly established a naval base at Taganrog, setting the stage for the ultimate transformation of the Black Sea into a Russian lake before the end of the next century.

In the face of these setbacks, the Ottomans were simply unable to continue the struggle along such an extended front and were compelled to seek terms with the coalition of European powers. This resulted in the Treaty of Karlowitz (signed on January 26, 1700), which for the most part provided that each country retain the territories that they were in control of at the time of cessation of hostilities. However, the sultan had to accept full Polish domination of Podolia and the Ukraine and to surrender his claims of suzerainty over the Cossacks. In addition, the sultan had to allow freedom of worship for Catholics, which gave the Hapsburg emperor the opportunity to intervene in Ottoman affairs, ostensibly on behalf of his coreligionists. Negotiations over the extent of the Russian foothold on the Black Sea dragged on somewhat longer and were finally concluded in a separate treaty at Istanbul on July 15, 1700.

The Treaty of Karlowitz marked the definitive transition of the Ottoman regime from an offensive to a defensive posture. From this point onward, the empire went into unrelenting decline. Indeed, it was evident from the outset that the treaty marked not the end of the conflict between the European powers and the Ottoman Empire but rather the point of departure for a new round of encroachments. These would begin whenever the European states felt ready to resume their campaign to drive the Turks out of Europe.

NOTES

1. John P. Spielman, *Leopold I of Austria*, p. 50.
2. Lavender Cassels, *The Struggle for the Ottoman Empire, 1717–1740*, p. 45.
3. Thomas M. Barker, *Double Eagle and Crescent*, p. 223.
4. De la Croix, quoted by William B. Munson, *The Last Crusade*, p. 17.
5. Ibid., p. 20.
6. John B. Wolf, *Louis XIV*, p. 444.

4

Beginnings of the Russo-Ottoman Conflict

The political environment in the Ottoman Empire immediately after the Peace of Karlowitz was quite volatile. It became increasingly obvious to some in Ottoman leadership circles that further serious damage to the viability of the empire was certain unless drastic steps were taken to reform and restructure the state. It was evident that the European powers were growing stronger as the Ottoman Empire grew weaker. This was clearly demonstrated by the recent loss of substantial territories long considered as integral components of the empire.

A restructuring and modernization of the Ottoman military machine was seen as particularly critical, and a serious effort in this direction was undertaken by the grand vizir, Husain Pasha. The army was overhauled and streamlined, and greater attention began to be paid to the professionalism, training, and combat-readiness of its standing forces. Similarly, a serious effort was undertaken to modernize the Ottoman navy, which was essentially obsolete when compared with its European counterparts. It was only at this time that the Ottomans changed over from the traditional oar-powered to sail-powered vessels, building a new fleet and restructuring its organization for modern naval warfare. However, once Husain Pasha attempted to reform the government administration as a whole, he quickly ran afoul of a variety of vested interests in the capital that sought to undermine his efforts. Frustrated and ill, he resigned from office in September 1702, effectively bringing the much-needed reforms to a close. By the time that Sultan Mustafa—who had secluded himself in Edirne throughout the immediate postwar period, giving himself over entirely to self-indulgence—recognized the need to take action, it was already too late. He was faced by a military rebellion that soon got out of hand, and when his own guards joined the rebels he was deposed and replaced on August 22, 1703, by his brother Ahmed III (1703–1730).

Under the new sultan, the military and naval reforms continued, and the new grand vizir, Chorlulu Ali Pasha, sought to avoid involving the empire in any further European conflicts of the sort that had helped deplete the treasury during the preceding century. Accordingly, despite efforts by France to induce the sultan to intervene in the War of the Spanish Succession (1701–1714) against Austria, and by Sweden and the khan of the Crimean Tatars to join in the Great Northern War (1700–1721) against Russia, the Porte opted for neutrality. Indeed, in the latter instance, Tsar Peter had delayed proceeding against Sweden (his goal was to break through the Swedish grip on the Baltic coast that had kept Russia landlocked) until he was certain that he would not be attacked in the south by the Turks. Two-front wars had proven disastrous for Russia in the past, and Peter had no intention of running such a risk now. The onset of the war was thus delayed while Peter negotiated laboriously with the Porte. As one historian observed: "These negotiations were conducted personally by Peter in the utmost secrecy under the very noses of a special Swedish embassy to Moscow. He succeeded in fobbing off the Swedes with protestations of friendship and the solemn reconfirmation of the previous Russo-Swedish treaties, though his duplicity stopped short of renewing his oath to abide by them."[1] However, while Peter stalled, waiting for the negotiations with the Porte to be completed, the war with Sweden was initiated by his ally Augustus of Saxony in January 1700. Even so, Peter waited. The Turkish treaty was eventually signed on July 14, but Peter did not learn of it until August 19. That same day, Russia declared war on Sweden.

Ottoman nonbelligerence had the effect of leaving Peter free to defeat Charles XII of Sweden and thereby shift the balance of power in Eastern Europe in favor of Russia. The vizir subsequently granted refuge to the Swedish king and the Cossack hetman in Ottoman territory as they fled across Poland in the wake of the Swedish defeat at Poltava on June 28, 1709. Flushed with victory, Peter decided to move against the Ottomans and began to stir up insurrections by their Christian subjects and vassals. After receiving promises of support from the princes of Moldavia and Wallachia, Peter used the pretext of the fugitive Swedish king's presence in Ottoman territory as the basis for issuing an ultimatum to the sultan, which arrived in Istanbul on December 20, 1710. The Ottoman imperial council declared war that same day, triggering the conflict between Russia and the Ottoman Empire that continued sporadically over the course of the next two centuries.

Peter's plans for a rapid drive through Moldavia and Bulgaria to Istanbul ran aground almost as soon as the campaign began. The Tatars and Cossacks formed an anti-Russian alliance on February 5, 1711, and began attacking the Russian lines of communication through Poland, causing severe shortages of supplies at the front. The Russian army crossed the Pruth into Moldavia on July 1 but was soon trapped against the river on July 20 by the Ottoman army, which had entered Moldavia from Wallachia. Surrounded by Turkish forces, and unable to retreat, Peter was compelled to sue for peace. Although the Ottomans were in a dominating position, they too were anxious to bring the conflict to a rapid close; the Turkish forces were also plagued by inadequate supplies and there was some uncertainty as to how much longer they could remain in the field as an effective fighting force. Accordingly, the Ottomans declined to use their immediate military advantage to demand unconditional surrender. Instead, the terms of the Treaty of Pruth (July 21, 1711) were not nearly as harsh as they might have been and therefore were soon accepted by Peter.

The treaty provision of greatest consequence was Article 1, which stipulated: "The fortress of Azov shall be returned to the Ottoman Empire in the state in which it was captured, with all its dependent lands and jurisdictions."[2] Compliance with this provision would have removed the Russian bridgehead on the Black Sea coast. When Peter subsequently refused to fulfill this condition of the treaty, the Turks declared war again in December 1711. The brief struggle that ensued was ended by a second agreement on April 17, 1712. Once again the Russians failed to comply and war was declared a third time. A new and more definitive peace treaty with Russia was finally signed on June 5, 1713, at Edirne (Treaty of Adrianople). It required the abandonment of the Russian gains in the Azov region, and the elimination of Peter's new Black Sea fleet. Compliance with the treaty effectively forced a Russian withdrawal from a dominating position in the Black Sea region for more than another sixty years. Nonetheless, this was to be the last time that the Ottomans confronted the advancing Russian Empire and emerged victorious.

The Ottoman success in the conflict with Russia lent great support to those elements in Istanbul who were pressuring the sultan to go to war against Venice in order to regain the Morea. Additional support for this position came in the form of appeals for Ottoman assistance from the Greek Orthodox inhabitants of the peninsula, who were seeking relief from domination by the Catholic Venetians. However, it was not until Venice lent its support to the large-scale insurrection against Ottoman rule in Montenegro that had broken out in 1711, and after it began raiding Ottoman shipping between Istanbul and Egypt, that war was declared on December 8, 1714. The Venetians turned to Austria for help, but the latter had little interest in going to war with Turkey so that Venice might be able to preserve its position in Greece, particularly since the Hapsburg treasury had been virtually bankrupted by the recently concluded War of the Spanish Succession.

An Ottoman land-sea expedition that was launched in the summer of 1715 quickly brought the Morea back under Turkish control, and the Ottomans stood poised to take the campaign into Croatia and Dalmatia, if they so chose. Although it is by no means certain, it seems most likely that it was the threat of the latter that led the Austrians to renew their alliance with Venice on April 13, 1716, and demand a rollback from the recent Ottoman conquests. The Austrians had considered seeking to bring Russia into the alliance, but concluded that such a move might prove counterproductive in the long run. Prince Eugene of Savoy, president of the Hofkriegsrat and most important member of the Privy Conference, presented the issue to the emperor in realistic terms.

It is easy to recognize that an alliance with the tsar would force the Turks to divide their forces and thereby make it easier and more advantageous for us to fight a Turkish war. But we also have to fear that the tsar would make this alliance very costly for us. . . . We should not doubt that the tsar follows only his own interests and will involve himself in nothing else.[3]

The Austrians decided to take on the Ottomans without the assistance of any other major power.

As it turned out, the Ottomans themselves contributed the benefits that might have accrued to the Austrians from a Russian involvement. The easy conquest of the Morea appears to have made the Turks overconfident and the grand vizir split his army, sending large forces to Albania to attack Corfu while leading the rest, some one hundred thousand men, northward into Hungary. This proved disastrous as the vizir's troops were easily overwhelmed by the superior Austrian forces under Eugene at Petrovaradin on the Danube, on August 5, 1716. This defeat was followed by a series of military debacles that took place during the following year, culminating in the loss of Belgrade to the Austrians on August 18, 1717. The string of defeats experienced at the hands of the Austrians forced the Ottomans to seek to bring the war to an end, something that was much desired by the Hapsburgs at this time because of the concurrent assault on Hapsburg Sardinia by the Spanish fleet. With the diplomatic assistance of the British and Dutch ambassadors, a peace agreement was reached at Passarowitz on July 21, 1718, on the basis of the existing situation. This meant that the Austrians effectively abandoned the Venetians, on whose behalf they had ostensibly entered the conflict in the first instance, by allowing the Ottomans to retain possession of the Morea.

It was clear from the course of the war that, in general, the Ottoman armies were becoming less and less of a match for the more technically sophisticated armies of Europe, which made devastating use of modern artillery. In effect, the Turks were no longer considered to be a serious military threat, at least not to their European neighbors. The situation was somewhat different in Asia where, despite the fact that the sphere of real Ottoman control had contracted significantly during the preceding century, the Turks still represented a formidable though declining power.

To a large extent, the efficacy of Ottoman writ varied in accordance with the distance from Istanbul. Beyond Anatolia, the empire was held together only rather loosely. Further east, the Kurdish chieftains were gaining ever-increasing autonomous control of the northern Turkish-Persian frontier region. In Iraq the extent of Ottoman control was almost wholly dependent upon the ability of the pasha of Baghdad to keep a rein on the desert Arabs, seminomadic Kurds, and others who roamed the region freely, frequently interrupting the important caravan routes between Aleppo and Baghdad. This activity forced the diversion of trade northward, from Trebizond on the Black Sea coast to Erzerum and then Persia. Although Turkish control in the Arab zone was perhaps strongest in Syria, it did not really extend to the turbulent region of Mount Lebanon, which was left alone for the most part, even though the governors of Sidon and Damascus were held responsible for collecting its taxes. In Egypt also, by the outset of the eighteenth century, the Ottoman grip was evidently slipping. Tribute payments to the Ottoman treasury rarely exceeded two-thirds of what was demanded, and the Turkish viceroys in Cairo were confronted by repeated military insurrections spurred by the institutional survival of the Mamluk beylicate. The latter consisted largely of Bosnian and Circassian grandees who seemed constantly to be plotting against the sultan and his representatives. In Arabia, even though the Ottomans still had firm control of the Red Sea ports, the sherif of Mecca, the hereditary ruler of the Hejaz, conducted affairs in barely disguised defiance of the sultan's authority. It seemed that the task of keeping the empire from unraveling might well exceed the still significant capabilities of the Porte.

The successful outcome to the War of the Polish Succession, at least as far as Russia was concerned, left Poland in the hands of the pro-Russian Augustus III (1734–1763). The Russian empress, Anne (1730–40), was able therefore to redirect her attention to the achievement of Peter's aims in the Black Sea region. These were twofold. First and foremost, as observed earlier, since many of Russia's major trade-bearing rivers emptied into the Black Sea, it was essential that the delta regions be brought under Russian control. Second, the Russians were determined to eliminate the threat from the Tatars, who had repeatedly attacked Russian settlements over a very long period of time. Furthermore, during the course of the Polish war, Russia concluded a treaty with Austria that committed the emperor to join any Russo-Ottoman war, although it was clearly understood that such a conflict should be the result of Ottoman aggression, not Russian.

There were intimations that, if the Hapsburg emperor joined in the conflict, he would share the spoils equally with the Russian empress. Russia would obtain the Crimea and Azov, while Austria would take Bosnia and Herzegovina, as a preliminary to further advances in the Balkan region at the expense of the Ottomans. Although the Austrians were not eager to seek territorial expansion at the time, they were concerned that a failure on

their part to support the Russians could cost them their only reasonably reliable ally, an ally whose support had proved critical in the recent past. For
their part, the Ottomans were also somewhat inclined to resolve their outstanding issues with Russia on the battlefield. Indeed, had they not been
preoccupied with their war with Persia, the Ottomans would most likely
have initiated the conflict in 1734 when Augustus was placed on the Polish
throne instead of the French candidate whom they supported. The French,
for reasons of their own, were also urging the Porte to initiate hostilities
against both Austria and Russia.

The stage for the conflict was set by a Russian ultimatum that denounced the sultan for repeated violations of the Treaty of the Pruth, that is,
for the Tatar raids that the Russians knew the sultan could not prevent. At
the beginning of 1736, the Russian commander Field-Marshal Burchard
Muennich presented his operational plan to the tsarina. It called for the
conquest of the entire northern littoral of the Black Sea and the occupation
of Moldavia and Wallachia, to be followed by the conquest of Istanbul. As
Muennich himself described it to the tsarina, in a flight of rhetoric:

The banners and standards of the Czarina will be erected, where? . . . In Constantinople! The Czarina will be crowned Empress of the Greeks in the oldest Greek
church, in the renowned cathedral of Santa Sophia, and will bring peace—to
whom? . . . to the whole world. . . . Who will then question whether the Imperial title
belongs to him who is crowned in Frankfurt, or to her who is crowned and
annointed in Stamboul?[4]

Since the Russians attacked before the Ottomans were fully mobilized
for war, the initial advantage was theirs. The Russians invaded the Crimea
and placed Azov, at the mouth of the Don, under siege. Azov fell on July 13,
1736, after having been invested for three months. However, once again the
Russians made the error of overextending their lines of communications.
Chronically short of supplies, and unable to live off the land which had
been devastated in the process of conquest, the Russian army was eventually defeated there by famine and sickness, losing some thirty thousand
men of which only about two thousand were killed by the enemy.

The Russians also intended to drive across the Dniester into Moldavia in
the summer of 1737, but were blocked at Bender by a heavily reinforced Ottoman army. The Austrians finally declared war on July 14, 1737, and
quickly appeared to be making better headway than their Russian allies.
Receiving supplies and support from the local populations, they invaded
Bosnia and Wallachia and soon spread out into southern Serbia, taking
Nish on August 1. By the end of the summer, however, the Ottomans had
regrouped and counterattacked. They retook Nish on October 20, and
blocked any further Austrian advance into Macedonia or Bulgaria. They
also defeated the Austrians near Bucharest and forced them to withdraw
into Transylvania for the winter. The Austro-Russian alliance never

seemed to regain its initial momentum and the tide of battle clearly seemed to have shifted to the Ottomans.

With the war apparently destined to result in a stalemate, diplomatic efforts were undertaken on all sides to find a way of bringing the conflict to an acceptable conclusion. In the meanwhile, in a series of hard fought campaigns, the Ottomans pushed the Austrians generally back across the Danube, except for the Belgrade salient, and reestablished the river as the forward defense perimeter of the empire in Hungary. By the end of 1738, the Austrians were becoming frantic to bring the war to an end. The finance minister, Gundaker Starhemberg, observed:

The condition of things is as bad as could be. The crownlands are desolate, the treasury deep in debt. One can do nothing against the Turks. If one battle is lost, all is lost. It would be a stroke of good luck to make peace by any means. In another campaign Austria could win nothing, but might lose everything.[5]

Other Hapsburg statesmen were not as pessimistic as Starhemberg and believed that an accord could be reached with the Ottomans on the basis of the restoration of the situation on the ground that had prevailed before the initiation of hostilities, an arrangement that would still leave Belgrade in Austrian hands. The Ottomans, who were also hurting badly from the conflict, their resources stretched to the breaking point, were equally anxious to bring an end to what increasingly appeared to be a pointless war. However, no one seemed to know quite how to bring it to a conclusion. Since none of the belligerents were interested in agreeing to abide by an armistice while negotiations continued, the war was destined to drag on into 1739.

The Ottomans appeared to give highest priority to the Austrian front. They deployed the bulk of their forces there, leaving the Principalities essentially defenseless against a Russian advance. At this point the Austrians fully recognized that a continuation of the conflict, of which they were bearing the brunt, would only benefit the Russians at Austria's expense. Nonetheless, there were many in the Privy Council who still believed that peace could be made with the Ottomans on the basis of a restoration of the prewar state of affairs. In fact, because the Austrian commander, Field-Marshal Oliver Wallis, did not believe that Belgrade could be defended adequately, and therefore was prepared to surrender it in return for a peace agreement, his negotiating authority was transferred to one of his subordinates, Reinhard Wilhelm Neipperg.

There is some irony in the fact that it was Neipperg who unilaterally concluded a separate peace agreement with the Ottomans on August 29, 1739, under which the Austrians yielded all the territorial gains they had achieved by the Treaty of Passarowitz, including Belgrade. The treaty thus reestablished the Sava and Danube as the boundary between the two empires. Although the government in Vienna was tempted to repudiate the agreement, by the time they learned of it and could react, the Turks had already occupied Belgrade. Another factor that caused them to have second thoughts about rejecting the agreement was the fact that the French had been instrumental in facilitating the negotiations. Prudence prevented them from taking a step that would be interpreted as a major diplomatic snub to France, their traditional antagonist in the struggle for supremacy in Europe, particularly at a time when they urgently needed peace. Accordingly, they apologized to the Russians for making a separate peace, suggesting that the emperor had no realistic choice other than to accept the treaty.

The defection of Austria from their alliance was a severe blow to the Russians. When Russian commander Muennich learned of the Austro-Ottoman agreement, he was outraged and expressed his chagrin to Prince Lobkowitz, the Austrian commander in Transylvania:

While the Russians take fortresses from the enemy, the Austrians raze or surrender them to him; while the Russians seize provinces, the Austrians give up whole kingdoms; . . . while the Russians continue the war, the Emperor signs an armistice and concludes peace. I ask what will become of that indissoluble alliance? I dare assure you, sir, that even had the Emperor's army been absolutely destitute, the Empress my sovereign would have secured for him a peace far more honorable than Vienna has obtained.[6]

By arrangement with Poland, the Russians had marched through Polish territory to attack Hotin and Bender, breaking through the Ottoman Carpathian defense line. They then invaded Moldavia, taking Jassy on September 14, 1739, and stood poised for an invasion of Wallachia. Now, without a diversion of Turkish troops to the Austrian front, they had to face the probability of a full scale Ottoman counteroffensive in the spring of the coming year. At the same time, they were again afflicted by overextended lines of communication and began to suffer from the identical supply problems that had turned the earlier Crimean campaign into a debacle. Accordingly, with French mediation, the Russians too made peace reluctantly with the Ottomans on September 18, 1739, the same day that the formal Austro-Ottoman treaty was signed.

Under the terms of the Treaty of Belgrade, the Russians agreed to destroy the fortress at Azov and withdraw their fleet from the Black Sea and the Sea of Azov. Furthermore, their maritime trade in the Black Sea region would have to make exclusive use of Ottoman vessels. In return, the sultan agreed to place restraints on the Tatars, a condition that he was unlikely to be able to fulfill and which was the ostensible reason for the just-concluded conflict in the first place. In effect, the war had accomplished nothing of any real consequence for Russia and had cost Austria both loss of territory and considerable prestige.

NOTES

1. B. H. Sumner, *Peter the Great and the Emergence of Russia*, p. 53.

2. See J. C. Hurewitz, ed. *The Middle East and North Africa in World Politics: A Documentary Record*, p. 56.

3. Karl A. Roider, *Austria's Eastern Question, 1700–1790*, p. 47.

4. Lavender Cassels, *The Struggle for the Ottoman Empire, 1717–1740*, p. 100.

5. Roider, *Austria's Eastern Question, 1700–1790*, p. 82.

6. Roider, *The Reluctant Ally: Austria's Policy in the Austro-Turkish War, 1737–1739*, p. 174.

5

Decline and Fall of the Safavid State

It was noted earlier that, toward the end of the seventeenth century, Persia's Kirman frontier had been seriously destabilized and subjected to incursions by Baluchi tribesmen, aided and abetted by the Moghuls of India. Order in the region had been restored only by the intervention of the Kartlian prince Georgi XI (Shah Nawaz). Now, in 1703, similar incursions took place in the province of Qandahar, home of the Ghalzai Afghans, which was ravaged by the Baluchis under the leadership of Mir Samandar. Once again Shah Sultan Husain turned to Georgi to deal with the problem. After extracting a suitable political price, the naming of his nephew Wakhtang as vali of Georgia and his own designation as governor-general of Qandahar, Georgi left Kirman at the beginning of May 1704 with his troops and soon forced the submission of Mir Samandar and the Baluchis.

As ruler of Qandahar, Georgi appears to have been rather severe with the Ghalzais. His Georgian troops treated the populace with considerable brutality, soon triggering a rebellion. Georgi made short work of the insurrection and sent the leader, Mir Wais, who was the mayor of Qandahar, to Isfahan as a prisoner. The Ghalzai leader, however, was an exceptionally shrewd politician and was soon able not only to gain his freedom but also to obtain access to the shah. He then devoted himself to undermining Georgi's position at the court, where he found natural allies among the Georgian's enemies. Mir Wais made the case to the court that Peter the Great was about to invade Persia, and that he was planning to annex both Georgia and Armenia with the cooperation of Georgi and his Georgian troops. The Ghalzai chieftain was subsequently sent back to Qandahar in honor to keep an eye on Georgi, who had by now lost much of his influence in Isfahan.

Mir Wais was determined to bring about the overthrow of Georgi, and the opportunity to do so came in April 1709 when the majority of the Georgian troops, under Georgi's nephew Alexander, were away from Qandahar on a punitive expedition against a tribe that had been raiding in the province. Georgi, who remained in the city with only a small contingent of troops, was assassinated, and Mir Wais (1709–1715) seized the reins of power in Qandahar.

Another of Georgi's nephews, Kai Khusraw, the governor of Isfahan, was dispatched with an army of Persians and Georgians to retake Qandahar in November 1709. However, the effort was soon undermined. There were powerful men in the capital who were opposed to the inordinate influence of the Georgians at the Persian court, and who therefore made it very difficult to find the necessary financial resources for the expedition. Accordingly, progress was very slow, and it took a full year before the relief army arrived at Farah, some 225 miles northwest of Qandahar. Then, for reasons that remain a mystery, a truce was arranged with the Ghalzais that lasted until the summer of 1711. The Ghalzais were ultimately forced back into Qandahar, which was placed under siege. Two months later, Mir Wais was prepared to discuss terms, but Kai Khusraw insisted on unconditional surrender. This proved to be a fatal error, since the Ghalzais chose to continue to fight while appealing to the Baluchi tribes of the south to come to their aid. The Baluchis, with their own score to settle with the Georgians, responded favorably and began to attack the Persian and Georgian lines of communications, cutting off the flow of supplies to the siege army. It was not long before the Georgian position became precarious and, on October 26, Kai Khusraw ordered a retreat from Qandahar. The Ghalzais fell on the retreating army, inflicted heavy casualties (Kai Khusraw was killed in the process) and transformed the nearly successful expedition into an unmitigated military disaster. As a practical matter, the province of Qandahar henceforth became virtually completely independent of Safavid Persia.

The success of the Ghalzais in ridding themselves of the Persian yoke inspired a similar attempt on the part of the Abdalis of Herat, who had previously fought alongside the Persians against the Ghalzais. Under the leadership of Asadullah, the Abdalis succeeded in defeating Mansur Khan, the governor of Mashad, and then Fath Ali Khan Turkman, who was sent into Khorasan with an army to restore order in 1716. Yet another army was sent to Khorasan from Isfahan under Safi Quli Khan. However, before it could engage the Abdalis, it was forced to turn northward to meet an invasion of Khorasan by the Uzbeks under Shir Ghazi Khan, who was soon joined by the Teke and Yamut Turcomans. Safi Quli Khan succeeded in turning back these incursions and then moved on to Mashad before heading for Herat. However, by the time the Persian army began to move against the Abdalis, the latter were fully informed of the Persian movements and attacked them en route. The battle turned into a disaster for the shah's forces, and Safi Quli Khan committed suicide.

The news spurred the shah to organize yet another expedition to restore the lost territories and, ostensibly to facilitate the recruitment of new troops, the capital was moved temporarily from Isfahan to Qazvin. However, once there, nothing of any consequence happened. As the contemporary Persian historian Muhammad Muhsin observed:

The leaders and pillars of the state, each one by reason of his vain personal interests and hypocrisy against the others, veiled his eyes to what was expedient for the state. Whenever anyone wished to move [against the enemy], each [of the others] would make an excuse and prevent anything from being done. They postponed their departure and occupied themselves with pleasures. For three years they remained in Qazvin, practising the selling of offices and the receiving (of bribes).[1]

Largely as a consequence of Persian indolence and incompetence, much of Afghanistan had become autonomous by 1717.

It was at this time that Peter the Great began to demonstrate a serious interest in Persia. Ostensibly, his primary concern was commercial; he wanted to divert the lucrative silk trade between Persia and Europe from the traditional routes that passed through Syria and Anatolia to a route that passed through Russia. Toward this end he dispatched a mission to Persia in July 1715 under Artemii P. Volynsky. His instructions were to convince the Persians, through bribery if necessary, that it was to their advantage to make use of the extensive river and canal system of Russia to reach Europe, in preference to the lengthy and slower overland route through Aleppo and Smyrna. If Volynsky was not successful in this, he was to find a means of interfering with the flow of trade along the overland route. In addition, it appears that Peter's interest in Persia went beyond the matter of trade. He also instructed his emissary to collect comprehensive information on the military capabilities, resources, and communications of Persia, specifically including information on the rivers that flowed into the Caspian Sea. He also wished to know specifically if any of the rivers originated in India.

By the time the Volynsky mission arrived in Isfahan in March 1717, Peter had already sent an expedition under Prince Alexander Bekovich Cherkassky to lay the groundwork for a secure trade route from Russia to India across the Caspian, and from there overland either through Persia or Khiva and Bukhara. Bekovich began the construction of forts on the Caspian coast near the mouth of the Oxus, an act that alarmed the khan of Khiva and subsequently resulted in the massacre of virtually the entire Russian force of some eight hundred men by the Khivans.

When Volynsky returned to Russia from Isfahan in 1719, he reported on the incompetence of the shah and prophesied that the Safavid dynasty would be overthrown soon unless the shah was replaced. He urged the tsar to annex the provinces bordering the Caspian before the Afghan rebels overran them. In his estimate, the Persian military was so demoralized that it would require only a small Russian army to conquer the entire country in the event of a war. Volynsky's estimate proved prescient; however, Peter's armies were still too committed to the Great Northern War for him to consider mounting a simultaneous campaign in Persia. Nonetheless, the tsar continued to maintain a high level of interest in the country and sent Volynsky to Astrakhan as governor in order that he should be able to keep a sharp eye on developments in Persia.

The Safavid state was indeed in an advanced stage of decline. This condition was clearly evidenced by the growing instability along its several frontiers. The situation in the south, for one example, was highly volatile. The imam of Oman, Sultan ibn Saif II, captured the islands of Bahrain, Qishm, and Larak, and had placed Hormuz under siege in 1717. There was a real threat that the Omanis might also seize Bandar Abbas, dealing a severe blow to Persia's income from the customs and trade revenues that derived from the port. The governor-general of Fars raised a Persian army and negotiations were undertaken with the Portuguese to provide a fleet to transport this army to the other side of the Gulf so that it could attack the Omanis in Muscat. At this point the French, who were anxious to establish their own alliance with Persia against Muscat, successfully intervened to prevent an Ottoman-Portuguese alliance. The net result was that the negotiations with the Portuguese came to nothing, while the French failed to provide the needed naval support. By 1720 the shah put aside the plans for an assault on Muscat to deal with the more serious and more imminent threat to the Safavids that was emerging in Afghanistan.

In Qandahar, Mahmud, the eldest son of Mir Wais, became leader of the Ghalzais in 1717 and began building a power base that was clearly directed against the Persians. He was aided in this by the process of disintegration that was taking place to the east in Moghul India, especially after the death of the emperor Aurangzeb a decade earlier. Although the latter's great-grandson Raushan Akhtar ascended the Moghul throne in 1719, it soon became evident that it was quite unlikely that he would make any attempt to recover Qandahar, leaving the Ghalzai eastern flank secure. Accordingly, in late summer 1719, Mahmud decided to probe the defenses of Persia and marched into Kirman with a force of some eleven thousand tribesmen. Upon his approach to the capital of the province, the governor-general, who had very few troops, abandoned the city to the Ghalzais. Mahmud remained there for nine months before withdrawing to Qandahar to deal with a local rebellion.

In the northwest, the Kurds rose in revolt and seized Hamadan, raiding as far as the outskirts of Isfahan. Further north, the Sunnis of Shirvan and Daghestan began to appeal to the Ottoman sultan to relieve them of the religious oppression they were being subjected to under Shiite rule. To make matters worse, the Lazgis of southern Daghestan struck into Shirvan, where the Lazgis of the Qaniq valley east of Tiflis joined them. They ravaged the country and completely defeated the forces of Hasan Ali Khan, the Safavid governor of Shirvan. They then turned to Georgia, which they also laid waste.

The depredations into Georgia aroused the ire of Wakhtang VI, who had been reinstated as king of Kartli and vali of Georgia by the shah in 1719, after he agreed to accept Islam. Wakhtang amassed an army of some sixty thousand men to attack and possibly wipe out the Lazgis. The shah, however, was convinced by his counselors that if he permitted Wakhtang to do this, the latter would be in a very strong position to pose a deadly threat to the security of Persia itself, especially if he were to receive Russian support. The shah therefore ordered Wakhtang to cease operations against the Lazgis just at the point when he was prepared to deliver a decisive blow. As observed by a historian of the period, the abrupt manner in which he was instructed to stand down was soon to have far-reaching consequences:

Tis more easy to imagine, than to express how much the Prince Vachtanga was enraged at an Order so imperious and unseasonable. He was provoked to see certain victory snatch'd out of his Hands; and that he should be brav'd in such a haughty Manner in the sight of those very Barbarians, that he was ready to crush to Pieces. It was thought that in his Vexation he would have gone farther, notwithstanding the Orders of the Court, if he could have been sure of the chief Lords of his Nobility, whose troops made great Part of his Army; but mistrusting that the Court had gain'd them, and fearing to be abandoned by them, as the Prince Georgi-Kan formerly was, if he contraven'd the King's Orders, he took the only Course he had to take, which was to declare that he would obey. He made the Declaration, indeed, but in a Manner that was truly worthy of his great Soul; for having sent for the Courier, which had brought him the Order, he drew his Sword before him, and pointing him to it, made an Oath that he would never draw it for the Service of the King, or the Defence of Persia; an Oath which he observed afterwards too religiously, to the great Prejudice of the King and Kingdom.[2]

Notwithstanding the fact that he had saved them from near certain destruction, the shah did not earn any gratitude from the Lazgis who continued to keep the Caucasus in a boil. The only recourse left to the shah was to offer the Lazgis bribes in return for their cooperation in restoring order to the region. In effect, he was paying them tribute that, however, did not always reach them because of the corruption of the Persian officials entrusted with its delivery. Before long, with nothing to fear from Wakhtang, the Lazgis staged another revolt against Persian authority. The Sunnis of Shirvan joined them in the rebellion, in addition to several other tribes of the region. The Lezgi coalition mobilized some fifteen thousand tribesmen and laid siege to Shamakhi, the capital of Shirvan, on August 15, 1721. The city fell on September 9 and was sacked. Shirvan was completely overrun by the rebels, who now appealed to the Ottoman sultan for protection. The sultan, seeing an opportunity to expand into Persian territory, acceded to the request and accepted the Lazgis as Turkish subjects, designating one of the rebel leaders, Daud Beg, as the Ottoman governor of Shirvan.

During the sack of Shamakhi, the Lazgis also looted the stores of the numerous Russian merchants in the city, causing them very substantial losses. Volynsky reported to the tsar that this was a clear violation of the 1717-trade treaty with Persia, wherein the latter guaranteed to protect Russian nationals. Since the shah was obviously unable to carry out that treaty provision, Volynsky urged that the tsar take advantage of the opportunity to invade Persian territory on the pretext of intervening to restore order. He assured Peter that the Russian army would be welcomed and supported by the Georgians and the other Christian peoples of the Caucasus. Peter, however, placed little reliance on the support he might receive from the peoples of the Caucasus. Moreover, he would have preferred to wait another year, in order to recover fully from the long war with Sweden which had finally come to a close in 1721 with the Treaty of Nystad, before undertaking another campaign. Nonetheless, the Afghan leader Mahmud spurred him to early action by the renewed interest and involvement of the Ottomans in Persian affairs, as well as by the second invasion of Persia.

Peter arrived in Astrakhan at the end of June 1722 and began preparations for an assault on Persia. He had a manifesto drafted that asserted that the Russians were intervening as friends of the shah and Persia for the purpose of assisting in their struggle against the Lazgis and Afghans. He also sent a message to Wakhtang in Georgia advising him of the impending arrival of Russian troops and cautioning him against any actions that might precipitate an untimely Ottoman intervention.

The tsar left Astrakhan on July 29 with a force of some one hundred thousand troops loaded on 274 ships and proceeded south along the western Caspian coast, while about ten thousand regular cavalry and Cossacks moved southwards overland. The entire force arrived at the head of Agrakhan Bay in early August and began marching on Persia by mid-month. Some indication of Peter's aims is reflected in a remark made at the time by the tsar to a young naval officer. Pointing to the distant mountains, Peter asked: "Have you ever been in the gulf of Astarabad? You must know that these mountains extend to Astarabad and that from there to Balkh, Bukhara and Badakhshan it is only 12 days' journey with camels. Bukhara is the commercial centre of those parts, and on that road to India no one can interfere with us."[3]

The invasion met with little opposition. The strategically important town of Derbent opened its gates and welcomed the Russians on September 3. At this point, however, nature intervened and wreaked havoc with Peter's plans. On September 5, a sudden gale wrecked a supply fleet of thirteen ships, leaving the army seriously short of essential supplies, while it was already too late in the season for another supply fleet to be provisioned and sent from Astrakhan. At the same time, an Ottoman envoy arrived in his camp with a warning from the grand vizir against marching inland to Shirvan, if the Russians wished to avoid a collision with the Turks who had now extended their suzerainty over the province. Given his supply problem, Peter concluded that prudence was the wisest course and decided to withdraw, leaving a strong garrison in Derbent. Although the campaign did not achieve any of Peter's main goals, it did extend Russian control of the Caspian littoral for an additional 150 miles and blocked the Ottomans from taking Derbent.

As mentioned earlier, one of the factors that caused Peter to accelerate his timetable for a thrust into Persia was the second invasion of the country by Mahmud of Qandahar. The latter departed Qandahar toward the end of August 1721 and reached Kirman about October 22 with a relatively modest force of perhaps eighteen thousand tribesmen. That Mahmud contemplated conquering Persia with such a small army is a tribute to Afghani military capabilities as well as a clear indication of the state of decay of the Safavid regime and the sorry state of its army. Although Mahmud easily took the town of Kirman, he could not break into the citadel, which was strongly defended. When he tried a frontal assault, it cost him some fifteen hundred men, an unacceptable loss given the total size of his army. Accordingly, he settled down to a siege of the well-provisioned citadel, something that his Ghalzai tribesmen were psychologically ill equipped to carry out. Fortunately for Mahmud, the death of the determined Persian commander Rustam Muhammad Sadlu in January 1722 enabled his successor to offer Mahmud a substantial bribe for abandoning the siege. Faced by some desertions of his men who returned to Qandahar, Mahmud accepted the offer and marched off to attack Yazd instead, arriving there in mid-February 1722. Running into unanticipated resistance from the garrison at Yazd, and without the artillery necessary to break through the town's defenses, Mahmud decided to bypass the city and move on to the Safavid capital at Isfahan.

The Persian capital was in frenzy when it was learned that Mahmud had bypassed Yazd and was on his way to attack Isfahan. Instead of preparing to defend the city, a move that probably would have produced the same result as the defense of Yazd, namely the withdrawal of the Ghalzais, the shah was persuaded by his counselors to meet the Afghan force on the battlefield. Mobilizing an army that outnumbered that of Mahmud by more than two to one, the shah met the Afghans at the Battle of Gulnabad on the morning of March 8, 1722.

Although the Persians seemed to be in control of the battle in its early stages, by late afternoon the tide of battle changed and soon turned into a debacle for them, forcing the Persians to flee back to Isfahan. Mahmud hesitated to attack the city for at least two days, presumably still smarting from his lack of success in investing Yazd and the citadel at Kirman. However, when a peace feeler came from Isfahan two days later, he apparently concluded that the state of the city's defenses was such as to justify an assault. Still proceeding cautiously, he first took the suburbs of Julfa and Farahabad, delaying the attack on Isfahan until March 20. To his surprise, his assault was successfully repelled and once more he was forced into a siege. This, however, was actually an unrealistic course of action for Mahmud, because the perimeter of the city was simply too large for the relatively small number of troops that he had at his disposal. Consequently, the most he could do was to establish a series of posts around the city that made exit from it dangerous but not impossible. Nonetheless, the siege took its toll on the Persian populace, which faced starvation as their supplies ran out. On about October 20, after a siege of six months, Shah Sultan Husain concluded that he had no alternative other than to surrender to Mahmud. The Afghan chieftain entered Isfahan on October 25, 1722, effectively bringing an end to the Safavid state.

The siege of Isfahan by the Afghans, and the anticipated collapse of the Safavids, spurred the Ottomans to invade Persia as well. On May 15, 1722, the grand vizir, Damad Ibrahim Pasha, met with the imperial Divan and concluded that action was necessary before the rebellion against the shah reached the borders of the Ottoman frontier provinces, further destabilizing the region. In order to strengthen the eastern frontiers of the empire, the Porte decided that it was desirable to extend Ottoman control to the frontier cities of Erivan, Ganja, Tabriz, and Tiflis. However, because of concerns about the Russian reaction to such a move, and the desire to avoid an unnecessary conflict with the tsar, it was decided to hold off an invasion of Persian territory until Mahmud's intentions became clear. In any case, it was deemed necessary to wait at least until Isfahan had fallen to be able to justify an Ottoman intervention. An additional restraining factor of some importance was French influence at the Porte. The ministers of Louis XV were determined to prevent a war between the Ottoman Empire and Russia. French interests required that Ottoman strength not be sapped by a conflict that might render it an ineffective threat to Austria. The mission of the French ambassador, the Marquis de Bonnac, was to assure that the Ottomans remained a constant source of concern to the Hapsburgs, and that they not become involved in adventures that would detract from that purpose.

Matters were further complicated by the son of the shah, Tahmasp, who had been sent out of Isfahan by his father in early June and established himself at Qazvin. Upon the fall of Isfahan and the abdication of Sultan Husain, Tahmasp declared himself shah on November 10, 1722. However, he was unable to organize any effective resistance to the Afghans and was soon forced to flee. Instead of going to Luristan, where he had a significant number of loyal followers that could constitute a viable military force, for some reason he went to Tabriz instead. This was a particularly poor choice, given its proximity to the Ottoman frontier. Although he had some reliable troops garrisoned in Tabriz, Erivan, and other important northern out-posts, he had no reserve forces to speak of. Under the circumstances, he was desperately in need of allies and probably should have devoted his ef-forts to building support in those parts of the country not yet in the hands of the Afghans or the Russians. Instead, following the incompetent advice of his counselors, he created additional problems for himself. Thus, when he learned that Wakhtang had been in contact with the Russians, Tahmasp dismissed him from his posts as vali of Georgia and king of Kartlia, and ap-pointed his rival Constantine III (Muhammad Quli Khan) of Kakhetia in his place. Wakhtang refused to give up his positions without a struggle and at-tempted to prevent Constantine from reaching the provincial capital at Tiflis. This effort proved indecisive and Wakhtang turned to the Ottomans for help. The Ottomans, who seized the opportunity to attack Tiflis in April 1723, drive Constantine out, and reinstall Wakhtang, welcomed his appeal. Constantine turned for assistance to the archenemies of Wakhtang, the Lazgis. The latter were only too pleased at the opportunity to discomfit Wakhtang and joined Constantine with some seven thousand men in an at-tack on Tiflis, which they took on May 8. Wakhtang managed to escape and appealed once again to the Ottomans, who were marching toward Persia from Kars.

Because of the conflict between Wakhtang and Constantine, the Turkish forces encountered no opposition as they crossed the frontier into Persian Georgia, where Wakhtang joined them. When the Ottoman force arrived at the walls of Tiflis on June 10, 1723, Constantine immediately surrendered the keys to the city. Furthermore, to buy their favor, he not only offered the Ottomans a large monetary payment but also a promise to arrange for the surrender of the fortresses of Erivan and Ganja. Delighted at the prospect of gaining such important objectives without a fight, the Ottoman com-mander, Ibrahim Pasha, accepted Constantine's offer, notwithstanding his prior commitment to Wakhtang. The latter, to preserve his position, of-fered Ibrahim Pasha an even greater bribe that was also duly accepted. However, Ibrahim Pasha made Wakhtang's reinstatement as king of Kartlia contingent upon his reconversion to Islam, something Wakhtang refused to do. The upshot of the affair was that Wakhtang's son Bakar was given the throne in his place. However, it was not long before Ibrahim Pa-sha's avarice drove both Bakar and Constantine to take up arms against the Turks. It was Constantine, in particular, who was able to launch a guerrilla war that kept the Ottomans from enjoying the fruits of their conquests for the next several years.

In the meantime, Tahmasp also appealed to the Ottomans for help against the Afghans, but the Porte demanded as a price of its aid the cession of all the provinces that had once been under their control. This extreme de-mand was completely unacceptable to the Persians and nothing came of the negotiations. Nevertheless, the volatile situation did present an opportunity for further Russian intervention, ostensibly to protect Tahmasp as the legitimate Safavid heir to the Persian throne. When he abandoned Tabriz and moved further north to Ardabil in July 1723, Tahmasp dispatched an envoy to St. Peterburg to negotiate a treaty with Russia as an offset to the Ottomans. As it turned out, the Russians had already decided to move into Persian territory and had taken Baku on the 25th of that same month, while simultaneously conducting negotiations with the Porte that were intended to prevent a war between the two powers over Persia. It was perhaps a sign of the growing desperation of the Persians that Tahmasp's envoy to the tsar was prepared to grant the Russians much of what had been refused to the sultan.

The Russo-Persian treaty of September 23, 1723, committed Peter to the defense of Tahmasp against the Afghans, in return for which Tahmasp was to agree to cede to Russia the cities of Derbent and Baku in perpetuity, as well as the provinces of Astarabad, Gilan, and Mazanderan. This was in accordance with the Russian view that, since it had established its supremacy in the Caspian, it was only reasonable that it should also have possession of the coastal areas. Although Tahmasp subsequently refused to ratify the treaty, as a practical matter it was too late. He had given his envoy plenipotentiary power to negotiate and sign a treaty, and the Russians treated it as a *fait accompli.*

The key provisions of the Russo-Persian treaty were implicitly incorporated into the subsequent Turco-Russian agreement over the partition of northwestern Persia that was concluded on June 24, 1724. In addition to the partition of territories in the Caucasus region (Armenia, Daghestan, Georgia, and Shirvan) between Russia and the Ottoman Empire, Article 3 of that treaty provided that a line be drawn from a point one hour's ride to the west of Ardabil to Hamadan and then to Kirmanshah. All the territory west of that line was to be incorporated within the Ottoman Empire. In return for Tahmasp's agreement to hand over these territories "without difficulty" through the mediation of the tsar, the Porte was to recognize him as shah of Persia. However, in accordance with Article 6:

If Tahmasp should refuse to surrender the provinces which, through the mediation of the Tsar, are to fall to the Sublime Porte or which have forever surrendered to the Tsar, the two Powers will each first take the share belonging to it and, after pacifying Persia, will transfer the absolute and independent government of Persia to a Persian-born individual whom they consider worthy of the position, and they will strengthen him on the throne; . . . and in order that he might be able to reign in peace and without fear, the two powers undertake to reject any representation from Mir Mahmud and to make no arrangement whatsoever with him.[4]

Notwithstanding the negotiations with Russia, the Ottomans were not prepared to await Tahmasp's voluntary renunciation of the territories they coveted and took steps to secure them directly. Thus, an Ottoman army of some thirty-five thousand men under Arif Ahmed Pasha left Kars in June 1724 to attack Erivan, which he was ordered by the sultan to conquer at any cost. Another army of some twenty-five thousand men under Abdallah Koprulu Pasha of Van had been sent to take Tabriz, while yet another force of some size under Hasan Pasha (who was succeeded as governor of Baghdad after his death during the campaign by his son Ahmed Pasha) was to capture Hamadan. Although these major fortresses were strongly defended, causing the Turks to take heavy casualties, they all fell within the next year. By early 1725, the Ottomans had succeeded in reaching, by force of arms, the boundary as defined by the Turco-Russian partition treaty of 1724. And, with the death of Peter the Great early in the year, and the subsequent loss of immediate Russian interest in the region, the Ottomans felt free to cross the boundary into the areas originally designated as part of the Persian zone, occupying Ardabil. Tahmasp was forced to flee, first to Qazvin and then to Tehran.

The Ottomans justified their actions on the basis that it was necessary to occupy Ardabil to prevent it from falling into the hands of rebel forces. This elicited protest from the Russians, who were concerned about the implications of the Turkish move for the security of their own nearby territories, but the Porte ignored it. Indeed, by late summer 1725, the Ottomans were in control of all Armenia, Georgia, Azerbaijan, and Shirvan, except for the small areas of the latter two provinces that were held partly by the Russians and partly by Constantine and some Armenian chieftains. In early 1726, the sultan dispatched a force of one thousand Turkish troops on an "unofficial" raid into Gilan, presumably to probe the Russian defenses in the province. The Russians reacted by strengthening their frontier defenses and by sending Wakhtang, who had taken refuge in Russian territory, into Gilan to conduct a propaganda campaign there against the Ottomans.

While this game of encroachment was taking place in the north, an Ottoman army had also been dispatched from Hamadan by Ahmed Pasha, the governor of Baghdad, to occupy Luristan, even though none of that province came within the Ottoman zone as defined by the 1724 treaty. It appeared likely that the Ottomans might attempt to extend their zone of control to encompass much if not all of Persia. Given the change in the situation on the ground, the Ottomans were no longer eager to demarcate the boundaries in accordance with the partition treaty and began to give consideration to repudiating it entirely.

Whatever the Ottoman ambitions in Persia may have been, they were soon to find that dealing with the decaying regime of the Safavids was one thing, but that it was quite another matter to smash the Afghans. The latter had now consolidated their grip on the region of Isfahan and were the *de facto* rulers of most of Persia, including most of Persian Iraq, Fars, Kirman, Qumis, Sistan, and a good part of western Khorasan. Afghan control of the country seemed especially solid after the increasingly demented Mahmud was replaced by his cousin Ashraf as shah on April 26, 1725.

NOTES

1. Laurence Lockhart, *The Fall of the Safavi Dynasty and the Afghan Occupation of Persia*, p. 99.

2. Judasz Tadeusz Krusinski, *The History of the Late Revolutions of Persia*, vol. 1, p. 269.

3. Lockhart, *The Fall of the Safavi Dynasty*, p. 180.

4. See J. C. Hurewitz, ed., *The Middle East and North Africa*, pp. 68–69.

6

The Era of Nadir Shah

The Ghalzais presented a particularly difficult problem for the Porte. By contrast to the Safavids, the Afghans were Sunnites, a fact that made them popular with the sultan's subjects. Secondly, the sultan was prevented from joining forces with Ashraf out of concern that such an overt act might cause a serious breach with Russia. Ashraf understood that he was at risk from the Ottomans and sought to reach a settlement with them that would prevent a war, but he was not prepared to act as a supplicant. Indeed, the ambassador he dispatched to Istanbul made it quite clear that in return for his acknowledgment of the sultan's suzerainty, he wanted the latter to turn over to him all the Persian provinces that had been seized by the Turks. Furthermore, he asserted that although the sultan was quite properly considered as the imam or spiritual head of the Ottoman Empire, that fact did not preclude Ashraf from serving as imam in Persia.

The Porte was understandably upset by Ashraf's challenge to the sultan's religious authority among Sunnis. It convened a general meeting of the Muslim *ulema* that concluded that, in the opinion of the major religious authorities, there could not be two imams reigning simultaneously unless their territories were separated by a major natural barrier. Since such was not the case in the instance of the sultan's domains and those of Ashraf, the latter could make no legitimate religious claim to a distinct imamate, and was therefore to be considered as a rebel against the religious authority of the sultan. With this decision by the religious authorities of the empire in hand, the Ottomans formally proclaimed Ashraf a rebel and outcast and declared war against him. Hostilities began in May 1726.

The war turned out to be an unmitigated fiasco for the sultan. While the Turkish troops in the Caucasus region were engaged in a series of skirmishes with local Georgian and Armenian guerrilla forces, as well as with the remnants of Tahmasp's army, the main strike against the Afghans was intended to come from the west. Ahmed Pasha set out from Hamadan in the autumn of 1726 with an army of more than seventy thousand men to challenge Ashraf, who had a force of no more than seventeen thousand. Since he was overwhelmingly outnumbered, Ashraf resorted to psychological warfare to reduce the odds against him. He sent agents to the large Kurdish contingent in the Ottoman army who offered lavish bribes in exchange for a change in their allegiance. He also sent several members of the *ulema* to the Ottoman camps to dissuade the Turkish troops from any further fighting against their coreligionists, urging them instead to join forces against the Persian Shiite heretics. Furthermore, they argued that Ashraf was dismayed by the unholy alliance between the Ottomans and the Christians (Russia) against the Muslim Afghans.

This propaganda campaign proved more devastating than Ashraf's troops and soon took a significant toll in terms of the readiness of the sultan's forces to carry on the war. Most of the Turkish troops refused to advance against the Afghans when ordered to do so, and some twenty thousand Kurdish cavalry, under Bebek Suleiman Oglu, switched sides. When Ahmed Pasha restructured his significantly reduced active forces and managed to launch an attack against Ashraf, it was repulsed, as were two other follow-up efforts. At that point, Ahmed Pasha withdrew from the field, having lost some twelve thousand men without having achieved anything. To make matters worse, the defecting Kurds, who seized most of the Ottoman artillery and supplies, had pillaged his camp. The Porte saw little alternative to reinforcing and replenishing Ahmed Pasha's army, and by the end of the summer 1727, he was ready for another campaign against Ashraf.

The prospect of a renewal of the war with the Ottomans was something that Ashraf now clearly wished to dispel. Throughout the year Ashraf had found himself beset by rebellions in the east, as well as by the emergence of a new and potent protagonist of a Safavid restoration, Nadir Quli Khan (Nadir Shah). Given these problems, Ashraf concluded that he had more to gain from peace with the Ottomans than war and offered terms at the beginning of October. By this time, the Turks were also quite ready to bring a halt to the conflict, which had become very unpopular, largely because of its religious aspects. By mid-October 1727, a peace treaty was concluded that acknowledged the sultan's primacy in the Muslim world and confirmed in perpetuity Ottoman control of the Persian lands they had taken previously. Ashraf was formally acknowledged as shah of Persia, granting him the mantle of legitimacy that the Afghans had sought earlier without success. Nonetheless, the days of the Afghan regime in Persia were numbered.

It was noted earlier that the rapid Russian penetration of Persia came to a halt with the demise of Peter in 1725. Russia's primary concern became that of holding on to the territorial gains he had achieved. This, however, ran counter to the intentions of Ashraf, who was determined to force the Russians to withdraw from all Persian territory. Apart from a few minor skirmishes, only one battle of any consequence took place between the Afghans and Russians at the end of 1727, in which the Afghans were defeated and subsequently forced to evacuate Gilan. A few days after the battle, the Russian commander, a General Levashev, went to Qazvin, where he agreed to a truce that was subsequently transformed into a peace treaty signed at Rasht by Levashev and the Afghan commander, Muhammad Saidal Khan, on February 24, 1729. The treaty incorporated a number of provisions that seemed to resolve all the outstanding issues between Russia and Persia but, as a practical matter, it was never put into effect. By the time the pact was signed, Ashraf's regime was already on the verge of being overthrown by Nadir Quli Khan.

As commander of Tahmasp's army, Nadir, who had earlier wrested control of much of northern Khorasan, succeeded in forcing the Abdalis of Herat to come to terms and accept Tahmasp's sovereignty in the spring of 1729. Recognizing the danger to continued Afghan control of Persia from Tahmasp and his powerful general, Ashraf left Isfahan with as large an army as he could mobilize to meet the challenge on the battlefield. The opposing armies clashed on September 29, and the Afghans got the worst of it, Ashraf being forced to retreat to Isfahan. Threatened by an attack by Nadir's forces that he could not prevent and might not be able to withstand, Ashraf appealed for help from the Ottoman governor of Baghdad, Ahmed Pasha, who responded by sending some troops and artillery to assist him. The Afghans and Persians soon clashed again, and once more the Afghans were defeated. Ashraf abandoned Isfahan on November 13 and moved his government to Shiraz. Nadir then placed Tahmasp back on the throne in Isfahan, although it was clearly the general who was in command of the restored Safavid state. The final blow to the Afghan position in Persia came on December 24, when Ashraf was decisively beaten by Nadir near Shiraz. He subsequently fled to the east and soon met his fate as a fugitive.

Having successfully disposed of the Afghans, Nadir then turned his attention to the restoration of the Persian lands seized earlier by the Ottomans and the Russians. He directed himself first to the Turks, apparently according them the higher priority. The Persian ambassador, Reza Quli Khan, arrived in Istanbul in June 1730 and demanded the return of all Persian territory ceded to the Turks under the treaties of 1724 and 1727.

Nadir, however, was not one to rely on diplomacy alone and, while negotiations with the Porte were under way, he launched a military campaign to reconquer the claimed territories. Hamadan fell quickly, followed by Ardelan and Kirmanshah. He next moved against Azerbaijan, taking Tabriz on August 12. His easy conquest of the provincial capital was facilitated by a mutiny that broke out in the Ottoman army, which resulted from longstanding grievances that had been neglected by the Ottoman authorities and threatened to spread throughout the region. A major revolt broke out on September 28, 1730, for a variety of internal economic, political, and social reasons, but this time it took place in Istanbul rather than in the provinces. Nadir's conquest of Azerbaijan, which had first been taken by the Ottomans at great cost in resources and blood, helped set off the popular rebellion, which was led by Patrona Halil, an Albanian janissary. The sultan was soon forced to abdicate and was succeeded on October 1 by Mahmud I (1730–1754), who soon managed to suppress the revolt and restore order.

The Abdali Afghans in Herat prevented Nadir from taking advantage of the confusion in the Ottoman ranks by the simultaneous outbreak of a revolt against Persian rule. He was thus forced to leave Tabriz only a few days after having taken the city and was unable to return for almost a year, leaving the western frontiers under the control of the not very competent Tahmasp. Within a few weeks of Nadir's departure, Tabriz was lost once again, and Ottoman forces under Ahmed Pasha succeeded in inflicting a serious defeat on Tahmasp near Hamadan. This left the way to Isfahan open, and Ahmed Pasha could probably have taken the Persian capital had he elected to do so. However, for reasons that are not clear, although there are some suggestions of possible collusion with the Persians, he chose to return to Baghdad instead. Under the circumstances, Tahmasp had little choice but to agree to a treaty negotiated with Ahmed Pasha on January 10, 1732, that left western Persia and Azerbaijan, including Tabriz, in Persian hands, but acknowledged Ottoman control of Persian territories in the Caucasus region. When Nadir returned from his successful campaign in Khorasan and learned of the terms of the treaty agreed to by Tahmasp, he refused to be bound by them.

At the same time, it seemed quite evident to the Russians that, if Nadir succeeded in his campaign against the Ottomans, it would be just a matter of time before he turned against them as well. Nonetheless, seeing him as a far lesser threat to their significant interests than the Ottomans, the Russians were quite pleased to see the Turks becoming preoccupied with the pressures that could be applied by Nadir's forces and decided to wait and see what happened before addressing the Persian threat themselves.

Nadir had a good understanding of Russia's concerns and interests, and saw an opportunity to exploit the situation to Persia's advantage. Were he to choose to observe the treaty concluded by Tahmasp, it would leave the Ottomans free to threaten the Russian southern flank. Accordingly, he turned to the Russians and offered to abrogate the treaty with the Ottomans. This effectively eliminated the immediate concerns of the former about the likelihood of being forced to conduct a two-front war, in exchange for a satisfactory territorial settlement with regard to the Persian lands occupied by the Russians. Given the prospect of an untimely conflict with the Ottomans if they refused, the Russians had little choice but to accede to Nadir's terms.

Under the terms of the Treaty of Rasht (February 1, 1732) the Russians renounced all claims to the provinces of Astarabad, Gilan, and Mazandaran, that is, to all the territories of Transcaucasia south of the Kura River. They further agreed to withdraw from Persian territories north of the river, including Baku and Derbent, once the Ottomans were ejected from Armenia, Georgia, and the other Safavid territories that they had seized in the Caucasus region. As it was stated euphemistically in the treaty:

The other provinces and places located on this [northern] side of the Kura will remain under the domination of Her Imperial Majesty, as they are at present, for the sole purpose of preventing the restless nations along the frontiers from joining the evil-intentioned subjects of the Shah and causing new troubles, if Her Imperial majesty should withdraw her troops, by seizing forcibly the places now under Russian occupation.[1]

The Russians subsequently withdrew from both Baku and Derbent, and the Treaty of Ganja of March 21, 1735, formally retroceded the towns to Persia. That agreement, which dealt mostly with commercial matters, stated in its final article: "Unless Ottoman and Tatar forces which are upon the borders of Persia, Georgia, and Moscow were withdrawn, it is decided not to abandon the war against the Ottomans."[2]

After concluding the Treaty of Rasht with the Russians in 1732, Nadir informed the Porte that the earlier agreement signed by Tahmasp was unacceptable and that the Ottomans "must relinquish all of the territories taken from Persia or prepare for war."[3] The Porte suspected, with good reason, that Russia was covertly providing military assistance to the Persians despite the Russo-Turkish treaty of 1724. On at least one known occasion, a number of Russian artillery officers disguised as Persians were sent to lend a hand to Nadir's forces. There was no question that the Ottoman Empire was Russia's primary antagonist in the region, and the Russians were prepared to offer substantial concessions to Persia in order to encourage Nadir to sustain and even intensify his campaigns against the Ottomans. It was clearly in Russia's interest to keep the Turks engaged in a long-term struggle to maintain their positions along the Persian frontiers. The Russians attempted, with little success, to convince the Porte that it was not being double-crossed by them. They justified their abandonment of the Persian provinces on the basis of their inability to sustain the heavy expenditures involved in maintaining their occupation and defense, which in itself was quite true. However, Russia's overriding geopolitical purpose in the treaty became rather evident in 1733 with the outbreak of the War of the Polish Succession (1733–1735). The latter made it highly desirable for Russia to keep the Ottomans preoccupied in a war with Persia at a time when it was itself fully committed to a struggle on its own western flank in Europe.

Notwithstanding his ability to turn it to his advantage, Nadir was quite upset by Tahmasp's negotiation of the treaty with the Ottomans in his absence. He subsequently deposed the shah and placed the latter's eight-month-old infant son Abbas III (1732–1736) on the throne on July 7, 1732, thereby assuring his own undisputed control of the country. He then turned to the matter of the reconquest of the Persian territories that had been lost to the Ottomans. As the Ottomans prepared for the expected Persian attack in Iraq in 1733 that cost them Baghdad, Nadir seized the initiative and struck into the Caucasus region, taking Shirvan and Daghestan with Russian help, and placed Tiflis under siege with the help of the Georgians. He later defeated an Ottoman relief army on June 14, 1735, which left him free to complete the conquest of Georgia and Armenia that summer. He even made an unsuccessful attempt to capture Erzerum, the gateway to Anatolia, before bringing his campaign of reconquest to a halt.

Having retaken all the territories he wanted to, Nadir proposed peace to the Ottomans. He was acutely aware that the Persian-Ottoman wars were ruining his country's economy, particularly because of the loss of revenues from the lucrative silk trade, which was shifting to the Ottoman-controlled Levant. Persia's deteriorating commercial position was clearly reflected in the difficulties encountered by Nadir in amassing the resources needed for his military campaigns. He needed a respite from these costly conflicts, and to some extent this was made easier for him by the early death of the infant Safavid heir. Nadir had himself proclaimed shah on March 6, 1736, bringing a definitive end to the Safavid dynasty, which was now replaced for a relatively brief period by the Afshars.

Anticipating the outbreak of a new war with Russia, the Ottomans were also quite eager to bring the conflict with Persia to a close. Doing so was made much easier for them by the fact that during his coronation Nadir proclaimed a religious policy that favored Sunnism, a move that was designed primarily to limit the power of the Shiite *ulema* in Persia. He declared: "If the people of Persia desire that we should reign, they must abandon this doctrine which is opposed to the faith of the noble predecessors and the great family of the Prophet, and (they must) follow the religion of the Sunnis."[4] The Ottomans suspected that Nadir was using this revolutionary religious policy to lay the groundwork for an ultimate attempt to wrest the caliphate from the sultan. Nonetheless, the Ottomans exploited Nadir's apparent "conversion" to Sunnism to make it much more acceptable for the sultan to agree to sign away the Persian territories originally conquered at high costs in Turkish lives. Nadir proposed that the following religious terms be incorporated into the peace treaty:

(1) The Persians, having given up their former beliefs and chosen the religion of the Sunnis, were to be recognised as a fifth sect, to be known as the Ja'fari. (2) Since each of the Imams of the four existing sects had a column in the Ka'ba assigned to them, a fifth column was to be provided for the Imam Ja'far. (3) A Persian Amiru'l-Hajj (leader of the Pilgrimage), with a position equivalent to that of the Amirs of the Syrian and Egyptian pilgrims, should be appointed, and to be allowed to conduct the Persian pilgrims to Mecca.[5]

The Ottomans, however, firmly rejected these religious clauses because, as suggested, they believed them to be intended to lay the groundwork for a Persian encroachment upon the sultan's position as the head of Islam.

The treaty between the Persians and Ottomans was finally signed in September 1736, after extensive negotiations regarding religious and trade issues, but Nadir subsequently refused to ratify the accord in the absence of an agreement on the religious clauses he had proposed, which he considered essential to Persian interests. Moreover, once war broke out between Russia and the Ottoman Empire on May 28, 1736, a new geopolitical situation emerged and it seems that Nadir preferred to keep open his future options, both religious and economic, with respect to the Ottomans. Although the Russians attempted to induce Nadir to attack the Ottomans, for reasons that are unclear, Nadir preferred to await the outcome of the struggle between his two powerful neighbors before taking any initiative that might affect the balance of power between them. It was also apparent that he did not trust the Russians any more than he did their antagonists. Finally, with the prospect of a long war between the Russians and Ottomans, he concluded that his western frontiers would be sufficiently secure from attack by either power for some time to come, thus leaving him free to direct his attention eastward, where indigenous rebellions were being hatched once again. Ali Murad Khan had risen in revolt in Baluchistan, the Abdalis were up in arms once more in Herat, and it also became necessary to reconquer Qandahar. Moreover, Nadir had his eyes set on the wealth of India, which he hoped to harvest by a campaign of conquest and thereby refill the coffers of his treasury that were depleted by the loss of revenue from trade with Europe.

The settlement of the Russo-Ottoman war in Europe once again exposed Persia's western frontiers to encroachment from its imperial neighbors, and it was at this time, perhaps by coincidence, perhaps by design, that Nadir returned to Persia in May 1740 from his campaigns in India. The latter had fulfilled Nadir's every expectation in terms of the wealth he was able to bring back to Persia, which was estimated to be the equivalent of some nine million pounds sterling, an extraordinary sum at the time. Bolstered by this influx of wealth, and supplemented by the merciless taxation of the Persian people, Nadir now felt he had the needed resources to undertake a major drive into the Caucasus. He would also renew his pressure on the Ottomans for recognition of his religious demands, which, if agreed to, would have significantly diminished the status of the sultan in the Muslim world.

In March 1741, Nadir launched his campaign into the Caucasus with an incursion into Daghestan, ostensibly to punish the Lazgis for the death of his brother Ibrahim at their hands. However, the campaign, which lasted two years, soon became bogged down as his forces were defeated repeatedly by the tribesmen who took full advantage of their intimate familiarity with the rugged terrain. The campaign turned into a quagmire, in which the Persian forces seemed to be trapped. To make matters worse, the protracted conflict and the extensive destruction of the land forced Nadir to turn to the sea in order to bring supplies to his beleaguered army. Since he had no fleet of his own, he had to rely on Russian merchantmen to keep his forces supplied. For a while it appeared that Nadir had intended to march into the Crimea and Russia, but whatever thoughts of such an expedition that he may have entertained were soon dispelled by the significant increase of tensions along the Ottoman frontier, where the sultan had begun to mass forces. The Porte had watched events in Daghestan with great interest and took careful note of the inability of the Persian forces to suppress the guerrilla war being waged against them. It was taken as a clear indication of Nadir's growing weakness. Accordingly, the Ottomans consciously ignored the provisions of the 1736 treaty and began to deliberately harass Persian traders and officials.

One unmistakable lesson that Nadir learned from the Daghestan fiasco was that it was essential for him to build his own naval capability so that he would not again become dependent on foreign shipping to sustain his forces in the field. Accordingly, and notwithstanding the escalating tensions with the Ottomans, Nadir elected to begin the buildup of a fleet in the Persian Gulf, where he had been almost completely dependent on the ships of the British East India Company. This was a massive undertaking that required lumber to be hauled overland some six hundred miles from Mazandaran to Bushire, where the ship construction was to take place.

At the same time that he had committed himself to a war in Daghestan, Nadir also launched an ill-conceived attack against Oman. He had originally intervened there in 1738 at the request of the Omani imam, Saif bin Sultan II, who solicited the shah's help in suppressing an anticipated rebellion against his ineffectual rule. At the time, Nadir's attempt to take Muscat proved a failure and he was forced to withdraw. It appeared that the purpose of the new invasion was to establish Persian control of the Gulf and thereby impede the flow of the Basra-Baghdad trade, which in fact was soon brought to a halt. By 1742 the Persians under Taqi Khan were in control of Muscat and the surrounding area and had laid siege to Sohar, which yielded after holding out for nine months. It was not long, however, before the Persian garrison at Muscat was decimated through desertions resulting from nonpayment of wages and the subsequent slaughter of the Persian troops by the Omani populace which was brought about through outright treachery.

Despite the failures of his campaigns in Daghestan and Oman, Nadir decided to launch an attack on Iraq. He began withdrawing his troops from Daghestan for this purpose in late fall 1742. It seems that Nadir's primary target was northern Iraq, but he wanted to create the impression that he intended to take Baghdad. To give credibility to this perception, he invaded Ottoman territory around Basra and Baghdad in 1743, while directing the bulk of his forces to the north. According to Jonas Hanway, an English observer of Persian affairs at the time, Nadir's true intention was to march on Van with a "design to hem in the Turks at Erzerum, and force them to a battle, and then to attack the Ottoman dominions in two different parts at the same time, and push his conquest as far as the capital."[6]

After taking the northern town of Kirkuk by mid-August 1743, the Persians laid siege to Mosul on September 14 and began a massive bombardment of the city on the 25th. Despite the ferocity of the Persian assault, the city held out as the attackers were repulsed with heavy losses. Once again Nadir found himself bogged down in a struggle he could not win. Accordingly, he took the initiative to arrange a truce and lifted the siege of Mosul on October 23, 1743.

His failure to take Mosul had serious domestic consequences for Nadir, who was now faced by a significant upsurge of discontent and rebellion throughout Persia, instability triggered to a large extent by his heavy exactions from the populace to support his expansionist military campaigns. It appears that the shah was not prepared to use the large fortune he amassed in his Indian campaigns for this purpose. He now found himself in desperate need of a face-saving device to restore his sagging prestige both at home and abroad. Unable to achieve any gains in this regard through negotiations with the Porte, whose position was significantly strengthened by his failure at Mosul, Nadir sought to vindicate himself on the battlefield once again.

The Ottoman and Persian armies clashed once more at Kars, which Nadir placed under siege in July 1744. However, as was the case with Mosul, the Persians failed to take the town after investing it for eighty days. At the same time, the Persian position in northern Iraq was being undermined by Ottoman support and encouragement of the Lazgis, who attacked the Persian rear and harassed Nadir's lines of communication. Undaunted by this setback, the shah regrouped his forces during the winter and returned to the battlefield in June 1745 with an attack on Erivan. This time the tide of battle went in favor of the Persians, who inflicted a serious defeat on the Ottoman army, forcing it to retreat. However, for reasons that are unclear, although perhaps reflecting Nadir's determination that prudence was the wiser course of action, the shah did not seek to take immediate military advantage of the situation and allowed the Ottoman forces to withdraw unmolested to Kars. Presumably, he hoped to use the altered situation on the battlefield to negotiate a territorially advantageous peace agreement with the Porte. If such was his expectation, he was to be disappointed. The Treaty of Kurdan, which was finally concluded on September 4, 1746, merely reaffirmed the prewar territorial arrangements. The preamble of the treaty asserted: "The terms of peace concluded (at Zuhab) in the time of Sultan Murad IV (in 1639) were to be observed, and the frontier between the two states was to be as laid down in that instrument."[7]

In effect, Nadir never really recovered from his defeat at Mosul in 1743, which proved decisive for the history of the region. Robert W. Olson aptly summarizes the geopolitical significance of that event:

The failure of Nadir Shah to conquer Mosul ended his hope of extending his rule from the Indus to the Bosphorus. The repulsion of his forces at Mosul expelled the Persian threat to the Mosul-Aleppo and the Erzerum-Diyarbekir-Aleppo trade routes. Nadir, like Abbas, would not reach the Mediterranean. The Ottoman Empire would not be severed; the eastern provinces would not be detached from Anatolia. The Porte was saved from the threat of three and a half centuries, and Persia was never again to be a danger to the sovereignty or economic integrity of the Ottoman Empire—a threat which the long sword of Nadir nearly realized.[8]

It seems certain that Nadir became increasingly demented in his later years and given to tyrannous excesses that engendered rebellions throughout his empire, even among his close associates. For example, his nephew Ali Quli Khan, whom the shah sent to Sistan to quell an uprising, soon joined forces with the rebellious Sistanis, Baluchis, and Afghans and marched on Herat in April 1747. Nadir, who was engaged at the time in suppressing revolts in the western parts of the empire, hurried east to Mashad only to find himself confronted by an insurrection by the Kurds of Quchan, and he turned northward to deal with the problem. At that point, Nadir sealed his own fate through a highly imprudent move against his own officers. For some time, he had been favoring the Afghans and Uzbeks in his entourage over the indigenous *qizilbash*, who made up the traditional core of the Persian army. On June 20, he decided that he could no longer trust the *qizilbash* at all and instructed his Afghan lieutenants to arrest all the principal Persian chiefs the following day. However, their spies at the shah's court quickly revealed the secret instructions to the Persian commanders and Nadir was promptly assassinated.

When the young Abdali leader of the four thousand-strong Afghan cavalry force, Ahmed Khan Durrani, learned of the preemptive coup, he had good reason to believe that he and his men would soon be attacked by the *qizilbash*. Mobilizing his men, he fought his way out of the Persian camp, seizing the army's artillery in the process. Heading south by a circuitous route to avoid Mashad and Herat, both of which were now under the control of Ali Quli Khan, he proceeded to Qandahar, calling upon the chiefs of the seven Abdali subtribes to assemble there. The moment was opportune for the Abdalis to assert their independence and form a state of their own. Their chief rivals, the powerful Ghalzai, were still recovering from the mauling they had received at the hands of Nadir Shah, and there was little to fear from the Persians, whose forces were in disarray, or from the Moghuls of India, who were also in the process of political disintegration. In October 1747, Ahmed Khan was elected shah of the Afghans, founding the Durrani dynasty and modern Afghanistan.

Back in Mashad, Ali Quli Khan mounted the throne of Persia under the name of Adel Shah on July 6, 1747. Adel Shah's reign was brief. Unlike his uncle, the new shah did not have the force of character to command the respect of the independent-minded chiefs and was barely able to keep the Persian Empire intact. Moreover, he was faced by a revolt by his brother Ibrahim, who succeeded in overthrowing him in June 1748, after a reign of less than a year. Ibrahim was subsequently proclaimed shah in Tabriz on December 8, 1748. His reign was also to be a very brief one. While he was establishing himself in western Persia, the fourteen-year-old grandson of Nadir Shah, Shah Rukh Mirza, was proclaimed shah in Mashad on October 1 by a junta composed mainly of Kurdish and Bayat officers.

Ibrahim took a few months to consolidate his own forces and marched against Mashad in the spring of the following year. However, by early July 1749, while Shah Rukh was still far off in Astarabad, the festering dissent in Ibrahim's camp broke out into open revolt. When his advance guard elected to switch sides, the effect was devastating, and Ibrahim's army effectively disintegrated. Ibrahim fled to Qazvin, where he was subsequently captured and blinded, soon meeting his end on the way to Mashad. Shah Rukh's reign was as brief as was his predecessor's. Mir Sayyid Muhammad, a grandson of the Safavid shah Suleiman, who ascended the Persian throne two weeks later as Suleiman II Safavi, overthrew him on December 30, 1749. He in turn lasted an even shorter time than Shah Rukh and was overthrown on March 20, 1750, by a coup carried out by his own officers in collusion with his wife. Shah Rukh was then restored to the throne as the puppet of Mir Alam Khan, who formed an alliance with the powerful Kurdish tribes of Khorasan.

While Persia was in such political disarray, Ahmed Shah, the ruler of the new Afghan state centered in Qandahar, seized Herat in late 1750 and, despite the onset of winter, laid siege to Nishapur in January 1751. This proved to be a serious tactical error. He was unable to take the city and was forced to withdraw, compelled to remain satisfied with the earlier conquest of Herat. Persia received a reprieve for the next three years as Ahmed Shah was preoccupied with his Indian frontiers to the east. However, Ahmed Shah returned to the offensive in Khorasan in the spring of 1754, promptly winning over the Kurds and other dissatisfied elements in the province. Mir Alam Khan was betrayed by his Kurdish troops and was soon executed. Ahmed Shah placed Mashad under siege in July, and the provincial capital was starved into surrender five months later. He took Nishapur the following spring and began to march westward towards Astarabad, the stronghold of the Qajar clan.

After the advance guard of Alam Khan's forces ran into an army sent by Muhammad Hasan Khan Qajar to stop them, and was severely mauled, it was forced to flee back to Nishapur. This, in turn, precipitated a rebellion there, one which was suppressed only with great brutality. In reviewing his situation, Ahmed Shah concluded that any attempt to extend the Afghan frontiers further westward into Persia would leave his critical lines of communication, which passed through barely pacified territories, seriously overexposed and subject to interdiction. Accordingly, he ceased any further attempts to expand farther westward. He designated his frontier ally Amir Khan Qarai as military governor of Khorasan, while the blind Shah Rukh remained the formal ruler of the province, perpetuating the Afsharid dynasty there. Ahmed Shah withdrew to Qandahar in the fall of 1755, from where he directed his attention eastward to Kabul and India.

In effect, for the next four decades Nadir's empire was partitioned along a north-south line, with the eastern part coming under Afghan suzerainty. In addition to Khorasan, Sistan also came into the Afghan sphere of influence as its Brahoi chief, Nasir Khan Baluch, also asserted his independence of Persia. In western Persia, Gilan and Mazandaran fell quickly to the Qajars, as the southern Caucasus and Azerbaijan came under the control of Azad Khan Afghan. However, it was in the heartland of the country, the Zagros region between Fars and Kurdistan, where the primary struggle for western Persia began among the numerous contenders for political power. All of western Persia soon came under the control of Karim Khan (1750–1779), chief of the Zand tribe from the Luristan-Kurdistan frontier, who ruled the country as regent (*vakil*) from Shiraz, while the pretender Ismail III was permitted to reign as shah in Isfahan.

The political chaos in Persia following the death of Nadir Shah offered numerous opportunities for Ottoman intervention and expansion, and the governors of the frontier regions repeatedly urged the Porte to authorize action to retake the territories previously lost to the Persians. However, the Ottomans were exhausted from wars, and the sultans had no wish to become embroiled in yet another one with the Persians. Accordingly, the last years of Sultan Mahmud's reign, as well as those of his successors, Osman III (1754–57) and Mustafa III (1757–74), provided the longest period of peace in Ottoman history. They adopted a policy of peace it would seem, primarily because of an inability to make war.

NOTES

1. See J. C. Hurewitz, *The Middle East and North Africa*, p. 70.
2. Robert W. Olson, *The Siege of Mosul and Ottoman-Persian Relations, 1718–1743*, p. 100.
3. Ibid., p. 92.
4. Laurence Lockhart, *Nadir Shah*, p. 99.
5. Ibid., p. 101.
6. Olson, *The Siege of Mosul*, p. 123.
7. Lockhart, *Nadir Shah*, p. 255.
8. Olson, *The Siege of Mosul*, p. 185.

7

Russian Imperialism under Catherine the Great

Between 1747 and 1768, the Ottoman Empire experienced a rare interval of relief from external conflicts. This period of relative peace in the region was brought to a close as an immediate consequence of a new resurgence of Russian imperialist activity under the empress Catherine the Great (1762–1796). Following the death of Augustus III of Poland in 1763, Catherine seized the initiative and took steps to ensure the election to the Polish throne of her favorite, Stanislas Poniatowski (1764–1795). An able ruler, Poniatowski sought to provide religious equality in Poland for non-Catholics, that is, for the Protestant and Orthodox minorities. This aroused the wrath and hostility of the Roman Catholic clergy and nobility, which in turn soon precipitated an armed intervention by Russia on behalf of the minorities.

By early 1768, the negative indigenous reaction to the Russian presence in the country was manifested in the emergence of the Confederation of the Bar, a Catholic paramilitary force dedicated to expelling the Russians from Poland. Seeking external help, and reflecting a sophisticated awareness of the prevailing geopolitical environment, the Confederation appealed to the Ottoman sultan, Mustafa III (1757–1773), for assistance in obtaining a Russian withdrawal from the country. At the same time, the khan of the Crimean Tatars, who was under unrelenting Russian expansionist pressure, as well as the French, who were acting for strategic reasons of their own relating to the balance of power in Europe, were pushing the sultan in the direction of conflict with Russia.

The scales tipped decisively in favor of war in mid-July 1768. Reports were received in Istanbul that the Ottoman town of Balta, on the Polish border, had been attacked and its populace massacred by a perhaps overzealous detachment of Russian Cossacks in search of Polish members of the Confederation. This led to an uproar in the Ottoman capital, which was fueled to some extent by large infusions of French money, and public demand for action against the Russians. The sultan responded on October 6 by issuing an ultimatum that the Russians immediately evacuate Poland. When the Russian ambassador was unable to offer a firm commitment in this regard, he was arrested and imprisoned. This action was equivalent to a declaration of war and hostilities began. It was clearly a war that no one really wanted, including the French, who had gone out of the way to help precipitate it. Historian Albert Sorel observed: "The declaration of war surprised and disconcerted all men—the Turks who had made it, the Russians who had provoked it, the French who had prompted it, the Prussians who had discouraged it, the Austrians who had lived in perpetual dread of it, even the English, who pretended to be indifferent to it."[1]

In theory, it appeared that the Ottomans were in a much better offensive position than were the Russians. They controlled the Crimea, from which they could fan out into Russia in a number of directions. The Turks also had undisputed control of the Black Sea and its littoral, which gave them the capability to resupply their forces anywhere along its extensive coast, thereby permitting them to conduct widespread military operations. Finally, the Ottoman lines of communication between their armies and principal bases were considerably shorter than those of the Russians, whose armies would have to operate far from their home bases and whose long lines of communications were more vulnerable to attack and interruption. Nonetheless, from the outset, the war did not seem destined to go well for the Porte. For one thing, it became very difficult to coordinate the war effort effectively with the Crimean Tatars, the traditional allies of the Ottomans. The Russians had already taken active measures to destroy much of the military potential of the Tatars by arranging the assassination in January 1769 of their khan, Qirim Giray (1758–1764, 1768–1769), who had shaken the Russians with a devastating foray into southern Russia earlier that same month. The incompetent Devlet Giray IV (1769–1770, 1775–1777) replaced him as khan. The Russians also undertook a clandestine destabilization campaign designed to exacerbate the internal divisions between the Crimeans and the other Tatar hordes of the region, particularly the Nogays, who were settled in the area between the Danube and the Dniester. This left the Crimean Tatars barely able to defend their traditional homelands, let alone play a major role in an Ottoman expeditionary army. To make matters worse, the Turkish grand vizir, Mehmed Emin Pasha, was also militarily incompetent and incapable of properly organizing the necessary war effort, thereby creating a serious problem of morale in the Ottoman army.

The Russians, on the other hand, irrespective of the fact that they too had their share of problems, including a divided military command and inter-

ference by the imperial court in the conduct of the war, were far better prepared for a major conflict. Russian armies were positioned north of the
Caucasus, at Azov near the Black Sea, and in the Ukraine, ready to pounce
on the Ottomans from all three points simultaneously. At the same time,
Russian agents were fomenting insurrections in the Principalities,
Montenegro and Serbia, destabilizing much of the periphery of the Ottoman Empire in Europe and making it difficult for the Turks to conduct a co-
hesive campaign.

The Russian and Ottoman armies converged on the fortress of Hotin
near the Dniester where a major battle took place on September 17, 1769.
The Janissaries fought ferociously and took very heavy casualties. When
the other Turkish troops realized that the elite contingent of the Ottoman
army had been severely mauled by the Russians, panic surged through the
ranks and the Ottoman army in the field virtually disintegrated, abandoning the highly defensible fortress to the invaders. With the Ottoman troops
in a disorderly retreat, the Russian armies swept down into Moldavia, taking the capital, Jassy, on October 7. Meeting only light resistance, the Russians continued the drive southward into Wallachia, entering its capital of
Bucharest on November 17. They now seemed poised to cross the Danube
and to march through Bulgaria to Istanbul.

These developments had a profound impact on the Austrians, who
came to believe that if the Ottoman Empire collapsed under the pressure of
the Russian advance, their own longstanding political position in the Balkans would be usurped by the Russians, a prospect they could not contem-
plate with equanimity. The Austrian chancellor Wenzel Anton von
Kaunitz indicated to his ambassador in the Ottoman capital on January 5,
1770, that he had assumed "that the war would be conducted and ended so
that neither side would have any advantage and everything would return
to its former balance." Indeed, he had originally thought that the war
would serve Austria's interests. "Nothing could be more helpful for securing and lengthening [our] peace because both sides would require a period
of time to recover from their losses and thus would have to postpone their
desires to foment new troubles," he believed. However, the scope and ra-
pidity of the Russian advance shattered this illusion and raised a fearful
prospect. As Kaunitz explained, "If the Turks are compelled to conclude a
disadvantageous peace, the Russian court would win so many advantages
through its conquests that it would have little or nothing to fear from the
Turks for a long time and would have completely free hands in that area
[the Balkans]."[2]

The Austrians clearly preferred a weak Ottoman Empire to a powerful
Russian Empire on their immediate frontiers and seriously began to think
about intervening to prevent a complete Ottoman collapse. One significant
stumbling block to pursuing such a course was the opposition of Empress
Maria Theresa to collaboration with the Muslim Turks against a fellow

Christian state, a position that Chancellor Kaunitz understood but did not necessarily agree with when the geopolitical stakes were so high. As he observed, "when self-preservation is demanded, such qualities as differences of religion cannot be taken into consideration."[3]

Given the substantial differences in opinion among the Austrian leadership, the policy they actually adopted was that of merely increasing their troop deployments along the Carpathian frontiers with Moldavia and Wallachia. This device was intended to convey the unmistakable message that Austria would be unlikely to accept a Russian presence across the Danube. At the same time, Austria attempted to extract concessions from the Ottomans for the actions that it was going to take in support of its own interests anyway, without actually joining in an alliance with the Turks. In other words, the Austrians proposed that they be compensated by the sultan for pursuing their own national interests, while effectively giving him nothing tangible in return. Nonetheless, perceiving its position as desperate, the Porte was willing to offer concessions to obtain whatever additional Austrian help might be forthcoming. After extensive negotiations, an Austro-Ottoman treaty was signed on July 6, 1771, that ceded Little Wallachia to Austria, provided for an increase in the Ottoman subsidy, and offered certain commercial concessions as well, including freedom of navigation for Hapsburg vessels in the Black Sea. In return, Austria committed itself to the preservation of the territorial integrity of the Ottoman Empire.

Since neither the Russians nor the Austrians were anxious to go to war with each other, by April 1771 the Russians began to hint that they never really intended to establish their hegemony over the Principalities. They also subsequently informed Vienna of the Russo-Prussian agreement to partition Poland. The Austrian chancellor saw in this situation an opportunity to make greater gains in terms of security and compensation by abandoning Austria's commitments to the Ottomans and negotiating new arrangements with both Berlin and St. Petersburg. Negotiations were subsequently initiated and, in December 1771, the Russians secretly agreed to return the Principalities to the Ottomans. Since Austria's primary concern was to keep the Russians out of the Balkans, and the Russians had agreed to this, the Austrians no longer had any interest in bringing about a general peace agreement between the Ottomans and the Russians. They were not interested in the Russo-Ottoman struggle for domination of the northern Black Sea coast and the Crimea, since it was well beyond their frontiers. Kaunitz advised his representative at the Porte, on April 8, 1772, to inform the Ottoman government that Austria no longer considered their agreement of July 6, 1771, as binding.

In the meantime, the Russians sought to create a second front for the Ottomans in the southwest. Catherine sent a naval squadron from the Baltic fleet into the Mediterranean, with the cooperation of the English, who hoped to use the Russians as a counterweight to French influence in Middle

Eastern affairs. The Russian and Ottoman fleets finally confronted each other near the island of Chios at the beginning of July 1770. It quickly became apparent that the tsar's fleet was tactically superior to that of the sultan, and the engagement soon turned into a debacle for the latter. The Ottoman fleet fled for safety into the harbor at Cheshme, where it was set afire by the Russians and utterly destroyed. However, even though the entire eastern Mediterranean was now open to the Russians, disputes between them and their English allies prevented the former from taking full advantage of the situation. The most the Russian fleet was able to achieve was to partially disrupt Ottoman trade in the region and to lend some support to the Mamluk rebellions against the sultan that were taking place at the time in Egypt and Syria. At the same time, Russian agents arrived in the Morea for the purpose of fomenting a revolt against the Ottomans, which broke out in March 1771. The revolt, which was launched in anticipation of tangible Russian assistance, soon spread to the islands of Zanta and Cephalonia, where the Greeks attacked both the Ottoman garrisons and the Muslim population. But the Russians never delivered on their promises to the insurgents, and the rebellions were soon quelled.

The summer of 1771 also saw a full-scale Russian invasion of the Crimea. The assault was facilitated by the fact that the main Tatar force was still supporting the Ottomans in Moldavia and Wallachia. Moreover, many of the Crimean chiefs defected to the Russians once it became apparent to them that the latter would prevail in the conflict. As a consequence, the Russian invasion encountered only token resistance. They immediately established an autonomous Tatar state under Russian domination and installed their own protege, Sahip Giray (1772–1775), as khan. Nonetheless, the Russians were unable to stabilize the region to their satisfaction. The Crimeans again demanded suzerainty over the Nogays and the other Tatar hordes of the northern Black Sea littoral and rejected Russian demands for the right to garrison their troops in the Crimea. Religion also became a destabilizing factor in the relationship as Muslim clerics inflamed popular resentment over the cooperation of their leaders with the infidels. Before long the Russians were confronted by a series of uprisings directed against their presence, and many Crimean notables now fled to Ottoman territory, where they set up the equivalent of a government-in-exile under a khan of their own choice.

By the spring of 1772, the Russian advance had definitely become bogged down, and further gains at Ottoman expense seemed unlikely. With little prospect of achieving any gains worth the cost of continuing the conflict, both sides were ready to find a way to end it, and negotiations for a ceasefire began. A truce was reached on May 30, and peace talks began on August 8. The peace negotiations soon foundered, however, over the fundamental question of the status of the Crimea. The Russians insisted on its remaining independent, that is, under Russian control, while the Ottomans were unwilling to accept anything less than the restoration of their suzerainty, albeit nominal, over the territory. The peace talks were broken off on August 28, and it seemed that hostilities would begin again. However, the Russians had compelling reasons for trying to prolong the truce. The onset of the Russo-Ottoman peace negotiations and the impending partition of Poland had raised the concern of Gustavus III of Sweden that Russia might soon be sufficiently unencumbered to move against him. He appeared determined to preempt the Russians, but first had to gather the reins of power into his own hands, something that required the suspension of the Swedish constitution. Accordingly, Gustavus organized a *coup d'etat* on August 19 and seized complete power in the country. Now faced by the strong possibility of a new war with Sweden, the Russians were anxious to prevent the outbreak of any further hostilities in the south. They wanted to remain free to deal with Gustavus without having to conduct simultaneous campaigns on their northern and southern flanks. Since Russia and Turkey both were anxious to stop any further hostilities, each for its own reasons, the truce was eventually extended until March 20, 1773, and peace negotiations were resumed at Bucharest.

While the Russians negotiated with the Ottomans over the disposition of the Crimea, they also continued to negotiate separately with the Crimeans. They reached an agreement with the latter in November 1772, which was set forth in the Treaty of Qarazubazar. The Russo-Tatar pact formally recognized the independence of the Crimea, but also authorized the Russians to establish garrisons in Kerch, Yenikale, and Kinburn. Control of the Straits of Kerch was of particular strategic significance since it would permit the Russian fleet that was undergoing construction in the Sea of Azov to break out into the Black Sea. When this occurred, there would be a fundamental change in the balance of power in the region.

However, it was not long after this that the Porte learned of Gustavus's coup in Sweden. Recognizing its strategic implications for the Russians, the Ottoman government hardened its negotiating position. The Porte now refused to accept the validity of the Treaty of Qarazubazar and again insisted on Ottoman suzerainty over the Crimea. Furthermore, it rejected the aforementioned Tatar concessions to the Russians and refused to allow the tsarina's fleet freedom of navigation in the Black Sea. When she learned of the Ottoman position, Catherine became livid. She told the imperial council on January 14, 1773,

On no account do I wish that the Turks should dictate to me what ships I may or may not have on the Black Sea. The Turks are beaten, it is not for them to lay down the law to us. . . . As for Kerch and Yenikale, we have not received them from the Turks, we have conquered them from the Tatars, and the Tatars have ceded them to us by treaty. What need have we of Turkish consent?[4]

She also instructed the council to advise the Ottomans that she would not agree to an extension of the truce beyond March 20, 1773. Nonetheless, her councilors prevailed on her to be more conciliatory in order to nullify the Ottoman naval threat to the Crimea. After all, they argued, it really didn't matter if they were restricted to having only merchant ships in the Black Sea since these were easily converted into warships.

While peace negotiations were continuing, on March 1 the Russians decided to launch an attack on the main Ottoman army south of the Danube. The Russian forces crossed the Danube between June 17 and June 22 and mounted a major assault on the fortress at Silistria, an attack that failed, leaving the Russian lines of communications seriously exposed and threatening to trap the Russian army south of the Danube. However, the Ottoman army was not in a position to take advantage of the situation and failed to mount the counteroffensive that might have devastated the Russian forces. Instead, peace negotiations were resumed but soon foundered once again because of continued Ottoman unwillingness to concede its suzerainty over the Crimea. As a result, the war lingered on for another year.

On June 20, 1774, the advance guard of the Russian forces stumbled onto the main Ottoman army near Koludzhi and succeeded in putting it to rout, as well as capturing its base. The Ottoman headquarters were now cut off from the principal forward positions, and the grand vizir saw little alternative to seeking peace terms. This time, however, the Russians refused to negotiate and insisted that the Ottomans accept the terms they were being offered.

The treaty of peace between Russia and the Ottoman Empire, signed on July 21, 1774, at Kuchuk Kaynarja (a village near Silistria), set the framework for Russo-Ottoman relations for the next 140 years, until the outbreak of World War I. The Crimea was made independent, denying the Ottomans the valuable military assistance they had come to rely on for centuries from their Tatar vassals. The other territorial provisions of the treaty, which awarded control of the mouth of the Dnieper to Russia along with Azov but required a Russian withdrawal from the Principalities, the Caucasus, and the Aegean, were significant but not far-reaching. More consequential was Article II, which formally established Russia as a Black Sea power for the first time and guaranteed free passage through the Turkish Straits for Russian commercial vessels. With the end of exclusive Ottoman domination of the Black Sea, Russian ambitions with regard to control of the Straits became a perpetual bone of contention between the two states.

The Treaty of Kuchuk Kaynarja was quite unequivocal about the Crimea—the Tatar peoples of the northern Black Sea region, without exception, were to be recognized "as free nations, and entirely independent of every foreign Power." It stipulated further that, neither the Court of Russia nor the Ottoman Porte shall interfere, under any pretext whatever, with the election of the said Khan, or in the domestic, political, civil and internal affairs of the same; but on the contrary, they shall acknowledge and consider the said Tatar nation, in its political and civil state, upon the same footing as the other Powers who are governed by themselves, and are dependent upon God alone.[5]

This was a bitter pill for the sultan, Abd al-Hamid I (1774–1789), to swallow since it formally deprived him of the services of a valued vassal. Nevertheless, given the prevailing balance of power, he had little choice but to accept the loss and be satisfied that the region would become, prospectively, a neutral buffer zone between Turkey and Russia. However, it quickly became quite evident that Catherine had no intention of abiding by the terms of the treaty. Her appetite for imperial expansion had been whetted and was to be indulged. Almost before the ink on the treaty was dry, the Russians imposed their suzerainty on the Nogays and began to meddle in Crimean politics in the attempt to secure the khanate for someone amenable to their interests and susceptible to their influence. This Russian intervention served to encourage the emigration of many of the Crimean Tatars to Anatolia, initiating a refugee movement from lost Ottoman lands that was to reach into the millions in the following century. It also created pressures on the Porte from the wealthier of the refugees, who put their resources behind those in Istanbul who were resentful of Ottoman discomfiture at the hands of the Russians and who demanded action, war if necessary, to restore Ottoman suzerainty over the Crimea.

While the prowar party in Istanbul made some political headway, the Ottomans simply were in no position at the time to resume hostilities with the Russians. For one thing, they were still locked in struggle with the Persians under Karim Khan along their Anatolian frontiers and in Iraq. Furthermore, their longstanding European ally, France, was preoccupied with developments in North America, where the American colonists had revolted against British rule. The Porte was urged by Paris to react with extreme caution to any Russian provocation. On the other hand, and for the very same reasons, it was an opportune moment for the Russians to ignore the provisions of the Russo-Ottoman treaty and to intervene directly in the Crimea, awarding the khanate to their own protege, Shahin Giray (1777–1783). However, his effectiveness was severely hampered because the Russians did not trouble to replace the subsidy to the khan, now discontinued, that was traditionally provided by the Ottomans. Since it was primarily through the distribution of largesse derived from the subsidy that the khan was able to keep the highly independent Tatar chiefs subservient, he was soon faced with a rebellion against the central Crimean regime.

The Porte saw this development as an opportunity to restore the sultan's authority in the Crimea and sent a number of pro-Ottoman Tatars to attempt to seize control there at the beginning of January 1778. This soon triggered another Russian military intervention that quickly suppressed the rebellion. This time, however, the Russians occupied most of the Crimea before the Ottomans could react. Once again the Porte could do little to alter the situation and was forced to acknowledge the reality of Russian hegemony in the Crimea. Under the Treaty of Aynali Kavak (March 10, 1778), the Russians agreed to withdraw their forces from the territory in return for a commitment by the sultan to recognize Shahin Giray as khan for life. As it turned out, Shahin Giray was only able to maintain control of the peninsula with substantial Russian military and financial support. Consequently, it was not long before Catherine decided to put an end to the charade of Crimean independence and openly annexed the territory in August 1783.

Once again the Porte was confronted by a *fait accompli* and had little practical recourse other than to accept this major Russian expansion at its expense. The formal Ottoman acceptance of the annexation of the Crimea is reflected in the Treaty of Constantinople (January 9, 1784), which essentially confirmed the terms of the two earlier treaties except that the provisions for the independence of the Crimean Tatars were omitted entirely. The only concession made to the Porte was the formal recognition of the sultan as the religious leader of the territory's Muslims.

The annexation of the Crimea by no means satisfied Catherine's imperialist ambitions in the region. As early as 1782, the empress had conceived a grandiose scheme for driving the Ottomans out of Europe entirely and reconfiguring their territories into two new political entities. Moldavia, Wallachia, and Bessarabia were to be unified in the independent Orthodox state of Dacia, while Rumelia, Thrace, Macedonia, Bulgaria, and northern Greece were to be incorporated within a reconstituted Byzantine Empire, with its capital at Constantinople, and ruled by Catherine's grandson Constantine. For its cooperation in this scheme, Austria was to be rewarded with Serbia, Bosnia, Herzegovina, and those parts of Dalmatia still held by Venice, thus giving it most of the western Balkans. As compensation for its loss of Dalmatia, Venice was to be awarded the Morea, Crete, and Cyprus, which would effectively enhance its position of power in the Aegean and eastern Mediterranean. Even France, heretofore the sultan's staunchest European ally, but which had realigned itself with Russia and Austria since the accession to the throne by Louis XVI and his Austrian queen, Marie Antoinette, was to have a share of the spoils. It was to receive Syria and Egypt, which would place it in a position to dominate, if not completely control, trade in the Middle East.

The two major European powers left out of the Russian scheme, England and Prussia, took a dim view of the shift in the balance of power that was to be achieved at Ottoman expense. England did not want to see any enhancement of the French or Russian positions in the Middle East, which was too close to India for comfort, while Prussia was opposed generally to any growth in Austrian power. Accordingly, England and Prussia now adopted the argument that the continued territorial integrity of the Otto-man Empire was essential to their interests and encouraged the sultan to actively contest any further Russian encroachments on his territory.

The Crimea under Russian rule was soon transformed into a forward base for further territorial expansion at the expense of the Ottomans. Grigory A. Potemkin, governor of the province and Catherine's choice to be ruler of the future state of Dacia, established naval bases at Sevastopol in the Crimea and at Kherson at the mouth of the Dnieper. At the same time, agents from the Russian consulates at Jassy, Bucharest, and Scutari, autho-rized by the Treaty of Kuchuk Kaynarja, fomented dissent and insurrection throughout the Balkans and also encouraged Greek pirates to raid Otto-man shipping in the Aegean. In view of these Russian provocations, the sentiment in favor of war soon became pervasive in Istanbul, particularly after the formal visit in May 1787 of Catherine, accompanied by Joseph II of Austria, to Kherson and Sevastopol, only a short sailing distance from the Ottoman capital. The tough-minded grand vizir, Koja Yusuf Pasha, in-duced the sultan and the Imperial Council to issue an ultimatum to Russia threatening to declare war unless it promptly evacuated both the Crimea and the Caucasus, where they were also encroaching on Ottoman territory.

Catherine, of course, had no intention of doing either, and negotiations soon broke down. The sultan declared war on September 4, 1787, and Rus-sia reciprocated with its own declaration of war on September 15. Austria, notwithstanding its treaty obligations, was reluctant to enter the conflict on the side of Russia and therefore hesitated to declare war. However, that did not stop it from attempting, unsuccessfully, to take Belgrade by surprise at-tack on December 2, before it announced its belligerency. Austria formally initiated hostilities on February 19, 1788.

The war began rather slowly since none of the parties involved were re-ally prepared for a major conflict, and the initial campaigns were short and indecisive. Both Russia and Austria were faced by problems within their respective empires that demanded priority attention, while the Ottomans were diverted by the need to send an expedition against the Mamluks in Egypt and by internal squabbles over the conduct of the war. In addition, Russia and Austria felt the need to proceed cautiously because of uncer-tainty about the implications of the new Triple Alliance between Great Brit-ain, Prussia, and the Netherlands that came into being on June 13, 1788. At the same time, Sweden sought to take advantage of Russia's preoccupation in the south and attempted to seize Finland once again.

In late August 1788, Austria's intelligence service intercepted messages from the Prussian chief minister, Count Ewald von Hertzberg, to his am-bassador at Istanbul that discussed the desirability of a Prussian-Ottoman military alliance for the purpose of mounting a joint invasion of Hapsburg territory. The Hapsburg emperor, Joseph II, took this proposal very seri-ously. He was convinced that if Austria had to fight on two fronts, "the

Monarchy is lost, because it will be necessary to diminish the number of troops on the Turkish front to prevent the king of Prussia from occupying all of Bohemia and Moravia and marching to Vienna. But in diminishing the actual forces against the Porte we are no longer in a state to defend ourselves."[6]

Evidently concerned about the possible implications of a Prussian-Ottoman alliance, the Austrian emperor began to give serious thought to making a separate peace with the sultan in order to extricate himself from what might develop into a militarily untenable situation. To make matters worse, the Austrians had hoped that the Russians would divert the Ottoman forces eastward to facilitate their own drive across the Sava and the Danube. Since this had not occurred, the Austrians continued to stall. Thus, although the war was on, not very much happened for some time. Even the Russians began having second thoughts about the wisdom of continuing the conflict. Indeed, once Potemkin had taken the strategically important Ottoman fortress at Ochakov, which dominated the estuary of the Dnieper and had effectively bottled up the Russian fleet there, Catherine let it be known in December 1788 that she was prepared to accept a general peace. Her only demands were that Russia be permitted to retain control of the fortress in addition to receiving payment of an indemnity from the Turks.

In the spring of 1789, while negotiations with regard to the Russian peace terms were taking place, the grand vizir, Koja Yusuf, finally took the offensive and succeeded in giving the Ottomans their first notable success of the war. However, the death of the sultan on April 7 and the immediate accession of Selim III (1789–1807) to the throne soon disrupted the campaign. Selim inaugurated his regime by attempting to eliminate those opposed to the reform and modernization of the Ottoman state, which included Koja Yusuf. Although Selim initially deferred mounting such a purge while the conflict with Russia was still raging, he fired the grand vizir on June 7 and replaced him with Hasan Pasha, who ordered a number of military moves that soon resulted in disaster for the Turks.

Learning that the Russian and Austrian armies were planning to join forces to attack Bucharest and seize Wallachia, Hasan Pasha sent a large Ottoman force to Fokhshani to prevent the enemy armies from converging. However, the Russians arrived earlier than anticipated and linked up with the Austrians before the Ottoman troops arrived. On the morning of July 30, 1789, the joint forces attacked the unsuspecting Turkish force and inflicted a costly defeat on it. Although the Russian-Austrian victory in the battle was of limited strategic significance, especially since the defeated Ottoman force was comprised mainly of reserve troops and auxiliaries, it did have a serious demoralizing effect on the main Turkish army, which began to disintegrate. This permitted the Russians to seize the initiative and launch an offensive that rapidly pushed through Moldavia into Wallachia, dislodging the Ottoman troops, which retreated in disorder. Regrouping his forces, Hasan Pasha mounted a counteroffensive through Wallachia and Moldavia in mid-September that attempted to break through to the Austrian base at Fokhshani. The Russians under Alexander Suvorov intercepted the Ottoman forces on September 21 at the Rimnik River, where the Turks were again defeated in what proved to be the decisive battle of the war.

The news of the battering of the Ottoman army on the Russian front helped trigger a virtual collapse of the Ottoman armies in Serbia and Bosnia as well, permitting the Austrians to capture Belgrade, the key to the Ottoman Danube defense line, on October 8, 1789, after a month-long siege. The only remaining major fortress between the advancing Austrian and Russian armies and Istanbul was at Nish, and the Austrians were sweeping through Serbia toward it. Further east, an Austrian army occupied Bucharest without resistance on November 9 as the Turkish garrison made a disorderly retreat to the south. The war was clearly turning into an unmitigated disaster for the Ottomans, who now had to face the prospect of a joint Russian-Austrian offensive in the coming spring that would attempt to break through their lines and capture Istanbul.

By the winter of 1789–1790, however, the overall political situation in Europe had undergone some drastic changes that forestalled a joint Austro-Russian drive in the direction of the Ottoman capital. Nationalist uprisings against the Hapsburgs had broken out in Hungary and the Netherlands, and the new Austrian emperor, Leopold II (who ascended the throne upon the death of Joseph on February 20, 1790), had to give these challenges his principal attention. To further complicate Austria's problems, Prussia now threatened to intervene on behalf of Turkey. In return for Ottoman support of its claims to the territories of Danzig and Thorn, as well as its demand that Austria return Galicia to Poland, Prussia proposed a treaty with the Porte that involved a commitment to go to war with Austria, thereby relieving the military pressure on Turkey. The formal Prusso-Ottoman alliance was signed on January 31, 1790, although the Prussians delayed ratification of the treaty for several months while they sought a negotiated end to the conflict. At the same time, Russia was diverted by another Swedish invasion of Finland, which was a matter of higher priority for Catherine than the campaign against the Ottomans far to the south. Finally, the radicalism introduced by the French Revolution drove the Triple Alliance to advocate the rapid termination of the war between the Ottoman Empire and Russia and Austria so that the latter conservative states might be free to join in preventing the spread of revolution in Europe.

Notwithstanding the reversals experienced on the battlefield, Selim sensed that the political advantage had shifted from the preoccupied European powers to Turkey, and he insisted on the return of all conquered Ottoman territory as the price of the peace that the European states now wanted so urgently.

Prussia, however, ignored Selim's demands and undertook to negotiate on the sultan's behalf, without his authority or consent. Prussian diplomacy was successful, and Austria was induced to desert the Russians and to agree to a separate peace with Turkey. Under the Prusso-Austrian Convention of Reichenbach (July 25, 1790), Austria agreed to abandon all captured Ottoman territory in exchange for an end to the conflict. When Selim learned of the agreement on August 24, he was outraged, but subsequently agreed to go along with the Prussian initiative. A nine-month truce between Turkey and Austria went into effect on September 17, laying the groundwork for the formal peace talks that were to take place at Sistova.

Potemkin also had proffered peace feelers on behalf of Catherine in the spring of 1790. He offered to return Moldavia and Wallachia to the Ottomans, destroy the fort at Ochakov, and to neutralize the contested region between the Dniester and the Bug Rivers. The Russians also promised to desist from further intervention in Georgia and to respect whatever arrangements the Ottomans made with the local rulers in the Caucasus. But the sultan, who still expected help from Prussia and Sweden and therefore believed that he had the leverage to extract more favorable concessions, rejected the proposed Russian terms. As a result, the opportunity for peace was lost, and the war between Turkey and Russia continued.

The withdrawal of Austria from the alliance forced Russia to make significant revisions in the scope of its planned military operations. However, even at a reduced scale of action, the Russians were to prove to be more than a match for the increasingly demoralized Ottoman forces. In addition to the reverses the Ottoman army experienced on the battlefield, the Turkish navy also suffered one defeat after another. The Black Sea fleet was severely mauled by the Russian squadron operating out of Sevastopol in both July and September 1790. It was forced to withdraw to the Bosphorus, thereby ceding control of the entire Black Sea to the Russians. The Russians similarly attained effective control of the Danube, clearing the way for an invasion across its banks at any time they chose. Nonetheless, for reasons that are not entirely clear, Potemkin hesitated to proceed further. He finally launched an attack in mid-October that resulted in the seizure of the remaining principal forts along the Danube, but by that time the season for campaigning in the region was almost at an end and the Turks were given another temporary reprieve that lasted throughout the winter. But the Ottomans did not exploit the respite they were given to regroup and strengthen their forces in the field. As a result, when the war was resumed in the spring of 1791, new defeats were inflicted on the weakened Ottoman army, leaving the empire virtually defenseless. However, Catherine was unable to take full advantage of the situation because of renewed pressures from the Triple Alliance, which raised the threat of a general European war if she did not relent and accept a compromise solution, albeit with the sultan bearing the major burden of the concessions.

Although the sultan continued to procrastinate in the vain hope of getting some help from his European allies, the defeat of the Ottoman forces at Machin, which was taken by the Russians on July 9, seemed to be the proverbial straw that broke the camel's back. Selim could hold out no longer and on July 15 instructed his envoys at the Austrian peace talks at Sistova to prepare for similar negotiations with the Russians. The grand vizir was ordered to seek an immediate truce, and one was concluded at Galatz on July 31. The principal stipulation of the truce agreement was that the Treaty of Kuchuk Kaynarja would constitute the basis for peace negotiations, except that the Russian border was to be relocated further along the Dniester so that Ochakov and Bessarabia would come within its bounds. It was only a few days after this that the Treaty of Sistova (August 4, 1791) formally ended the war with Austria, essentially on the basis of the situation that had prevailed before the initiation of hostilities.

The final peace treaty with the Russians was concluded at Jassy on January 9, 1792. Under its terms, Selim was obliged to formally recognize the Russian annexation of the several Tatar khanates in the Black Sea region and that "the Dnestr shall serve forever as the boundary separating their two Empires."[7] In addition, he had to accept a new boundary in the northern Caucasus that was set at the Kuban River. As a practical matter, this was equivalent to acknowledging Russian suzerainty over Georgia. In return for these concessions, the Russians retroceded all the other Ottoman territory taken by them in the course of the war, including Bessarabia and Moldavia. Summarizing the principal outcomes of the conflict, Stanford J. Shaw wrote:

The Ottoman Empire had entered the war to regain the Crimea but instead had seen its boundaries driven back to the Dniester and the Koban. Russia was finally and definitively entrenched on the shores of the Black Sea, with Kherson and Sevastopol established as great naval bases and the territory provided for the emergence of Odessa as the new instrument of Russian naval supremacy. Russia now controlled the mouths of most of the major rivers emptying into the Black Sea. The Porte had been saved from even greater damage by the grace of the French Revolution and the dictates of European concert diplomacy than by its own efforts.[8]

NOTES

1. Albert Sorel, *The Eastern Question in the Eighteenth Century*, p. 28.
2. Karl A. Roider, *Austria's Eastern Question, 1700–1790*, p. 113.
3. Ibid., p. 120.
4. Isabel de Madariaga, *Russia: In the Age of Catherine the Great*, p. 228.
5. See J. C. Hurewitz, *The Middle East and North Africa in World Politics*, vol. 1, p. 94.
6. Ibid., p. 107.
7. Roider, *Austria's Eastern Question*, p. 182.
8. Stanford J. Shaw, *Between Old and New: The Ottoman Empire under Sultan Selim III, 1789–1807*, pp. 67–68.

8

Developments in the Ottoman and Persian Spheres

The Russo-Ottoman war had major ramifications for the future internal cohesiveness of the Ottoman Empire. Abd al-Hamid I (1774–1789), who ascended the throne at this point, was confronted by an effective loss of centralized imperial authority. The power of the provincial governors had increased significantly, and they began to assert their relative independence from Istanbul. During the recent war, the central government had become heavily dependent on their support and assistance, and the provincial governors exploited this circumstance to further develop and enhance their own regional armies and governmental administrations, as well as their treasuries. While they were still willing to acknowledge the sultan's suzerainty, they increasingly became less inclined to accept his sovereignty over the territories that were actually under their control. In other words, in addition to the external threats it faced, the empire also was being threatened by disintegration from within, and not only from local indigenous leaders seeking autonomy but also from the Ottoman provincial officials themselves.

Although the nominal ruler of Egypt was a viceroy appointed by the sultan, since 1681 real power in the country rested with the Mamluks who filled most of the administrative and military positions. The leader of the dominant Mamluk faction in Cairo became the unofficial *sheikh al-balad* (chief of the city), the real ruler of the country for all practical purposes. However, the continuing internal power struggle among the Mamluk chiefs kept Egypt in an almost perennial state of political chaos. Then, in the late summer of 1768, one of the Mamluk chiefs, Ali Bey al-Kabir (1760–1773), attained supremacy over the other beys (governors of minor provinces) and began to act as if he were the independent sovereign of

Egypt. When the Ottoman viceroy attempted to have him overthrown in November 1768, Ali Bey deposed the viceroy and assumed the position himself, taking all political power in Egypt into his hands. Nonetheless, he was reluctant to make an open breach with Istanbul and continued to acknowledge the sultan's nominal suzerainty, especially since his own legitimacy as ruler of Egypt was tainted.

Preoccupied with the war with Russia, the sultan could pay little attention to provincial affairs. When a dynastic struggle broke out in 1770 among members of the Hashemite family, the traditional rulers of Mecca, over control of the holy city, Abd al-Hamid requested that Ali Bey undertake to resolve the dispute. As a practical matter, there was nothing unusual about this, since the viceroy of Egypt normally handled Meccan affairs. Ali Bey welcomed the opportunity to enhance his legitimacy by intervening on behalf of the sultan and marched into the Hejaz with a large expeditionary force. He not only resolved the dynastic dispute, but also removed the Ottoman governor of Jeddah and installed a Mamluk bey in his place. Ali Bey thus effectively succeeded in making both Egypt and the Hejaz independent from Ottoman authority. He also added to his personal prestige by being in control of the holy cities of Islam.

Inspired by his successes, Ali Bey then focused his sights on Syria, a major territorial component of the pre-Ottoman Mamluk Empire. Control of Syria was deemed necessary for the security of both Egypt and the Hejaz, since it would serve as a buffer between them and the Turkish heartland. The political situation in the region appeared particularly favorable for Ali Bey's pursuit of his ambitions. The authority of the Ottoman governor of Damascus, Uthman Pasha, was being undermined by the growing power and autonomy of Sheik Zahir al-Umar in northern Palestine, and the Porte was in no position to do anything about it. Ali Bey and Zahir soon formed an alliance to oust Uthman Pasha from Syria. Moreover, after the Russian fleet virtually destroyed the Turkish navy in July 1770, it remained on station in the eastern Mediterranean, eager to assist any insurgents who might help further weaken the Ottomans. Ali Bey proposed to take advantage of their offer of material assistance and established a relationship with the Russians.

Confident of his ability to seize Syria, given that the Ottoman armies were fully committed to a major conflict in Europe, Ali Bey took action in the summer of 1771. He dispatched an expeditionary force that, together with the irregulars provided by Zahir, seized control of all of Palestine, defeated Uthman Pasha's provincial army, and captured Damascus. Then, just when it appeared that Syria was his for the taking, the enterprise was undermined from within. Ali Bey's principal lieutenant Abul-Dhahab had developed ambitions of his own and, without warning, decided to abandon the Syrian campaign and convinced the Mamluk commanders to follow his lead. The Mamluk chiefs returned to Egypt in the fall of 1771 to contest Ali Bey's authority. With the support of the Mamluk factions previously suppressed by Ali Bey, Abul-Dhahab defeated his forces in April 1772 and replaced him as ruler of Egypt, professing loyalty to the sultan.

With the end of the Russo-Ottoman war in 1774, the Porte was free once more to direct its attention to developments in the provinces. Faced with the need to deal with newly autonomous rulers in both Egypt and Palestine, it decided to play one against the other. It called upon Abul-Dhahab to invade Palestine to suppress Zahir in 1775. At the same time, the Porte had no intention of allowing Palestine to fall under the control of the Egyptian Mamluks and sent an expedition under Hasan Pasha to occupy Acre and the surrounding region. Open conflict between the Ottomans and the Egyptian Mamluks was avoided only by the sudden death of Abul-Dhahab, upon which the Mamluk army abandoned the campaign and returned to Egypt. At the same time, the Ottomans contrived to have Zahir betrayed, and with his death that same year the autonomous state he created in northern Palestine came to an end. Upon Zahir's downfall, Acre was turned over to the Ottoman governor of Sidon, Ahmed Pasha al-Jazzar, who soon set about the task of transforming the region into his personal domain.

The formidable one-time Ottoman governor of Baghdad, Ahmed Pasha (1724–1747), who ruled the province with virtual autonomy, had recruited a personal force of mamluks, mostly from Georgia, which enabled him to free himself from dependence on the Ottoman garrison which was loyal to the sultan. As was the case in Egypt, in Iraq too the province soon came under effective domination by the Mamluks, who constituted both the administrative and military elite. In 1764 Baghdad came under the control of the Mamluk faction of Umar Pasha whose seizure of power was ultimately formally ratified by the Porte. It was during Umar Pasha's autonomous rule of the province that a small but consequential conflict broke out with Persia, ruled at the time by Karim Khan Zand. He not only led raids into eastern Anatolia but also captured Basra in April 1776, which the Persians held until Karim Khan's death in 1779. The loss of Basra had serious effects on the Persian Gulf trade route and generated heavy pressure by the Porte to remove Umar Pasha, who was in fact overthrown shortly thereafter.

In the Arabian peninsula, the Ottomans had established their control primarily along the Red Sea coast, which included the Hejaz along with its holy cities, and in the district of Hasa along the Persian Gulf coast. The remainder of the peninsula was effectively outside the Ottoman sphere of influence. Accordingly, it was from the emirs of the remote plateau of Nejd in central Arabia that a significant challenge to the Ottoman position in the peninsula originated. It was in Nejd that Wahhabism, the rigorously conservative religious movement founded by Muhammad ibn Abd al-Wahhab in 1691, gained the support of the emir of Dariyya, Muhammad ibn Saud (1746–1765). The latter founded a religiously militant Wahhabi state, which sought to extend its dominance to the entire peninsula from its position astride the two main routes that traversed the interior of Arabia and converged in Nejd. These were the southeastern route from Syria to Jabal Shammar and the important east-west pilgrimage route from the Persian Gulf to the Hejaz. By 1773 Saudi-ruled territory extended as far as Riyadh, which fell to the Wahhabis after a struggle that began twenty-seven years earlier. This set the stage for further Saudi expansion at the expense of the Ottoman Empire and posed a direct challenge to the legitimacy of the sultan's position as preeminent leader of Sunnite Islam, a claim disputed by the Wahhabis.

Because of the widespread character of the challenges to the central government of the empire, the Ottomans were ill equipped to do much about them. They resorted to bribery on a grand scale in an attempt to buy the loyalty of the provincial notables, but it was an approach that met with only limited success. They fared no better with the dispatch of expeditionary forces sent to restore military control of the provinces; there was a tendency by the troops to defect to the provincial notables who paid them more and offered them better living conditions than the sultan. Also, because of the fact that the provinces were the source of much of the wealth of the empire, the increasing drop in the amount of tax revenues remitted to Istanbul had serious impact on the central Ottoman treasury. This caused a further decline in the effective power and influence of the sultan's regime.

The era of Catherine the Great proved to be a blessing in disguise for Persia. Since the Ottomans were kept preoccupied by the Russians for most of the period with a struggle for the security of their European frontiers, the Porte could pay but scant attention to developments on the empire's eastern flank in Asia. Following the death of Nadir Shah in 1747, the Persian state began to disintegrate into autonomous provincial components which were seized by various military chiefs. In the east, Khorasan and Sistan came under the control of the new independent state that had emerged in Afghanistan. Western Persia underwent a complex series of power struggles, but ultimately came under the domination of the Zands, whose leader Karim Khan ruled as regent in Shiraz for the next three decades. With his death in 1779, western Persia entered another period of political instability and internecine strife as a struggle over the succession broke out among the Zands. Ali Murad (1779–1785) emerged victorious and seized the throne in Isfahan, while his rival Sadiq (1779–1781) established his independent reign in Shiraz.

The internecine struggle among the Zands also provided an opportunity for the Qajars, a tribal clan of Mongol origin that dominated Astarabad, to reassert their claims to power and challenge the Zands for supremacy in Persia. Under Agha Muhammad (1779–1797) the Qajars waged an increasingly successful struggle against the ruling Zands, conquering Mazandaran in 1780, taking Gilan in 1782, and forcing them to abandon

Isfahan during the reign of Ali Murad's successor Jafar (1785–1789). In 1786 Agha Muhammad relocated the Qajar capital to Tehran and launched a campaign for the conquest of southern Persia. The Zand fortunes took a brief turn for the better under their last ruler, Lutf Ali (1789–1794), who was an extremely able general. Nonetheless, he too ultimately succumbed to the unrelenting Qajar onslaught and was killed during the conquest of Kirman in 1794. All of western Persia was now under Qajar control.

It seems that Agha Muhammad nursed the ambition to restore the Persian Empire to what it had been under the Safavids, and he initiated a campaign to conquer Georgia and Armenia in 1795. With an army of some sixty thousand cavalry and infantry, he launched simultaneous assaults from Tehran in three directions; one column marched on Erivan, another toward Qarabagh, and the third against Shirvan and Daghestan. From his camp in the region of Ganja, Agha Muhammad sent a message to the governor of Georgia, Erakli Khan, that stated in essence:

Shah Esmail Safavi ruled over the province of Georgia. When in the days of the deceased king [his own father Muhammad Hasan Khan] we were engaged in conquering the provinces of Persia, we did not proceed to this region. As most of the provinces of Persia have come into our possession now, you must, according to ancient law, consider Georgia part of the empire and appear before our majesty. You have to confirm your obedience; then you may remain in the possession of your governorship. If you do not do this, you will be treated as the others.[1]

This ultimatum placed Erakli Khan in an unenviable position since the king of Kartlia and Kahetia (eastern Georgia) had earlier voluntarily accepted a Russian offer of protection against the Persians. This was memorialized in the Treaty of Georgiyevsk (July 24, 1783), under which the king acknowledged Russian suzerainty in return for a guarantee of Georgia's independence and territorial integrity. When Agha Muhammad was informed that the governor of Georgia was obligated by treaty to acknowledge only the suzerainty of the empress Catherine, he marched on Tiflis and quickly captured the capital of the province. He assumed that the Russian guarantee would prove to be valueless.

Having succeeded in conquering Qarabagh, Shirvan, and Georgia, the new shah undertook the reconquest of Khorasan from the Afghans and the reunification of eastern and western Persia under Qajar rule in 1796. Agha Muhammad entered Mashad on May 14, 1796, as Nadir Mirza, who had succeeded the blind Shah Rukh to the throne of the province, fled to Herat for safety. The shah was about to launch a campaign to take Balkh and Bukhara when he received word from his emirs in Azerbaijan that the Russians had intervened in Georgia.

Empress Catherine of Russia is said to have become very angry and to have sworn vengeance when she heard of the Persian invasion of Georgia, the capture of Tiflis, the slaughter of large numbers of Georgians, and the plundering of the country. After all, the Georgians had quite legitimately considered themselves to be living under the protection of the Russian Empire, and the tsarist government's credibility was at stake. The Russian empress is said to have ordered forty thousand infantry, twenty-two thousand cavalry, and one hundred cannon under the command of Qizil Ayagh [Valerian Zubov] to invade Persia.[2]

The Russian intervention, however, was motivated by concerns more far-reaching than a mere desire by Catherine to avenge the slaughter of the Georgians. Aside from long-standing commercial interests in Persia, the strategic position of the country as the gateway from Europe to India and eastern Asia gave it new significance within the context of the empress's imperial ambitions. Catherine explained her perspective to Zubov when she sent him on his mission to attempt to establish Russian hegemony over northern Persia:

The establishment of peace and order in Persia will open to us rich markets not only along the shores of the Caspian Sea but within the borders of the Persian provinces. By means of the latter it would be easily possible to open the routes to India and, attracting this very rich commerce toward us by much shorter routes than those which all the European nations follow, going around the Cape of Good Hope, it will be possible to turn to our benefit all the advantages being obtained by the Europeans.[3]

In response to the Russian incursion into his northwestern territories, Agha Muhammad promptly returned to Tehran from the east to prepare for a campaign to retake the region. However, a few days after the shah left the capital to begin the reconquest of Georgia in the spring of 1797, he received word of the death of Catherine on November 17, 1796, six months earlier, and the subsequent withdrawal of Zubov's army by Tsar Paul. Agha Muhammad soon met his own death by assassination on June 17, 1797, and was succeeded by his son Fath Ali Shah (1797–1834). Although the Russian withdrawal ended the immediate threat of full-scale war with Persia, it was not to be long before the resumption of Russian advances into the Caucasus drove the Persians out of most of the region permanently.

NOTES

1. Hasan-e Fasa'i, *History of Persia under Qajar Rule*, p. 66.
2. Ibid., p. 71.
3. Muriel Atkin, *Russia and Iran, 1780–1828*, p. 32.

9

Napoleon Enters the Middle East

The French Revolution and its aftermath in the Napoleonic era, which had such great impact on the subsequent history of Europe and the Western world, also set in motion developments which were to have highly significant geopolitical consequences in the Middle East. Indeed, the Napoleonic era may be seen as introducing a fundamental change in the history of the region. While it had been subjected to penetration by extraregional powers since ancient times, as a rule such intrusions were aimed at achieving gains, sometimes political but more often economic, within the region itself. However, as a consequence of Napoleon's imperial ambitions, for the first time the Middle East took on a major geopolitical significance that was essentially unrelated to anything that was to be found within the region. It now assumed a new global and primarily political importance because of its geostrategic position as the bridge between Europe and India and points farther east.

The Treaty of Jassy introduced a period of relative relief from external conflict for the Ottoman Empire that was to last for six years. Then, in 1797, as a result of political and military developments in Europe, Austria was forced to sign a peace treaty with France at Campo Formio (October 17, 1797). Under its terms, Austria was obligated to recognize the French conquests in Western Europe in exchange for certain territorial accommodations in the east. In particular, the venerable Republic of Venice ceased to exist, and its territories were divided between France and Austria. The latter obtained the Istrian Peninsula and Dalmatia on the Adriatic coast, while France took over several ports in Albania and northern Epirus as well as the Ionian Islands. Acquisition of these Balkan territories made France an immediate neighbor of the Ottomans for the first time, while control of the islands put France in a position to use them as bases from which to dominate the littoral of the entire eastern Mediterranean. Possession of the islands of Corfu and Zante, Napoleon told the French foreign minister, Charles Maurice de Talleyrand, would "make us masters both of the Adriatic and of the Levant. It is useless to try to maintain the Turkish Empire; we shall see its downfall in our lifetime. The occupation of the Ionian Isles will put us in a position to support it or to secure a share of it for ourselves."[1]

Although Napoleon disclaimed any territorial ambitions within the Ottoman Empire, Sultan Selim III (1789–1807) was forced to reconsider the traditional relations he maintained with the European powers. It was France, the Porte's longstanding ally, that now posed the most significant threat to the empire, whereas Russia, the longstanding enemy, now appeared far less intimidating, particularly after the death of Catherine and the succession of her seemingly less expansionist-minded son Paul. Indeed, Paul seemed anxious for a rapprochement with the sultan to offset France's expanding power and influence in the east. He was particularly anxious to gain the right of transit for Russian warships through the Turkish Straits to counter the French penetration of the Adriatic and the eastern Mediterranean. The primary Russian concern was that the French would use the Ionian Islands as forward bases for an invasion of the Balkans, and Russian strategists therefore gave high priority to the task of dislodging them from those key positions.

The threat from France to the security and territorial integrity of the Ottoman Empire derived primarily from its ongoing struggle for preeminence with Britain, which began to take on global dimensions. Growing British naval supremacy, and especially its control of the Cape Route around Africa to India and the Far East, effectively denied the French reliable access to the rich trade of those regions. Talleyrand and Napoleon hoped to strike at the British by interdicting the lines of communication between Britain and the sources of its wealth in Asia. Napoleon proposed to do this by opening a new sea route to India that would be under exclusive French control, and Egypt was the key to achieving that goal. As he put it to the French Directory on August 16, 1797: "Really to ruin England we must make ourselves masters of Egypt."[2] Thus, in the Directory's decree of April 12, 1798 (which Napoleon drafted), he was instructed to "have the Isthmus of Suez cut and shall take all necessary measures to insure to the French Republic the free and exclusive possession of the Red Sea."[3]

The concept was both bold and brilliant. A French-controlled sea route from the Mediterranean to the Red Sea and the Indian Ocean would make the British-controlled Cape Route obsolete and shift the bulk of the Oriental trade into French hands, with devastating effects on Britain's economy. However, it would take some time to carry out such a complex scheme. In the meantime, it was necessary to take more immediate steps to attack the British position in Asia. Accordingly, it was proposed that Talleyrand go to

Istanbul to convince the Porte that the sole purpose of Napoleon's forthcoming invasion of Egypt was to restore the sultan's authority over the un-
ruly Mamluks. The intervention would ensure the integrity of the Ottoman
Empire, something that France considered vital to its own national interest.
Then, with the sultan's cooperation, the French army would be able to
march directly across the Middle East to attack British India, or to proceed
to the Persian Gulf from where they would be transported by French ships
the rest of the way to their ultimate destination. Talleyrand also proposed
that as many as fifteen thousand troops could be embarked for India from
Suez. The Directory was aware that the scheme might prove to be too
far-reaching, but was willing to risk a small army of some thirty-five thousand men on the chance that Napoleon might produce yet another victory
against all odds.

As it actually turned out, the Porte was kept completely in the dark
about Napoleon's plans. When it was learned in Istanbul that a French expedition had taken Malta on June 9, 1798, and was proceeding eastward, it
was assumed that the probable objective was the Morea, or perhaps either
Crete or Cyprus. The Porte advised the French government in late July that
any move by its fleet against Ottoman territory would result in the immediate outbreak of war. Talleyrand assured the Ottomans that French operations in the Mediterranean were intended merely to eliminate the pirates
operating in the vicinity of Malta. He expressed the hope that the two states
might cooperate in containing Russian expansion in the Black Sea and
Adriatic regions, which constituted a threat to the interests of both states.
Talleyrand's duplicity became clear when the Porte learned that, at the
same time he was offering it assurances about France's benign intentions in
the region, a French expeditionary force had already reached Egypt, landing at Marabout, near Alexandria, on July 1, 1798.

The Mamluks did not oppose the French landings, perhaps expecting to
make short work of the invaders once they were ashore on open ground
where the Mamluk cavalry would cut them to pieces. As soon as he established a beachhead, Napoleon quickly dispatched a force of some five thousand men to seize Alexandria, which it entered without opposition. When
the Mamluks under Murad Bey, who ruled Egypt with Ibrahim Bey, finally
challenged the invading force at Rahmaniya on July 13, they discovered to
their dismay that they were woefully ill equipped to confront a modern European army. Their cavalry, the principal component of their army, was no
match for the French cannon and well disciplined infantry. It was repeatedly decimated as it attempted to charge the French positions. The French
proceeded to march toward Cairo, encountering the Mamluks again at
Imbabeh, northwest of the Egyptian capital near Giza. The famed Battle of
the Pyramids that took place there on July 21 was a far bloodier affair than
the earlier engagement. The Mamluks lost some two thousand cavalry in
addition to several thousand auxiliary troops, while French casualties

amounted to about a total of three hundred men. Cairo was taken four days later without further struggle.

Nonetheless, Napoleon failed to totally eliminate the Mamluks as a viable fighting force. Murad Bey and his followers retreated up the Nile to refuge in Upper Egypt, where they reconstituted themselves as a guerrilla army, working in cooperation with the major Bedouin tribes of the region. Although Napoleon dispatched several expeditions up the Nile, some reaching as far south as Aswan, he was unable to wrest control of Upper Egypt. At the same time, Ibrahim Bey and the troops loyal to him escaped Napoleon's grasp by withdrawing to Syria, where they joined forces with those of the Ottoman governor and awaited further developments.

Napoleon's self-satisfaction at having conquered Lower Egypt at minimal cost was to be short-lived. Only a few days after entering Cairo, he learned that a British flotilla under Admiral Horatio Nelson had destroyed the French fleet on August 1 at Aboukir Bay in the mouth of the Nile. Interestingly, notwithstanding the threat conveyed to Talleyrand regarding an immediate resort to war if French troops entered Ottoman territory, the sultan did not declare war until September 2, some six weeks after he learned of the attack on Egypt. It was clear that there was great reluctance by some at the Porte to take such a step since it necessarily meant aligning Turkey with Russia, a disturbing prospect at best. Accordingly, the pro-French peace party in the capital succeeded in convincing the sultan to postpone the proclamation of war while they attempted to settle the confrontation with France peacefully. However, the sultan was effectively forced to enter the war by the Russians when they moved their fleet from Sevastopol to Istanbul and pressed the Porte for permission to transit the Straits in order to attack the French. He could procrastinate no longer. On the one hand, Turkey ran the risk of a Russian attack if he refused to cooperate; on the other hand the French would have considered it a hostile act if the Porte acceded to the Russian demand. The sultan apparently concluded that the most prudent course of action, given the circumstances at the time, was to declare war on France. He could then negotiate the question of the passage of the Russian fleet through the Straits from the vantage point of being a *de facto* ally of the tsar.

The Ottoman declaration of war triggered a rebellion in Cairo against the French on October 21 that caught them by surprise. Although the uprising was quickly suppressed, it raised the question as to how secure the French position in Egypt really was. Uncertainty about this, as well as the extent to which Murad Bey might constitute a threat to the French rear from his sanctuary in Upper Egypt, caused a delay of more than a half year in Napoleon's timetable for the conquest of Syria, which was strategically necessary to protect the French position in Egypt.

The French invasion of Egypt served to put a damper, at least for the moment, on the longstanding mutual Russian-Ottoman hostility. It also caused the British, primarily because of their concerns for the security of India, to become interested in preserving the territorial integrity of the Ottoman Empire as a buffer zone between India and Europe. As a result of the temporary convergence of the interests of the three powers, a tripartite alliance was formed between Britain, Russia, and the Ottoman empire in the fall of 1798, which was subsequently formalized by treaties signed at Istanbul on January 3 and 5, 1799.

Unknown to Napoleon at the time, the British had also begun to take steps to thwart his goal of raising a serious challenge to their essentially undisputed domination of the Indian Ocean routes. Always concerned about assuring undisputed control of access to their far-flung Asian enterprises, the British specifically sought to limit the potential of any significant French presence in the region. On October 12, 1798, the East India Company entered into an agreement with the sultan of Muscat (Oman), Sultan ibn Ahmed (1792–1806), that precluded the French from establishing a presence in any of his territories. Moreover, the Omani sultan agreed to a security clause in the treaty that stipulated, "in case of hostilities ensuing here between the French and English ships, the force of this State by land and by sea, and my people, shall take part in hostility with the English."[4]

Napoleon subsequently wrote a letter to the sultan in January 1799, stating: "I am writing this letter to you to inform you of what you have without doubt already learned, the arrival of the French army in Egypt. As you have at all times been our friend, you may be convinced of the desire I have of protecting all the ships of your nation, and that you undertake to send them to Suez, where they will find protection for their commerce." The letter, however, was intercepted by the British agent at Mocha and was forwarded to Bombay. The British resident at Bushire, under instructions from the governor general of India, promptly advised the ruler of Oman "to look upon the friendship and esteem of the English Government as the soul by which Muscat breathes and has its being" and to flee from "the continuation of the French fraternity as you would the plague."[5]

Shortly after joining the Anglo-Russian alliance, the Porte allowed warships of the Russian Black Sea fleet to pass through the Turkish Straits into the Mediterranean for the first time, where they joined forces with the Ottoman navy to campaign against the French in the Aegean and the Adriatic. Since Talleyrand now gave up any further hope of keeping Turkey from becoming an active belligerent along with Britain and Russia, he proposed to facilitate the overthrow of the sultan by an invasion of the Morea and Macedonia. There he expected to enlist the support of the local rulers who were straining at the bit to become completely independent of Istanbul. However, the Ottomans, who moved first to reassert their control in the more vulnerable provinces of the empire, preempted these plans.

By November 1798, the French were driven out of the Ionian Islands by the combined efforts of the Turks and Russians, except for Corfu, where they held out until March 3, 1799. The islands were occupied by the Russians, who were intent on keeping them as a foothold in the Mediterranean and who augmented their garrisons there with some eight thousand additional troops in the fall of 1799. The need to provision and replenish the Russian garrisons on the islands was the pretext for the unrestricted movement of Russian naval vessels back and forth through the Straits. The Porte was adamantly opposed to this ploy. It insisted on stipulating in the Russian-Ottoman treaty of 1799 that the permitted movement of Russian ships through the Straits during the conflict with the French "may not establish the right or serve as a pretext for claiming future free passage through the Canal."[6]

It was already quite evident that the question of Russian rights of transit through the Straits would remain a fundamentally intractable legal and political problem for the foreseeable future, and it remains a matter of contention between Russia and Turkey to this very day. The issue of the status of the Ionian Islands was resolved by the Russian-Ottoman Convention of March 21, 1800, under which they were transformed into the autonomous Republic of the Seven United Islands (Septinsular Republic), under Ottoman suzerainty and a Russian guarantee of its territorial integrity. Under this rather unrealistic arrangement, the islands became simultaneously an Ottoman vassal and a Russian protectorate. In fact, however, the islands remained under Russian military occupation until 1807, when they were surrendered back to Napoleon.

It was not until February 10, 1799, that Napoleon finally began his planned conquest of Syria by marching into Palestine with some thirteen thousand men. El-Arish surrendered on February 20 and Jaffa was taken on March 7. From there Napoleon moved on Acre, which he placed under siege on March 19. The siege dragged on for two months, during which the French forces were weakened by an epidemic that had broken out in the area. Then, when Napoleon learned that a British naval squadron under Sir Sidney Smith was ferrying an Ottoman army to Egypt, he broke off the siege on May 20 and returned to Egypt with what was left of his expeditionary force. Although outnumbered three to one, the French subsequently inflicted a serious defeat on the Turkish forces under Mustafa Pasha at Aboukir in a battle that lasted from July 25 to August 2, 1799.

At that time, internal French political considerations led Napoleon to put an end to his personal involvement in the Middle Eastern campaign and return to France. He had already decided to terminate the overall enterprise before he departed, and he left the task of evacuating the French forces to General Kleber, who negotiated an agreement in this regard with the Ottoman grand vizir at El-Arish on January 24, 1800. However, since the French fleet had been destroyed, the implementation of the El-Arish agreement depended on the use of British ships to evacuate the troops to France, thereby making the agreement effectively contingent on British approval of its terms. However, the British rejected the agreement because they wanted to be able to take the full credit for forcing the French out of Egypt. It was their view that this would put them in a position later to make substantial demands upon the sultan as compensation for their efforts on his behalf. As a result of this British policy, the conflict in Egypt continued unnecessarily for another year and a half.

Unable to evacuate the country, the French fought on, inflicting another defeat on the Ottoman army at Heliopolis on March 20, 1800. They also managed to reach an agreement with the Mamluk leader Murad Bey that finally gave them control of Upper Egypt. Notwithstanding these gains, it was clear that the French were fighting a hopeless war in Egypt. Without the ability to replenish their dwindling forces, it was only a matter of time before they would be forced to capitulate. The beginning of the end came in March 1801, when a British expeditionary force landed at Aboukir and linked up with an Ottoman army at Rosetta, while another British force from India landed on Egypt's Red Sea coast and made its way overland to the Nile. At the same time, another Ottoman army was marching to Egypt from Syria. The French, bottled up in Cairo and Alexandria, surrendered the former on June 18, 1801, and the latter on September 3. They were then evacuated in accordance with the terms originally negotiated a year and a half earlier at El-Arish. The Treaty of Amiens formally concluded peace between France and the Ottoman Empire on June 25, 1802.

With his Egyptian adventure at an end, in 1801 Napoleon agreed to join in a bold scheme proposed by Tsar Paul I of Russia for a joint attack on the British in India with some seventy thousand troops. Among other complaints, particularly his resentment over the British occupation of Malta (the tsar was grand master of the Knights of Malta), Paul considered British actions in the Middle East to be encroachments on the Russian sphere of influence. He therefore withdrew from the alliance with Britain in September 1800 and negotiated a rapprochement with Napoleon.

The joint Franco-Russian plan called for the Russians to reach the upper Indus valley by marching across Turkestan, Khiva, and Bukhara. At the same time, the French forces were to make their way down the Danube to the Black Sea, from where they were to be ferried to the Caucasus by Russian ships. They would then drive through Persia into Afghanistan, take Herat and Qandahar, and cross into India and link up with the Russian forces at the Indus. The first phase of the plan was only partially attempted when Paul instructed the Cossack *ataman* Orlov to lead an expedition of some twenty-two thousand men through the Turkoman steppe in February 1801. The venture proved a failure, however, primarily because of inadequate preparations, and with the death of Paul shortly thereafter (on March 24), the whole scheme unraveled. Napoleon nonetheless continued to view Persia as a potentially useful instrument of his subsequent anti-Russian as well as anti-British policies.

As the French consolidated their grip on Egypt in the period immediately after their invasion, the British also became worried about a possible unilateral French attempt at an invasion of India, possibly with Persian collusion. At the same time, they had reason to be concerned about the apparent designs on northern India of Zaman Shah (1793–1800), the king of Afghanistan. Accordingly, in October 1799, the British governor of India designated a special ambassador, John Malcolm, to negotiate an agreement with Tehran that would prevent both threats from materializing. It was clear that the Persians were at odds with the Afghans over the question of the control of Khorasan and that an Anglo-Persian alliance could be of significant value in assuring the security of western India.

Malcolm's mission was to prevent Zaman Shah from invading India by creating a counterthreat on his Persian frontier. In the event that Zaman Shah was not deterred by the Anglo-Persian alliance, Malcolm was to make it difficult for him to sustain operations on the Indian front by getting the Persians to open a second front on his western flank. Secondly, Malcolm was to get the Persians to agree to block any French advance toward India through their country. After a delay of more than a year, Malcolm finally arrived at Tehran and succeeded in getting Fath Ali Shah to agree to the British terms in a treaty that was signed on January 28, 1801. The treaty also stipulated that in the event that the French or Afghans initiated hostilities against Persia, Britain would intervene in the conflict.

However, by the time the treaty was concluded, the immediate Franco-Russian threat to India had dissipated. Coupled with the death of Zaman Shah the previous year, which reduced the Afghan threat as well, Britain lost interest in the Persian alliance, notwithstanding the fact that Persia was now engaged in a war with Russia, which was expanding in the Caucasus region at Persia's expense. It was simply no longer expedient for the British to be overly concerned with the territorial integrity of the Persian Empire. Had the British been aware at the time of the Franco-Russian plan for the invasion of India, their attitude toward Persia might well have been different. However, since nothing came of it, it had no practical effect on British policy, which was soon to be reinforced by the consideration that the first phase of the Napoleonic wars was brought to an end by the Anglo-French Treaty of Amiens (March 27, 1802). Subsequent French intrigue in the volatile Balkans, in Albania and the Morea, precipitated the beginnings of an Anglo-Russian rapprochement in 1804, and the British were not going to jeopardize their broader European interests because of any concerns about Persia.

In the meanwhile, Russia annexed eastern Georgia in 1801, and the new tsar, Alexander I (1801–1825), soon turned his attention to the conquest of western Georgia, which he saw as the strategic key to the control of all the northern provinces of Persia. The Russian drive into western Georgia, Armenia, and Azerbaijan at the beginning of 1804, and the quick capture of

Tiflis and Ganja, was a cause of great alarm in Tehran, where it was correctly perceived as a threat to the very existence of an independent Persia. When the Russians seized the sultanate of Shurgel, in the khanate of Erivan, Persia went to war, albeit with an army that was sorely in need of modernization. Hard pressed, and abandoned by the British, Fath Ali Shah sought help wherever he could find it, and France seemed like a natural choice for an ally. Persia and France had different but compatible interests. Napoleon was still anxious to establish a forward position from which to launch an eventual assault on India, and Persia needed French assistance if it was going to recapture Georgia from the Russians.

Earlier, in the period between 1802 and 1805, France had tried three times without success to conclude an alliance with Persia, but Britain had always blocked these efforts. Now, British influence in Persia had diminished significantly as a consequence of the Anglo-Russian rapprochement, and Napoleon tried once more to establish such an alliance in the summer of 1806. This time, he found much greater receptivity to the idea in Tehran. Given the demise of the tripartite alliance of Britain, Russia, and the Ottomans, and locked in a war with Russia, the outcome of which was still uncertain at the time, Napoleon proposed the formation of a new tripartite alliance made up of France, Turkey, and Persia against Russia and Britain. While negotiations with the Porte toward this end dragged on, the Turks being quite wary of Napoleon's purposes as a result of their recent experiences with him, he was successful in concluding a deal with the shah.

The Treaty of Finkenstein formalized the new Franco-Persian alliance on May 4, 1807. Under its terms, France recognized the legitimacy of Persia's claims to Georgia and committed itself to do everything in its power to compel Russia to surrender the territory. In return, Persia was committed to declare war on Britain and to grant France a right-of-way through Persia if and when Napoleon decided to attack India.

Napoleon dispatched a military mission under General Antoine Gardanne to Persia for the purpose of assisting in the reorganization and modernization of the Persian army, as well as to survey the terrain with a view to determining the best routes through the country for an invasion of India. Gardanne was also to do everything possible to arrange for coordination of Persian and Ottoman efforts against Russia in the Caucasus region. However, by the time that Gardanne arrived in Tehran in December 1807, Napoleon had already effectively betrayed his new ally Fath Ali Shah. By entering into the Treaty of Tilsit (July 7, 1807) with Russia, France abandoned Persia for all practical purposes, leaving it exposed and vulnerable to Russian expansionism in the north and to that of the British in the east. Indeed, in response to the Franco-Persian Treaty of Finkenstein, the British negotiated a mutual defense treaty (June 17, 1809) between British India and Shah Shuja al-Mulk (1803–1809) of Afghanistan that was directed against Persia and France. Under the treaty, Afghanistan was obligated to prevent an attack on India through its territory. However, by the time the agreement was signed by the governor-general of India, Persia had already denounced its alliance with France. Furthermore, since Shuja was overthrown shortly after concluding the agreement, the treaty proved to be worthless.

Notwithstanding the severance of the Franco-Persian alliance, Napoleon offered to mediate an end to Persia's war with Russia, which was going badly for the shah. Fortuitously, it happened to be in Russia's immediate interest to reach such an agreement. Tsar Alexander I (1801–1825) was anxious to be free to give his full attention to dealing with the Turks, to whose defeat the Russians assigned higher priority than to Persia. Indeed, the tsar sought to open negotiations with Persia on his own initiative, and an envoy was dispatched to inform the shah of Russia's interest in reaching an accommodation. But Fath Ali Shah refused to budge, insisting that he would not agree to peace with Russia until the tsar relinquished control of Georgia. He told the Russian envoy that "as long as one square inch of Persian soil remains in the possession of the Russian Empire, we shall be enemies."[7] To engender further enthusiasm for the protracted conflict on his Caucasian frontiers, in early 1809 the shah got the Shiite *ulema* to declare the struggle with Russia to be a *jihad* or holy war, making participation incumbent upon all faithful Muslims.

The Russo-Persian war dragged on inconclusively, and in the spring of 1810 the tsar once again sought to initiate negotiations to end the conflict. However, General Tormasov, who was assigned the task, proposed that the negotiations take place in one of the districts of Azerbaijan, the region whose ownership was the subject of the dispute between Russia and Persia. It is not certain whether this was simply a naive suggestion or whether it was intended to impede a negotiated resolution of the conflict. In either case, the proposal was viewed with deep suspicion by the shah, who refused to allow his prime minister, Mirza Shafi, to participate in the peace talks. Although preliminary discussions were held with lower ranked Persian officials, nothing came of the Russian peace initiative and the fighting went on until 1812. In that year, the Persian army was virtually destroyed at the Battle of Aslandoz, and the shah was forced to come to terms with the tsar. The provisions of the subsequent Treaty of Gulistan (October 12, 1813) were very unfavorable for Persia, which lost most of the territory over which the war had been fought. Russia, on the other hand, acquired sovereignty over the Caucasian provinces of Mingrelia, Qarabagh, Shirvan, Derbent, and Baku. In addition, Persia had to concede to Russia the exclusive right to maintain warships in the Caspian Sea, effectively transforming it into a Russian lake.

With the resumption of the war between France and Britain in 1803, Napoleon tried hard to drive a wedge between the Ottomans and the British, but failed to accomplish much in this regard. When the sultan, acting largely under British and Austrian influence, refused to accept Napoleon's self-proclamation as emperor of France two years later, Napoleon severed diplomatic relations (December 22, 1805) with the Porte. However, Napoleon's successive victories at Ulm on October 17, 1805, and at Austerlitz on December 2, followed by the Treaty of Pressburg on December 26, under which Austria ceded the territories of Istria and Dalmatia to Napoleonic Italy, forced the sultan to reevaluate his position. Selim became concerned that the alliance with Britain was no longer effectively serving Ottoman interests and that he needed to reach an accommodation with the French if the empire was to be kept intact. Accordingly, Selim reversed himself and acknowledged Napoleon as emperor of France in February 1806, thereby bringing about a prompt reestablishment of diplomatic relations between the two countries.

The Russians, however, had taken a dim view of the possible reassertion of French influence at the Porte. They concluded that the only way to forestall such from taking place was to take steps that would force the Porte to attach greater importance to maintaining good relations with its northern neighbor than with France. Accordingly, the Russians began covertly instigating and orchestrating increased instability in the Balkan region, raising anew the threat to Turkey's northern frontiers. The French, well aware of the Russian game, sought to offset it by offering the sultan tangible support from their position in Dalmatia for a planned Ottoman attack against the Serbs. The Russians countered this move by blockading the Dalmatian coast and rendering material assistance to the Serbs. Although Selim truly needed the French help, he nonetheless hesitated to enter into an alliance with Napoleon against the tsar. For one thing, he harbored a deeply pessimistic view of Napoleon's true intentions with regard to the Balkans. He also had little confidence that the French would make good on their commitments and actually render significant support to the Ottomans in the event of a full-scale war with Russia.

The British also sought to limit the rise of French influence at Istanbul and, having renewed the Anglo-Russian alliance in April 1805, lent their support to Russian demands with regard to freedom of navigation in the Turkish Straits. On September 28, 1806, both Britain and Russia insisted that Selim permit Russian warships to transit the Straits in order to attack French positions in the eastern Mediterranean region. To emphasize their determination to resolve this festering issue on their terms, the Russians stood poised to invade the sultan's Danubian Principalities if their demands were not met. The sultan, who saw a greater immediate threat from the Russians on his northern frontiers than from the French in Dalmatia, reluctantly acceded to these demands two weeks later.

But, when news of Napoleon's victory over the Prussians at Jena on October 14 reached Istanbul in mid-November, suggesting the serious prospect of a French victory against the Russians, Selim reversed his position and began to actively seek an alliance with Napoleon. At the same time, Russia began to pressure the British to honor their alliance by entering the war on its side. The British wanted to preserve the Ottoman Empire from dismemberment by Russia in order to maintain it as a buffer zone between Europe and India. They therefore sought to limit the potential damage to its interests by coercing the Porte into acceding to the Russian demands, thereby eliminating the justification for a Russian invasion.

The Russians, however, were determined to invade and seize control of Moldavia, Wallachia, and Bessarabia irrespective of what the sultan said or did, and without regard for Britain's efforts to bring about an accommodation between the tsar and the sultan. On November 24, 1806, a Russian army crossed into Bessarabia and moved down the Dniester, quickly occupying the province, while another force moved across the Pruth into Moldavia, taking Jassy by the end of the month. The Russians then issued a proclamation stating that they had intervened in the Principalities solely for the purpose of protecting the integrity of the Ottoman Empire from the French.

In the meantime, back in Istanbul, the British were still trying to get the Porte to agree to the Russian demands, unaware that the Turks had already decided to declare war on Britain. On February 19, 1807, a British fleet forced its way through the Dardanelles into the Sea of Marmara and anchored off Istanbul on the following day. The Porte was caught completely unprepared for such a confrontation and turned to the French for help. Following the advice of Napoleon's representative, Francois H. Sebastiani, Selim pretended to negotiate while mobilizing what forces he could for a direct confrontation with the British. When he was ready, on February 22, the sultan rejected the British proposals, terminated the negotiations, and requested an immediate formal alliance with France.

The unanticipated and rapid fortification of Istanbul by the Turks left the British fleet in a highly vulnerable position. If the Turks also managed to fortify the Dardanelles before the British fleet was able to pass through them, it could remain trapped in hostile Ottoman waters. The British decided to withdraw on March 1, running a gauntlet of Turkish shore batteries before exiting the Straits two days later after suffering heavy casualties and damage. Soon thereafter, the British were joined in the Aegean by a Russian fleet, and it was proposed that they launch a joint operation to break through the Turkish defenses at the Straits. The proposal was rejected, however, because the British did not really want to see the Russians in control of the Straits, which might also allow them to seize control of the eastern Mediterranean region as well. Without British help, the Russians were not in a position to attempt the assault alone and the plan was abandoned. They had to satisfy themselves with a blockade of the Dardanelles, hoping thereby to starve Istanbul and force the Porte to capitulate.

French machinations, Russian territorial ambitions, and British strategic policy all appeared to have worked in concert to draw the Ottomans into renewed conflict with Russia (1806–1812) and with Britain (1807–1809) although it seems quite likely that the war with Russia would have taken place in any case. However, Napoleon's defeat of the Russians at Friedland, in East Prussia on June 14, 1807, made the Ottoman alliance superfluous as he began peace negotiations with the tsar, who was ready to abandon his alliance with the British in order to prevent a further French advance toward Russia. The resulting Treaty of Tilsit (July 7, 1807) upset the entire pattern of regional alignments. It brought an end to both the Anglo-Russian and the Franco-Ottoman alliances as Napoleon committed himself to convincing the Porte to make peace on Russia's terms. It was stipulated that if he failed to achieve this, he agreed to join the war against the sultan and to divide the spoils of the Ottoman Empire with the tsar. In return, Alexander agreed to withdraw from the Balkans and return the Ionian Islands to France. It was a major diplomatic coup for France, achieved largely at Ottoman expense. Although the treaty did keep Russia out of the Straits and the Balkans, it also assured France a dominant position in the eastern Mediterranean, something the British found quite unacceptable.

Even though the sultan was furious at his betrayal by Napoleon, the Porte ultimately accepted the settlement with Russia that the French had proposed. This was because, notwithstanding its sacrifice of some fundamental Ottoman interests, the arrangement at least assured a Russian withdrawal from the Principalities as well as a cessation of assistance to the Serbs. With French mediation, an armistice between the Ottomans and Russia was signed on March 21, 1808. Under its terms, the Russians were to withdraw from Moldavia and Wallachia within a month, while the Ottomans would move their forces south of the Danube. However, while the Turks observed the agreement, the Russians did not. Apparently, the tsar had extracted an oral commitment from Napoleon that he would not interpose any objection to a continued Russian occupation of the Principalities, notwithstanding the armistice agreement. Faced by this blatant duplicity, the Porte broke off peace negotiations, and hostilities with Russia began once again.

The Treaty of Tilsit also opened the door for a rapprochement between Britain and the Porte that culminated in the Treaty of the Dardanelles (January 5, 1809). Under this agreement, Britain became the first European power to formally acknowledge the right of the Porte to close the Turkish Straits to foreign warships. It also provided, under a secret clause, that Britain would use its good offices to negotiate an advantageous and honorable peace between the sultan and the tsar. This would assure the continued territorial integrity of the Ottoman Empire in the not unlikely event that Britain made peace and reestablished friendly relations with Russia.

By the summer of 1811, it became increasingly evident to both Russia and the Porte that Napoleon was preparing for an invasion of Russia. Tsar Alexander therefore became anxious to reach a settlement with the sultan before the outbreak of the coming conflict. But Mahmud II (1808–1839) continued to insist upon the withdrawal of Russian forces from all Ottoman territories in the Balkans and the Caucasus as a prior condition for peace. While these negotiations were under way, Napoleon made a last desperate attempt to get Turkey to protect his right flank in his forthcoming attack on Russia. He not only promised to assure the return of the Principalities to Ottoman control, he also offered the return of the Crimea. For their part, the British threatened to fight their way through the Dardanelles and burn Istanbul if the sultan accepted Napoleon's offer.

As it turned out, Napoleon's proposal came too late. Mahmud had already come to terms with Alexander, an accommodation that was reflected in the Treaty of Bucharest (May 28, 1812). In accordance with its provisions, Russia returned all the Balkan territories except for Bessarabia and surrendered a good part of the Black Sea coast including the major fortress of Anapa. The Russo-Ottoman frontier in the west was established along the Pruth-Danube line as far as the Black Sea. In the Caucasus, the situation reverted to that which prevailed before the recent conflict broke out.

Notwithstanding the Treaty of Bucharest, it was clear that at best it could provide but a brief respite for the Ottoman Empire. The Napoleonic era had witnessed the emergence of the Middle East as a critical regional pawn in an increasingly globalized political and strategic environment, and there was no prospect in sight that this would change in the future, as indeed it has not. Russia was sure to continue nibbling away at the northern frontiers of the declining Ottoman Empire. The other major powers, especially Britain and France, would continue to extend their seemingly interminable competition for power from the European continent to the frontiers of the Ottoman heartland in Southwest Asia and North Africa.

NOTES

1. See John A. R. Marriott, *The Eastern Question: An Historical Study in European Diplomacy*, p. 166.

2. Ibid., p. 164.

3. See J. C. Hurewitz, ed., *The Middle East and North Africa in World Politics*, vol. 1, p. 116.

4. Ibid., p. 125.

5. Wendell Phillips, *Oman: A History*, p. 71.

6. Ibid., p. 129.

7. Hasan-e Fasa'i, *History of Persia under Qajar Rule*, p. 120.

10

The Era of
Muhammad Ali

The invasion of the Middle East by Napoleon in 1798 and its aftermath had several immensely significant consequences for the subsequent history of the region. One was that for the first time in its history the region became important not because of its wealth or the trade routes that passed through it, but because of its strategic position as the overland gateway to south and eastern Asia from Europe. A second major but unintended consequence was the emergence of the powerful figure of Muhammad Ali in Egypt.

Muhammad Ali, an ethnic Albanian from the small seaport of Kavala in eastern Macedonia, first appeared on the stage of history as second-in-command of some three hundred Albanian irregulars conscripted in his hometown to participate in the Anglo-Ottoman expedition against the French that landed in Egypt on March 8, 1801. He soon rose to command of his unit and so distinguished himself in battle that the Ottoman commander Mehmed Khusraw quickly elevated him to the rank of major. Before long he was promoted to the position of second-in-command of the entire Albanian contingent. A shrewd and ambitious man, Muhammad Ali took careful note of the brilliant political career that occasionally opened to a man of military genius such as Napoleon. He aspired to such a career for himself and found the opportunity to realize that ambition in the Egypt of his day.

The British forces in Egypt succeeded in their primary mission of forcing a French withdrawal from the country in 1801. However, a divergence of view developed between the British government in London and the British military command in Cairo with regard to how best to deal with the existing Egyptian ruling class, the Mamluks. The government was primarily interested in strengthening its political relationship with the Sublime Porte in Istanbul. The military, on the other hand, tended to support the cause of

Mamluk autonomy from the sultan. As a consequence of the failure to rec-
oncile these inconsistent British policies, a compromise arrangement was
negotiated with the Porte. In return for the withdrawal of British forces
from Egypt, among other things, the sultan agreed not to take any punitive
measures against the Mamluk beys and to grant them autonomy in the
province of Aswan.

When the British commander, Sir John Stuart, evacuated his forces from
the country in March 1803, he took the Mamluk leader Muhammad al-Alfi
with him to England to plead the Mamluk cause against direct control of
Egypt by the Porte. Stuart also left behind in Cairo an unofficial British
agent, Major E. Misset, who actively promoted a policy that was diametri-
cally opposed to that being pursued by Drummond, the British ambassador in Istanbul. Drummond had taken the not unreasonable position with
the Foreign Office that

it can never be consistent with our policy to leave the Beys in independent possession of Egypt . . . any connexion which we may desire to keep with Egypt may be
more effectively and easily maintained through the medium of the Porte. . . . While
Egypt continues to be an integral part of the Ottoman Empire its invasion by a foreign Power is less likely to happen than if it were subject to the Mamluks.[1]

At the same time, Misset was actively encouraging a revolt by the Mamluks
against the Turkish viceroy, Khusraw Pasha, whom the Porte had just installed in Cairo. The viceroy had received, reportedly, "the most positive
orders from the court to carry out a war of extermination against the beys,
to thrust aside ruthlessly any attempts to come to an understanding with
them."[2]

Fighting broke out several weeks after the British evacuation between
the viceroy's troops and the forces of the Mamluks, which had withdrawn
to Upper Egypt, where they established their base of operations. However,
the Albanian contingent, which had come to Egypt to fight the French and
not the Mamluks, remained in the country as a virtually independent force,
splitting away from the Turkish ethnics in the Ottoman army. In May 1803,
the Albanians mutinied because of the failure of the Ottoman viceroy to
meet their pay demands, and Khusraw Pasha soon fled from Cairo, leaving
the capital to the mutineers. He headed for Damietta, where he was captured by the Mamluk bey Uthman al-Bardisi. With Cairo, in a state of chaos,
the Albanian commander Tahir Pasha was appointed military governor to
deal with the situation. Tahir was assassinated shortly thereafter, his successor being none other than Muhammad Ali.

Muhammad Ali's first task as military governor was to restore order in
the country, which had lapsed into anarchy. At the same time, he was determined to prevent anyone else from exercising political leadership in
Egypt. He therefore joined forces with Uthman al-Bardisi in a concerted effort to prevent a new Ottoman viceroy-designate, Jazairli Ali Pasha, as well

as his rival, Alfi Bey, who had returned from his political mission in London, from assuming control in Cairo. Then, in March 1804, Muhammad Ali turned on Bardisi, demanding that he make good on the arrears in pay owed to the Albanian troops as the price of their continued support of the Mamluks. But, when Bardisi tried to raise the necessary funds by taxing the populace of Cairo, Muhammad Ali incited a revolt against the extortion that forced Bardisi and his men to flee from the capital. He then contrived to join forces with Khurshid Pasha, the Ottoman governor of Alexandria, who had been appointed viceroy of Egypt. However, once they succeeded in forcing the Mamluks, who were blockading Cairo, to withdraw to their stronghold in Upper Egypt, the alliance between Muhammad Ali and Khurshid Pasha collapsed. The Porte subsequently attempted to dislodge Muhammad Ali from Egypt by giving him the title of pasha and appointing him as governor of Jeddah in Arabia, but he refused to budge. Instead, he turned for support to the Muslim clergy, particularly to the highly respected *naqib al-Ashraf* (marshal of the notables) Umar Makram, who had been alienated by the extortionist practices of Khurshid and the general misbehavior of the Ottoman troops.

On May 12, 1805, Umar Makram and his colleagues in the *ulema* acted to safeguard the interests of the Muslim community by supporting the stronger contender for power and deposed Khurshid. They invested Muhammad Ali with the powers of the viceroy, while Khurshid shut himself up in the citadel in Cairo and sought to rally the Mamluks behind him. Faced by Muhammad Ali's *de facto* seizure of power in Egypt, the sultan sought to mitigate the blow to Ottoman prestige by confirming the ousting of Khurshid and formally appointing Muhammad Ali as viceroy of Egypt on June 29, 1805. Without hope of any further help from the sultan, Khurshid finally gave in on August 3 and evacuated the citadel. In the course of just a few years, Muhammad Ali had risen from obscure junior officer to viceroy of Egypt (1805–1849) although it was to take another five years before he fully consolidated his control of the country.

While these developments were taking place in Egypt, war had broken out again in Europe. This time, however, largely as a result of Russia's barely concealed hostility toward him, the sultan switched his support to Napoleon, evoking British concern about the possibility of another French invasion of Egypt. They had placed their reliance on Alfi and his Mamluk chieftains to prevent a French landing in the country. When it became evident that this was no longer feasible, given the ascendancy of Muhammad Ali and his onslaught against the Mamluks, the British landed a force of some five thousand troops under General Alexander M. Fraser at Alexandria in mid-March 1807.

The British sought to take advantage of Muhammad Ali's preoccupation with a campaign against the Mamluks in Upper Egypt and attempted to get Alfi's faction to join forces with them to overthrow the viceroy. But

Muhammad Ali managed to forestall this by making lavish promises of his own to the Mamluks if they would but assist him in getting rid of the British. The net result was that the Mamluks were effectively immobilized, making it possible for Muhammad Ali to direct his full attention to dealing with the British forces. He successfully blocked Fraser's two attempts to seize Rosetta, and drove the British, who suffered heavy casualties, back to Alexandria. Nonetheless, and in spite of his militarily advantageous position, Muhammad Ali was wary of continuing an armed confrontation with the British. Since the British navy controlled the Mediterranean, a siege of Alexandria was impractical, and there was a risk that Egypt might be subjected to a British blockade. Accordingly, he dismissed the idea of pursuing a military option and sought to achieve the desired British withdrawal from Egypt through negotiations.

Muhammad Ali knew that the British were engaged at the time in a struggle with Napoleon's forces in the Iberian Peninsula and were desperately short of grain to supply their armies. This need was one of the principal factors that led the British to throw their support behind the Mamluks; it was their expectation that the Mamluks would be able to make up the grain shortfall by shipments from Egypt. Muhammad Ali now proposed to supply the much needed grain, in addition to offering the British a preferential trade position in Egypt as well as a secure line of communications to India, in return for British support and recognition of his independence from the sultan.

The British agent Misset duly reported Muhammad Ali's offer to Secretary of State George Canning on June 13, 1807, with the observation that British support of his bid for power might well result in a break between him and the French, who still enjoyed his partiality toward them. Misset, however, was enraged at Muhammad Ali for the defeat of his strategy of promoting the Mamluks as British proteges. He therefore expressed his concern that Muhammad Ali's strength was essentially dependent on his Albanian mercenaries, who were too undisciplined a force to assure stability in the country. Accordingly, he considered it necessary "that both Muhammad Ali and the Albanians should be compelled to evacuate this country and that the Mamluk government should be re-established."[3] It was to be assumed that the Mamluks would then provide all that Muhammad Ali was prepared to offer, while ensuring a greater degree of stability in Egypt. Misset's ploy worked and Britain rejected Muhammad Ali's terms, although it offered to buy the grain it so sorely needed from him. The British subsequently tried once more, again unsuccessfully, to take Rosetta.

While these negotiations were taking place, the situation in Europe underwent a dramatic change as a result of the conclusion of the Treaty of Tilsit (June 14, 1807) between Napoleon and the tsar. The net result in the Middle East of this new arrangement, which effectively assured the Russians a free hand against Turkey, was to force the Porte to quickly mend its fences with Britain. Under these circumstances, there was no longer any purpose to the Fraser expedition in Egypt, and the British withdrew their forces in September 1807.

Muhammad Ali emerged from his confrontation with the British with significantly enhanced stature. With the overthrow of the reformist Sultan Selim III in Istanbul on May 29, 1807, followed by the brief reign of his successor, Mustafa IV (1807–1808), and the ensuing revolt of the Janissaries in November 1808, the Porte was much too preoccupied with internal Ottoman affairs to pay much attention to developments in Egypt, let alone to attempt to intervene there. As a consequence, Muhammad Ali now became the ruler of an effectively independent Egypt, a position he sought to make secure through the ruthless suppression of every potential competitor for power in the country. Seeing the Mamluks as such a potential threat to his unchallenged authority, he decided to eliminate them entirely as a political and military force in Egypt.

On March 1, 1811, Muhammad Ali invited the Mamluk grandees to the citadel in Cairo to attend the investiture of his son Ahmed Tussun Pasha as commander of an expedition to Arabia on behalf of the new Ottoman sultan, Mahmud II (1808–1839). As the unsuspecting Mamluk chiefs approached the citadel with their retainers, they were slaughtered en masse. Muhammad Ali then dispatched his eldest son, Ibrahim Pasha, to attack the remnants of the Mamluk forces in Upper Egypt. Thus, through the lavish use of treachery and brutality, Muhammad Ali succeeded in wiping out the Mamluks and making himself the undisputed master of Egypt.

However, Muhammad Ali's ambition was far from sated by achieving control of Egypt. The country was to be but an instrument of his larger imperialist aims. In early 1811, he attempted to gain some insight into how the British might react to his expansionist goals. As reported by a Captain Waldegrave, who had come to Alexandria to negotiate the use of its harbor by British vessels: "The Viceroy's secret wish is that the Porte may be annihilated and that he may declare his independence and proclaim his sovereignty from Damascus to the Yemen."[4] There is also some evidence that Muhammad Ali was similarly attempting to sound out the French with regard to his broader objectives, which were threefold. First, he wished to make Egypt effectively independent of the sultan. In the interim, he chose to maintain the fiction of being a vassal to the sultan rather than run the risk of completely alienating the Sublime Porte in the absence of an alliance with one of the major European powers, whom he wooed toward that end without success. Second, he wanted to establish his hegemony over neighboring Sudan and Arabia. Finally, he aspired to the conquest of Syria, and possibly the entire Ottoman Empire, although the latter was certainly not an immediate goal.

Muhammad Ali took a number of significant steps over the next several decades to transform Egypt into a powerful instrument of his imperial ambitions. From his first exposure to modern European armies he was deeply impressed by their general superiority to those of the East, and he became determined to modernize the Egyptian army and navy along European lines. To raise the necessary funds for this purpose, he took over control of the country's export-import trade and established a system of state monopolies. Under this scheme, the government bought local products at an artificially and arbitrarily set price and sold them abroad for a profit, reversing the procedure with regard to imports. In order to build a massive army, Egyptian peasants were recruited from the villages for the first time. To train his new army, he employed European officers, many of whom became readily available for such employment after the end of the Napoleonic wars. He engaged one French officer, Colonel Seves (Suleiman Pasha), to establish and direct an infantry training base at Aswan, and another, Colonel Varin, to head the cavalry school at Giza. A Spanish officer, Colonel Sequera, established an artillery school at Tura. An iron foundry, intended primarily to manufacture cannon and cannon balls, was established at Bulaq under the direction of a British engineer named Galloway.

He also took steps to develop the naval capability that would be essential if he wished to project power into the regions where the European navies held sway. At first, Muhammad Ali ordered his naval vessels constructed in foreign shipyards. But, after most of his fleet was demolished at Navarino in 1827 (discussed below), M. de Cerisy, a naval architect from Toulon, was employed to rebuild it, while its armament and the training of its sailors were provided by another Frenchman, M. Besson. Two separate fleets were constructed and stationed in the Mediterranean and the Red Sea. A major dockyard and arsenal were built at Alexandria, and the Mahmudiya Canal was dug to connect the major port city with the Nile. In effect, Egypt was bled dry to pay for the military and naval infrastructure necessary to serve Muhammad Ali's imperial ambitions.

From the very outset, however, Muhammad Ali recognized that he would be unable to realize his ambitions without the tacit cooperation of Britain. He understood clearly that the British would not accept the emergence of a major hostile power along the land approaches to their empire in India. Accordingly, he made it an essential element of his policy never to display any overt hostility toward Britain, regardless of the provocation. As a practical matter, the British were quite prepared to accommodate themselves to a stable regime in Egypt under Muhammad Ali, especially since he appeared to be ready to acknowledge nominal Ottoman suzerainty.

Having consolidated his power in Egypt after eliminating the Mamluks in 1811, Muhammad Ali finally was free to turn his attention to expansionism abroad. His first move in this regard was directed against Arabia. As noted earlier, he had been formally requested to intervene there on behalf of Sultan Mahmud II.

The growth of the religiously conservative and expansionist Wahhabi realm in Arabia, founded by Muhammad ibn Saud (1746–1765), the emir of Dariyya, began to pose a serious threat to the sultan's claim to the universal leadership of Sunnite Islam. By 1773 the Saudis under Abd al-Aziz I (1765–1803) had succeeded in establishing control of most of Nejd in the Arabian interior and had reached as far as Riyadh, which fell to them in that year. The northern district of Ha'il came under their control in 1787, thereby extending the Saudi sway over the entire Jabal Shammar. In 1793 the eastern district of al-Ahsa came under Saudi rule as well.

Once in firm control of much of the heart of the peninsula, the Saudis began to mount serious incursions along the frontiers of Iraq to the northeast, Syria in the northwest, and the Hejaz in the west. The emir of the Hejaz, Ghalib ibn Musa'id, attempted to push the Saudis back into the desert, and hostilities between Ghalib's successors and the Saudis were to continue for more than a century. By 1797 what had earlier been considered merely a localized movement in remote Nejd came to be perceived as a significant threat to the sultan's control of the fringes of the Ottoman Empire in Arabia. In response to the threat posed by the Saudis, the governor of Baghdad, Buyuk Suleiman Pasha, sent troops to bolster the efforts of the Muntafiq tribal confederation to drive the Saudis from the Iraqi frontier. The joint expedition proved to be a conspicuous failure. The following year, an offensive launched against them from the Hejaz by Ghalib was similarly beaten back by the Saudis, as was another assault from Iraq by Buyuk Suleiman Pasha.

In 1803 the successor to the Saudi emirate, Saud ibn Abd al-Aziz (1803–1814), invaded the Hejaz once more and succeeded in seizing Mecca, forcing Ghalib to withdraw to Jeddah, where he managed to hold out. Two years later, Medina surrendered to the Saudis as well. The fact that the Wahhabis were now in control of the two holy cities of Islam was an intolerable embarrassment to the sultan, one that he could hardly tolerate since he was responsible for the security of the annual pilgrimage. For his part, Saud was concerned about the formation of an effective alliance between the sultan and his old enemy Ghalib for the purpose of driving him out of the Hejaz.

The principal instrument of an Ottoman offensive against Saud was to be the governor of Damascus, Abdallah Pasha al-Azm, who had been assigned responsibility for overseeing the pilgrimage from Syria to the holy cities. In 1807 Saud decided to forestall any aggressive move the Ottomans might attempt and effectively prevented the Syrian pilgrimage from entering the holy cities. He repeated this maneuver annually for the next three years and in 1810 mounted his own expedition into the frontier districts of Syria, creating a panic in Damascus that led to the deposition of the governor, Yusuf Pasha.

From the outset of the establishment of Ottoman suzerainty over Arabia, the problems of security in the Hejaz had normally been the responsibility of the governor of Egypt, who was in effect the successor of the Mamluk sultans. It was thus with some reluctance, since there was little interest at the Porte in further enhancing Muhammad Ali's stature, that the sultan requested that the governor intervene in Arabia to restore Ottoman control of the Hejaz and the holy cities. At best, Mahmud hoped to drain some of Muhammad Ali's energies and resources in the campaign that he would have to mount to rein in the Saudis. Muhammad Ali originally displayed little interest in expending his resources on behalf of the sultan. However, he eventually came to view the struggle with the Wahhabis as a means of honing his fighting force and, perhaps more important, of gaining a foothold in territories closer to the major overland trade routes over which he aspired to gain control. Indeed, at one point Muhammad Ali requested that he be given authority over Syria on the basis that this would facilitate the conduct of the campaign in the Hejaz.

Muhammad Ali dispatched his son Tussun to the Hejaz to deal with the Saudis, and he succeeded in driving them out of Medina in November 1812 and Mecca early in the following year. Nonetheless, Wahhabi power in the peninsula remained essentially intact, and it soon became clear that it would be necessary to carry the war into the Saudi heartland in Nejd, an invasion that Muhammad Ali intended to lead personally. As it turned out, it was not until January 1815 that the Arabian campaign actually got under way.

The Egyptian expeditionary army soon defeated the main Wahhabi force of some thirty thousand men on the road from Mecca to Nejd. However, upon learning of Napoleon's return from exile in Elba, Muhammad Ali interrupted the campaign and returned to Cairo to be in a better position to monitor and to react to events in Europe that might have implications for him. He left it to Tussun to negotiate an accommodation with Abdallah ibn Saud (1814–1818), who had succeeded Saud ibn Saud as emir in May 1814. The agreement they reached, which was actually only a temporary truce, essentially preserved the status quo; the Saudis retained control of Nejd and parts of the Hejaz, while Egyptian forces remained in control of the holy cities and assumed responsibility for the security of the pilgrimages. The truce lasted until 1816, when Tussun returned to Egypt to die. Given that the Wahhabis were perceived by Muhammad Ali as rivals for control of the Arab world, he was determined to crush them. The ailing Tussun was replaced by Ibrahim Pasha, perhaps the most capable of Muhammad Ali's sons, who resumed hostilities in Arabia in October 1817, after some two years of preparation for a new campaign. Ibrahim laid siege to the Saudi capital of Dariyya in April 1818, and its defenders capitulated in September of that year, bringing the war to an end. Abdallah ibn Saud was captured and taken initially to Cairo. He was subsequently transferred to Istanbul, where he was executed.

One unintended consequence of Muhammad Ali's Arabian campaign was that the defeat of the Wahhabis also served the immediate interests of the British government of India which, with the only significant naval force in the Persian Gulf region, had been engaged there in suppressing piracy and the slave trade. But, despite their best efforts, the British were unable to stabilize the area as long as the Wahhabis controlled the Arabian side of the Gulf. Upon hearing of the Egyptian victory, an emissary was sent from Bombay to Medina to congratulate Ibrahim and to propose an agreement between the British, the Egyptians, and the imam of Yemen to maintain the peace in the Arabian peninsula. The proposal was also submitted to the Porte by the British ambassador in Istanbul. The Porte, however, was deeply suspicious of British aims in the region. There was a concern that they were attempting to establish a British sphere of interest in the Yemen because of the strategic importance of Aden as a base for control of the Babal-Mandab Straits, as well as the lucrative coffee trade from the Red Sea port of Mocha. Accordingly, the Porte insisted that Muhammad Ali have nothing to do with the British proposal, a demand that he readily acceded to since he had his own plans for the Yemen.

Although the purpose of the Egyptian intervention in Arabia was ostensibly to uphold Ottoman suzerainty in the peninsula, the net effect, as feared by many at the Porte, was to further entrench Muhammad Ali's power over the eastern littoral of the Red Sea. For a time, his sway extended over most of Arabia as far as al-Ahsa on the Persian Gulf coast, and probably contributed to the willingness of the sheikdoms between Qatar and Muscat to accept protectorate status from the British in 1820. In any case, Muhammad Ali was unable to retain effective control of these distant territories for very long and he had to be satisfied with the Hejaz. Nejd was abandoned in 1824, when Turki ibn Abdallah (1823–1834) was able to reassert Saudi dominance over the tribes of the region.

With the generally successful conclusion of the Arabian campaign, Muhammad Ali next struck southward into the regions of Nubia, Sennar, and Kordofan, territories that would later constitute the Egyptian Sudan. His motives for this were complex. For one thing, he had a residual concern about the remaining Mamluks who had established themselves as far south as Dongola, and who remained a threat, no matter how remote, to Muhammad Ali's position in Egypt. However, his primary purpose appears to have been to capture slaves to serve in his army. We already noted his ardent desire to build an army along European lines, and his existing forces did not seem suitable for the purpose. He considered the Albanians, whom he knew only too well, to be unreliable. Moreover, there was a constant threat of mutiny should he attempt to introduce basic reforms in the military structure. He was particularly sensitive to the fact that it was just such an attempt at reform that had eventually brought down the Ottoman sultan Selim III.

The Sudan expedition was placed under the command of another of Muhammad Ali's sons, Ismail Kamil Pasha, who left Aswan with an army in July of 1820, reaching the Funj sultanate of Sennar the following June. Although the Funj sultan capitulated quickly, the Mamluks evaded Ismail's grasp by retreating from Dongola before his arrival. At the same time, another expeditionary force under Muhammad Ali's son-in-law, Muhammad Bey Khusraw, crossed the desert to Kordofan, which was also easily subdued. Although the Sudanese rose in revolt in the autumn of 1822, killing Ismail in the process, they were soon subdued and remained generally submissive for the next sixty years. The Turkish officials who were sent to administer the country set up their headquarters in the small fishing village of Khartoum at the confluence of the Blue and White Niles.

With the Sudan campaign behind him, Muhammad Ali proceeded to organize his slave army, but soon discovered that it simply was not an effective force, and he abandoned the project. Instead, he undertook the conscription of the Egyptian peasantry to form the bulk of his new European-style army that, while still quite deficient by European standards, was nonetheless the most modern military force in the entire Middle East. Indeed, it was because of its relatively great capabilities that the Ottoman sultan, who was faced by the renewed outbreak of hostilities on the Persian frontier, was once again forced to turn to Muhammad Ali for help, this time against the Greeks, who had revolted against Ottoman rule.

The Greeks had never lost sight of the fact that it was they who had once ruled much of what was now the Ottoman Empire. Encouraged by the successive victories of the Russians at Ottoman expense, as well as by the nationalist aspirations that swept through Europe after the French Revolution, an insurrection aimed at complete Greek independence erupted in 1821. The sultan was able to send sufficient forces into Macedonia and Thessaly to suppress the outbreaks there by 1823. However, the recent conflict with Persia had prevented him from amassing the armies and other resources he needed to break into the Morea against the determined Greeks, who had declared their independence in the peninsula. Once again, Mahmud II had little choice but to turn to Muhammad Ali for help.

To induce him to cooperate with the Turks in suppressing the Greek revolt, the sultan offered Muhammad Ali the *pashalik* of Crete as his compensation, providing, of course, that he first reestablish Ottoman control of the island. Muhammad Ali succeeded in accomplishing this by 1824. However, chronically rebellious Crete, whose continued pacification promised to consume most of the revenues that he might be able to raise there, was considered by Muhammad Ali as hardly adequate compensation for the services he was being asked to render to the sultan. He wanted to be awarded control of Syria as well.

It appears that subsequent to his experience in Arabia, Muhammad Ali's ambitions were increasingly channeled toward the Arab zones of the empire. Indeed, in May 1823, the British consul-general in Cairo, Henry Salt, reported that Muhammad Ali was "in secret correspondence with the Kurds and has the Pashas of Acre and Damascus and the Emir Beshir [Shihab of Lebanon] under his control."[5] Again in January 1825, Salt reported that "the possession of the Pashaliks of Acre, Aleppo and Damascus is certainly his first aim."[6] The sultan, however, would not consider giving the ambitious viceroy such strategic footholds in Syria and Palestine. Instead, Mahmud offered him the *pashalik* of the Morea if he were able to pacify the country first. Since Muhammad Ali was an Albanian, the idea of holding a *pashalik* in southeastern Europe had great appeal for him and he agreed to help. An Egyptian expeditionary force of some seventeen thousand men under the command of Ibrahim Pasha landed in the Morea in February 1825 and soon succeeded in overwhelming the rebels and restoring Ottoman control there, but they also devastated the country in the process.

The events that followed were significantly affected by a new European preoccupation with what became known as the "Eastern Question." That is, there was concern that the power vacuum that was being created in the European portions of the Ottoman Empire as a consequence of Ottoman decline should not be filled by the growing power of Russia. Each of the major powers had their own interests in the question. Thus, Austria strongly favored the preservation of the territorial integrity of the Ottoman Empire as a means of containing what it perceived as a looming Russian threat to its interests in Central Europe. The French, on the other hand, were ambivalent. Although they were interested in offsetting the growth of Russian influence in Istanbul, they also wished to reestablish their earlier power position in the eastern Mediterranean, which had declined as a result of the Napoleonic wars and had been supplanted by British naval supremacy in the region. The French evidently believed there was a strong possibility that the emergence of an independent Greece as well as an independent Egypt, both closely aligned with France, might present a better prospect for enhancing the French position in the Mediterranean region than the traditional policy of preserving the territorial integrity of the Ottoman empire. As a result, French policy tended to waver between these mutually inconsistent approaches, confusing everybody. As for the British, they pursued a nominally consistent policy of supporting the continued territorial integrity of the Ottoman Empire as the best means of both maintaining the European balance of power and assuring the security of their lines of communications through the Middle East to India. However, the cause of Greek independence had a special appeal for the public and became quite popular in England. As a consequence, the British position on the Greek insurgency was ambivalent and led the government to issue a declaration of neutrality in March 1823.

Muhammad Ali's military successes in Crete and the Morea must therefore be viewed within the context of their impact on the policies of the European powers. Obviously, they went counter to the interests of the Russians, who wished to supplant Ottoman power with their own and therefore became ardent supporters of Greek independence. Accordingly, the suppression of the Greek insurrection by Muhammad Ali came to be seen as a threat to the ambitions of the new Russian tsar, Nicholas I (1825–1855), who mounted the throne late in 1825. Given that Nicholas evidently was prepared to use force to gain his objectives in southeastern Europe, Britain began backing away from its overt support of the sultan and sought to mediate an agreement between the two that would prevent the outbreak of a new Russo-Ottoman War. Accordingly, when Russia issued an ultimatum to the sultan on March 17, 1826, demanding the restoration of the privileges formerly enjoyed by the principalities of Moldavia and Wallachia, as well as fulfillment of the commitment to show clemency in Serbia, as required by the 1812 Treaty of Bucharest, the British applied heavy pressure on Mahmud II to meet the tsar's demands.

Since the most effective of the Ottoman forces were those under the command of Ibrahim Pasha in the Morea, Britain tried to neutralize Muhammad Ali, thereby increasing the pressure on the sultan to be accommodating. The British ambassador in Istanbul, Stratford Canning, even offered to intercede on behalf of Muhammad Ali in helping him gain the Syrian *pashaliks* that he wanted, on the condition that he use his influence with the Porte in favor of accepting British mediation in the Greek conflict. Canning wrote to Salt in Cairo,

it would surely be better for him [Muhammad Ali] to look for a share of the tribute to be paid by Greece and to a Pashalik for his son in Syria than to persist in wasting his resources on the reduction of a stubborn population which must be exterminated, leaving an unproductive possession in his hands as an infallible subject of quarrel between him and the European powers. I have little doubt that the influence of the Embassy would reasonably be lent to him in return for his prevailing on the Porte to accept our mediation and to proceed at once to the pacification of Greece.[7]

In any case, further weakened by the mutiny and subsequent destruction of the Janissaries, which left the Ottoman military establishment in a temporary shambles, it was becoming particularly difficult for Mahmud to reject an accommodation with Russia and Britain. The sultan eventually gave in and signed the Convention of Akkerman on October 7, 1826. This not only reaffirmed the obligations undertaken in the Treaty of Bucharest, but also recognized Russian domination of the Caucasus and accorded the right of free access by Russian merchant ships to all Ottoman waters, including the Straits. The Russians, however, were not satisfied and continued to demand that the Porte also meet the demands of the Greek rebels, proposing that Britain participate with them in a joint intervention in

Greece. Britain, on the other hand, had no interest in seeing any further Russian penetration of the region and sought to prevent this from happening by joining with Austria in pressuring the sultan into accepting international mediation of the crisis.

Notwithstanding the poor state of the Ottoman military at the time, Mahmud leaned toward those of his advisers who insisted that he had no acceptable choice other than to defy the European powers and assert his mastery over Greece. Accordingly, he ordered the Ottoman and Egyptian forces to go ahead with the complete subjugation of the country. Following the capture of Athens in June 1827, Britain felt compelled to sign a new Treaty of London with both France and Russia on July 6, which called for direct joint intervention if either the Greeks or the Ottomans refused their mediation. When Mahmud rejected their interference, the allies moved their fleets into the eastern Mediterranean and blockaded the Dardanelles as well as the Morea to prevent the resupply of the Ottoman and Egyptian forces there. Then, when the Egyptian navy subsequently joined the Ottoman fleet in the Bay of Navarino, in what was interpreted as a demonstration of its intent to challenge the European blockade, it was annihilated in a brief battle that took place on October 20, 1827.

But, contrary to the expectation of Britain and France that the Navarino debacle would compel the sultan to accept their mediation in Greece, it had the opposite result. Mahmud effectively scrapped the Convention of Akkerman and, on December 18, 1827, appealed for an all-out Muslim resistance to both the Russians and the Greeks. He also closed the Turkish Straits to all foreign shipping on February 5, 1828. Unfortunately for the sultan, these forceful steps proved to be ill timed. The tsar was no longer preoccupied with a war with Persia, which had just come to an end, and was now free to pursue his aim of breaking up the Ottoman Empire. Nicholas declared war on Turkey on April 28, 1828.

NOTES

1. John Marlowe, *A History of Modern Egypt and Anglo-Egyptian Relations, 1800–1956*, p. 30.

2. A. J. Denain, *Histoire scientifique et militaire de l'expedition française en Egypte, Egypte Moderne*, 9:71.

3. Misset to Canning, June 13, 1807. FO 24/3.

4. Waldegrave to C-in-C Mediterranean, January 24, 1811. FO 24/4.

5. Salt to Foreign Office, May 3, 1823. FO 78/119.

6. Salt to Foreign Office, January 4, 1825. FO 78/135.

7. Canning to Salt, June 10, 1826. FO 78/147.

11

Anglo-Russian Rivalry in the Persian Sphere

As indicated in the preceding chapter, the sultan had been forced to call upon Muhammad Ali to assist in the suppression of the Greek struggle for independence. This was because of his need to deal simultaneously with a new crisis that had developed on the Ottoman eastern frontier with Persia in the fall of 1821. The crisis had its roots in the nine-year-long Russo-Persian War that was brought to an end by the Treaty of Gulistan (October 12, 1813), negotiated through the good offices of Sir Gore Ousley, of Great Britain, and Abbas Mirza, the Persian heir-apparent and governor-general of Azerbaijan. Apparently in return for a Russian commitment to assure his succession, Abbas Mirza agreed to terms that were disastrous for Persia. Under the provisions of the treaty, which the Persian ruler Fath Ali Shah (1797–1834) was pushed into ratifying, Russia obtained most of the Caucasus, including Derbent, Baku, Shirvan, Shaki, and Qarabagh. In addition, Persia abandoned all further pretensions to sovereignty over Georgia, Daghestan, Mingrelia, Imeritia, and Abkhasia, and ceded the right to Russia to maintain naval forces in the Caspian Sea. It would seem that a major determinant in convincing Fath Ali Shah to agree to these harsh terms was the pending agreement with Great Britain, which seemed to offer a defensive alliance against further Russian encroachments.

The definitive Treaty of Defensive Alliance (November 25, 1814) provided that, in the event of an invasion of Persia by any European nation, Britain would send troops from India to assist in the defense of the country, or provide a substantial subsidy instead. For its part, the Persian government agreed

not to allow any European army to enter the Persian territory, not to proceed towards India, nor to any of the ports of that country . . . Should any of the European powers wish to invade India by the road of Kharizen, Taturistan, Bokhara, Samarkand, or other routes, His Persian majesty engages to induce the kings and governors of those countries to oppose such invasion, as much as is in his power, either by the fear of his arms or by conciliatory measures.[1]

Moreover, Persia agreed to come to Britain's aid in the event of a war with the Afghans, whereas Britain was to maintain a hands-off policy in the event of a similar conflict between Afghanistan and Persia. As was to be demonstrated before long, the mutual defense treaty with Britain proved of dubious value to Persia since there was little evidence that the British took it very seriously.

It also appears that Fath Ali Shah had hoped that his alliance with Britain would result in the readiness of the Russians to restore some of the territories signed away by Persia in the Treaty of Gulistan, as a means of offsetting the growing influence of Britain in Persia. However, when the tsar finally sent a mission to Tehran under General Yermoloff, the commander-in-chief of the Caucasus, it was not to cede any territory but rather to make additional demands. The Russians sought a right of way for an army through Astarabad and Khorasan for an impending invasion of Khiva, a request the Persians rejected. At the same time, the Russians proposed an alliance with Persia against the Ottoman Empire. They encouraged Fath Ali Shah to take advantage of Mahmud's preoccupation with internal affairs and his perennial problems in the Balkans and to compensate himself for his losses of territory to Russia by retaking some formerly Persian lands from the Ottomans. Although the shah rejected this initial overture, it was ultimately accepted several years later by the ambitious Abbas Mirza, who was convinced by Mazarovitch, the Russian agent at Tehran, to invade the Ottoman domains.

The ostensible justification for the shah's decision and the ensuing conflict between Persia and Turkey that broke out in 1821 was the action taken by the Ottoman governor of Erzerum, who accorded protection to two nomadic tribes which had fled Azerbaijan. Abbas Mirza soon succeeded in occupying all the districts adjacent to Azerbaijan, including Kurdistan. An Ottoman attempt to outflank the Persians with an attack launched from the south by the pasha of Baghdad was defeated by Muhammad Ali Mirza, the shah's eldest son. It almost resulted in the conquest of that city, which was averted only by the outbreak of cholera among the Persian forces. The conflict was ultimately ended by the Treaty of Erzerum (July 28, 1823), which effectively restored the Ottoman-Qajar frontiers to what they had been prior to the outbreak of hostilities, that is, as they had been established by the Treaty of Kurdan (September 4, 1746).

The latent Persian hostility toward Russia resulting from the Treaty of Gulistan reached the boiling point in 1825. It was precipitated by a minor territorial dispute involving three districts lying between Erivan and Lake Gokcha, whose disposition was left unclear by the treaty. The Russians were anxious to obtain control of all the territory north of the Aras River, which they considered to constitute a more defensible frontier than that which existed at the time. Accordingly, they seized Gokcha and thereby provided the justification for war that Abbas Mirza anxiously sought in order to restore his tarnished reputation.

Having mobilized a substantial fighting force, Abbas Mirza struck at the ill-prepared Russians and made some dramatic initial gains. He captured an entire Russian regiment and raided in the Caucasus as far north as the gates of Tiflis. Within a month, the Persians had seized all of Shirvan, Shaki, Talish, and Ganja. The Russians, however, had been concentrating their forces at Tiflis and, although significantly outnumbered, they were soon able to wreak havoc with the superior Persian cavalry, which was demoralized by the powerful Russian artillery put into operation at Shamkar, near Ganja. The Persian cavalry disintegrated as an effective fighting force, and Abbas Mirza was compelled to proceed north with the bulk of his army, some thirty thousand men, to confront a Russian army half its size at the Akstafa River west of Ganja on September 26, 1826. The battle, which was grossly mismanaged by Abbas Mirza, turned into a debacle for the Persians, who were forced to retreat to the Aras River, about 150 miles to the south. The Persians were driven out of Derbent, and the Russians moved south to within striking range of Tabriz. Nakhichevan fell, and Erivan was placed under siege, falling in 1827 after Fath Ali Shah refused to spend the funds necessary to keep his army in the field. With Tabriz's subsequent surrender without a struggle to a small Russian force, the war came to an end.

It would have seemed that Britain was obligated to come to Persia's aid under the 1814 Treaty of Defensive Alliance, since the Russians appeared to have triggered the conflict by their seizure of Gokcha. However, Britain was on reasonably good terms with Russia at the time and would not be drawn into a conflict that did not serve its broader diplomacy. Accordingly, the British concluded that despite the Russian action at Gokcha, it was the Persians who were the aggressors, and that their obligation under the treaty to render assistance to Persia in the event of an attack by a European power did not come into effect. However, to smooth over the affair, Britain gave Abbas Mirza the sum of some two hundred thousand tomans in exchange for a modification of the treaty to eliminate those clauses calling for British intervention on behalf of Persia. Abbas Mirza needed the money desperately to purchase the Russian withdrawal from Tabriz, and he agreed to the revision of the treaty.

Although the Russians seemed to be in a position to impose very harsh terms in the subsequent Treaty of Turkmanchai (1828), in fact they were dissuaded from doing so by their preoccupation with renewed hostilities with the Ottomans over Greece. They were therefore reluctant to risk triggering a renewal of the conflict with Persia by making the terms of peace unacceptable. As for further territorial concessions, the treaty provided for the annexation by Russia of the provinces of Erivan and Nakhichevan and delineated the frontier west of the Caspian in considerable detail. Perhaps most significant, the treaty ceded certain extraterritorial rights to Russia in Persia that had the practical effect of directly impinging on the shah's sovereignty.

Traditional British policy with respect to the Ottoman Empire was to a large measure conditioned by its concerns over Russian expansionism. However, by contrast with the other European powers, which were primarily concerned with Russian ambitions in Europe, the British were even more focused on the tsar's ambitions in Asia. Of particular concern in this regard was Russia's tendency to encourage Persia to turn to Afghanistan to seek territorial compensation for the lands lost to the tsar. This policy threatened to further destabilize the already volatile western frontiers of British India. From the perspective of those responsible for India, the success of the Persian military campaigns against Afghanistan portended the appearance of Russian agents and political influence in the region south of the Hindu Kush, which Britain preferred to see as the limit of Russia's southward expansion in central Asia. Accordingly, the British Government of India was prepared to go to considerable lengths to keep Afghanistan outside the Russian or even Persian sphere of influence, even if it meant war with its erstwhile Persian allies, and even if this made the latter turn to the Russians for support. This British policy created an extremely awkward situation for the Persians, who had no wish to enter into a conflict with Britain, and had even less interest in becoming dependent on Russia for their external security. But they also saw the provinces of Herat, Kabul, and Qandahar as integral components of the ancient patrimony of Persia to which they were not prepared to abandon their claims in the interest of their ephemeral relationship with Britain.

Upon the death of the heir-apparent to the Persian throne, Abbas Mirza, in 1833, the shah's grandson, Muhammad Mirza, who was governor of Khorasan and commander of the Persian armies, interrupted his siege of Herat and returned to the capital to be appointed crown prince. But, with the death of Fath Ali Shah on October 23, 1834, two of his sons, Farman Farma, governor of Fars, and Zil-u-Sultan, governor of Tehran, became determined to contest the succession of Muhammad Mirza. This struggle over the Persian throne presented the British with an opportunity to significantly enhance their position and influence in Tehran.

At that moment, Sir John Campbell, the British envoy to Persia, was at Tabriz, and he threw his weight behind Muhammad Mirza, enabling the new shah to enter Tehran accompanied by a considerable British military force commanded by Sir Henry Lindsay Bethune. This precipitated the immediate submission of Zil-u-Sultan, who was abandoned by his supporters. The other pretender, however, posed a threat to the new shah, and to consolidate British influence in the capital the British commander was soon on the march to Isfahan to challenge Farman Farma. The latter's cavalry was subsequently decimated by artillery in a battle at Kumishah, and the threat to the new shah was eliminated. That same year a substantial British military mission, which included representatives of the various armed services, was dispatched to Tehran to attempt to influence the leadership of the Persian military. However, the British were unable to gain the same degree of influence with the new Persian ruler that they had with Fath Ali Shah. Despite their best efforts, Muhammad Shah (1834–1848) was clearly under the dominant influence of the Russians, and this promised to create significant problems for British imperial interests.

Shortly after consolidating his position in Teheran, Muhammad Shah undertook a second campaign into Afghanistan. The purpose of the operation was to conquer Herat and to eliminate its ruler, Kamran Mirza (1829–1843), who had seized and annexed Sistan, a traditionally Persian province. Britain, as already indicated, was concerned that a Persian advance into Afghanistan would also mean the penetration of Russian agents and attempted to get the shah to call off the expedition. However, its ability to achieve this was hampered by the fact that, under the Anglo-Persian treaty of 1814, Britain had formally committed itself not to intervene in the event of a Persian war with Afghanistan.

The campaign for Herat unleashed a complex of local forces that further complicated Anglo-Russian rivalry in the region. At the time, the ruler of Kabul was Dost Muhammad (1826–1863). His abiding ambition was to reconstitute a kingdom stretching from Herat in the west, which was under the control of Kamran Mirza, to Peshawar in the east, which had been conquered by Ranjit Singh and made a province of the Sikh kingdom in western India. Dost Muhammad hoped to realize this ambition, or at least part of it, through an alliance with the British. But Lord Auckland, the British governor-general in India, refused to consider any competing claims to territories conquered by Ranjit Singh. As a consequence, Dost Muhammad turned to the Russian agent, a Captain Vitkavich, who promised Russian support for his ambitions. However, he was not content to base his future on Russian promises, which turned out to be devoid of tangible value since Vitkavich was himself soon disowned by the Russian government. Dost Muhammad therefore also entered into an alliance with Muhammad Shah of Persia against Kamran Mirza, a move that was clearly counter to British interests but which seems to have been precipitated by British mishandling of the situation.

Strengthened by his alliance with Dost Muhammad, in the spring of 1837 the shah mobilized his forces at Shahrud and moved through Khorasan into the province of Herat. In anticipation of the arrival of the Persian army, Yar Muhammad Khan, the vizir and power behind the throne in Herat, collected most of the available crops into the city in preparation for the forthcoming siege, and then put the torch to everything within a dozen miles of the city. Much of the defense of Herat was undertaken successfully by a young British artillery officer, Eldred Pottinger, who had arrived there incognito. The siege proceeded without result until the spring of 1838, notwithstanding the military advice given by Russian General Perovski, who was killed in a vain general assault on the city. While the siege was under way, according to Persian sources, a British naval force entered the Persian Gulf and occupied Kharg Island after a failed attempt to establish a foothold at Busheir. The British general was reported to have warned: "If the Persian army does not raise the siege of Herat, we shall occupy the whole coast of Fars, even the whole province. We shall change the friendship between Persia and England to enmity and do what will be appropriate and suitable."[2] Ostensibly, after weighing the implications of an open conflict with Britain because of Herat, the shah concluded that it was in the greater interest of Persia to forego the attempt to take the city, and the siege was lifted on September 9, 1838.

However, while the siege was in process, the expectation of the fall of Herat led to rumors in India of a pending Muslim invasion that would bring an end to British rule, which had a devastating effect on the market value of public securities. To counteract the negative effects that this rumor was having, Lord Auckland decided to launch a counterattack in Afghanistan to dispel any illusions about the relative weakness of the British forces and their ability to hold onto the country. Since he and his advisers were already hostile to Dost Muhammad, it was decided to make an example of the Afghan ruler. For this purpose, they enlisted the aid of a refugee Sadozai prince, Shah Shuja, who had earlier been deposed from the throne of Kabul by the Barakzais, the family of Dost Muhammad. The original British plan was to get the Sikh leader Ranjit Singh to collaborate in the campaign by marching on Kabul through the Khyber Pass, while Shah Shuja attacked by way of Qandahar at the head of an army that he would recruit for the purpose. It soon became evident, however, that the scheme would probably not work unless the British themselves became directly involved in the campaign and broke the siege of Herat.

In fact, the British plan was incredibly naive and dangerous since the British army in India hardly had the necessary resources for such a campaign. The assembly point for the army was located at Karnal, some eleven hundred miles from Qandahar, which was itself about four hundred miles from Herat. To carry out the campaign, the British would have to march an army of twenty thousand men about fifteen hundred miles through very difficult terrain, with the possibility that they might find a relatively fresh Persian army, perhaps augmented by Russian troops, waiting for them when they arrived at Herat. Fortunately for Britain, the shah decided to withdraw from Herat, making the expedition unnecessary.

Nonetheless, the British decided to go ahead with that part of the plan that called for the overthrow of Dost Muhammad and his replacement by

Shah Shuja, who had been on their payroll since he was deposed as ruler of Kabul. A somewhat reduced British force ultimately made the difficult march, suffering heavy losses in men and camels, and arrived at Qandahar, which they discovered to be undefended. Indeed, the British forces encountered no resistance until they reached Ghazni, which they took easily through a stroke of luck. They managed to blow up the Kabul Gate of the city, the only entrance to the city that had not been fortified. This caused a general panic that resulted in the abandonment of the city's defenses, making the abundant supplies stored there available to the weary British troops. Now fully rested and replenished, the British force easily took Kabul in August 1839, with Dost Muhammad surrendering soon thereafter. By a combination of circumstances quite beyond their control, what could and perhaps should have been an unmitigated military disaster was transformed into a remarkable albeit short-lived achievement. Two years later, Kabul came under ferocious attack by Dost Muhammad's son, Akbar Khan, who dislodged the British from the stronghold. The struggle for Kabul cost the British about four thousand casualties and as many as twelve thousand indigenous followers, who were cut down while retreating to Jalalabad. Although the British regained control of Kabul in the spring of 1842, Shah Shuja had already been killed, and Dost Muhammad was soon permitted to return to his throne there as the British army evacuated Afghanistan after what proved to have been a bloody and pointless military adventure.

NOTES

1. See J. C. Hurewitz, ed., *The Middle East and North Africa in World Politics: A Documentary Record*, vol. 1, p. 200.

2. Hasan-e Fasa'i, *History of Persia under Qajar Rule*, p. 260.

12

The War of 1828 and Its Aftermath

The timing of the renewed conflict with Russia, the origins of which were described in an earlier chapter, could not have been worse from the Ottoman standpoint. Sultan Mahmud had recently undertaken the modernization of the Turkish army and had done away with the traditional Janissary corps. But his new army was still undergoing training, and he had just lost his and Muhammad Ali's navy at Navarino. Moreover, the Egyptian army under Ibrahim Pasha was now stranded in the Morea and little additional assistance could be expected from Egypt. Under these circumstances, it was extremely difficult to mount an effective defense against the Russian assault in the Balkans.

With one hundred thousand troops at their disposal, the Russians attacked on three fronts, advancing rapidly into Moldavia and Wallachia and challenging the Ottomans along a good part of the Danubian frontier. The Ottoman forces were able to hold their positions only in Silistria in central Bulgaria. In the east, the Russians had a virtually free hand, moving along the Black Sea coast and taking Anapa and Ahiska, and then invading eastern Anatolia, seizing Kars in July 1828 with the help of the Armenian populace.

At about the same time, on August 6, 1828, an agreement was successfully concluded without the sultan's knowledge between the British Admiral Codrington and Muhammad Ali that provided for the unhindered withdrawal of the stranded Egyptian forces from the Morea. In return, the Egyptian commander Ibrahim Pasha was instructed to turn over the key positions held by his troops to the new Greek government of John Capodistrias. It is noteworthy that Muhammad Ali did not make any attempt to place his forces at the sultan's disposal once he was free to do so.

Instead, in April 1829, he convened an assembly of the *ulema* and other notables in Cairo, over which he presided, to make a determination as to whether he was obligated to dispatch troops to aid the sultan. Not surprisingly, the assembly issued a unanimous declaration opposing the sending of any forces to the sultan's aid. The fact was that Muhammad Ali saw the Ottoman Empire as a mere shadow of its former self and was more interested in getting Britain to back Egypt as an alternative power center capable of securing the eastern Mediterranean zone against Russian penetration, the primary concern driving British regional policy. For the British, however, the geopolitical reality remained the fact that Turkey stood directly between Russia and the Mediterranean, and Muhammad Ali's Egypt was no adequate substitute for this. British policy continued to remain focused on Istanbul.

The war with Russia dragged on into the summer of 1829, but it was a lost cause for the Ottomans. Resistance soon collapsed after the Russians took Erzerum on July 8, and another Russian force swept through the Balkans to take Edirne after only a three-day siege on August 22. To forestall a complete disaster, Mahmud now eagerly sought international mediation of the conflict. Although Russia was well positioned to force its way through Thrace and to seize Istanbul and the Turkish Straits, the tsar was dissuaded from doing so for a number of reasons. The army that had crossed the Balkans and taken Edirne was far from its sources of supply and its lines of communications were therefore dangerously exposed. In the political arena, there was a real concern about the reaction that such a move on Istanbul might provoke from Britain and France. Finally, the special Committee of Seven, which Tsar Nicholas appointed in 1829 to propose options for Russian policy toward the Porte, recommended against the elimination of Ottoman rule in Europe. It was argued that a move to eliminate the Turks and to establish Russian dominance over the entire northern littoral of the Black Sea would prove counterproductive at the time.

The reasons given were several. Because of the simultaneous Russian expansion in the Caucasus and Transcaspia, there was a concern that the ejection of the Turks from Europe might precipitate the unification of all the Muslim peoples on Russia's southern periphery, under the sultan's banner. This could create a belt of serious resistance to the tsar's rule that might stretch across Asia as far as China. Furthermore, if the Ottoman Empire were to be partitioned, there was no effective way of preventing the other European powers, particularly Austria, Britain, and France, from demanding and taking their shares of the spoils. This would have resulted in replacing a weak neighbor on Russia's southern flank with three powerful ones, each with ambitions of its own in the region. Finally, while internationalization of the Turkish Straits would permit Russian ships to egress from the Black Sea into the Mediterranean, it would also allow the more powerful British and French fleets access to the Black Sea and Russia's soft underbelly. Because of these considerations, Nicholas decided not to press his military advantage and to allow the Ottoman Empire to remain intact, at least for the time being. However, he also clearly wanted it to be too weak to prevent any further Russian encroachment at some more propitious point in the future.

The subsequent Treaty of Edirne (September 14, 1829), which brought the conflict to an end, yielded some small but significant gains for Russia. The Russian frontier was moved from the northern mouth of the Danube to the southern, giving the tsar control of the entire delta region and placing the Russians in a position to dominate the regional trade and commerce. On the other hand, the Russians were required to withdraw from all their conquests south of the Pruth, causing them to evacuate Moldavia, Wallachia, Dobruja, and Bulgaria. However, the Pruth frontier was to remain unfortified, offering easy access to Russian forces in the event of a renewal of hostilities and, although the Principalities were to remain under the nominal sovereignty of the sultan, they were effectively left open to Russian intervention at will. In the east, Nicholas returned Erzerum, Kars, and Bayezid to the sultan in return for Ottoman recognition of Russian rights in Georgia, Circassia, and sections of Transcaucasia, including Erivan and Nakhichevan, which were recently acquired from Persia. Finally, the sultan was saddled with a gigantic war indemnity to be paid over a ten-year period that amounted to twice the imperial revenues for the decade. Because it was virtually impossible for Turkey to meet this heavy financial burden, the debt was subsequently reduced in exchange for further territorial concessions to Greece. In fact, in 1830 the sultan was forced to accept full Greek independence.

The peace treaty with Russia by no means ended the sultan's immediate problems. Foremost among these was Muhammad Ali of Egypt. The Ottoman loss of Greece cost Muhammad Ali the *pashalik* of Morea that he had been promised, and he now demanded Syria as compensation. Since Mahmud never had any intention of giving him a foothold in the heart of the empire, and was quite unhappy with his powerful vassal who had refused to come to his aid during the recent war with Russia, relations between the sultan and his viceroy became rather testy. Ironically, the mounting disdain with which the Mahmud treated Muhammad Ali only served to increase the probability of an Egyptian invasion of Syria, as well as the likelihood of an attempt to overthrow the sultan.

It was clear to the British officials in Cairo as early as 1827 that "the possession of Acre is evidently the goal to which he tends: that important fortress could effectively cover Egypt from attacks by land while his fleet would protect him from a blockade by sea."[1] Muhammad Ali was keenly aware that the security of Egypt, meaning primarily the militarily vulnerable region of the Nile delta, had always been directly linked to friendly control of the Asiatic land approaches through Palestine. Given the level of hostility between Cairo and Istanbul, it seemed only a matter of time before the Egyptians would move against Palestine and probably Syria as well.

Muhammad Ali, however, had to proceed in a manner that would not antagonize Britain, which had effective control of the eastern Mediterranean and was opposed to any further dismantling of the Ottoman Empire at the time. Accordingly, he decided to move into Palestine in a way that could avoid direct hostilities with the Porte. The opportunity for doing so resulted from some actions taken by Abdallah, the pasha of Acre, who was himself out of favor with the sultan. It seems that, as a consequence of Muhammad Ali's military conscription policies, a good number of men who refused to serve in his army, augmented by scores of deserters, were able to find asylum with the pasha of Acre. This gave Muhammad Ali a justification for taking steps against Abdallah, without necessarily appearing to be striking out at the sultan and the Ottoman state. Indeed, he tried his best to make it appear that he was preparing for an invasion of Palestine at the behest of the Porte.

The Egyptian expeditionary force, under the command of Ibrahim Pasha, finally began to move in October 1831 and soon laid siege to Acre, which fell on May 27, 1832, after putting up an unexpectedly strong resistance. It is noteworthy that the Porte did nothing to aid Acre, although it did encourage the local pashas to offer resistance as the Egyptian forces moved deeper into Syria. Following the fall of Acre, Muhammad Ali sent an emissary to Istanbul proposing a peace agreement and requesting that he be awarded the *pashaliks* of Acre and Tripoli, which would have given him effective control of the entire Mediterranean coast from Al-Arish in the Sinai to Latakia in northern Syria. As proof of his sincere wish to reach an accommodation with the Porte, he offered to waive his claim to Damascus. However, before his emissary reached Istanbul, Muhammad Ali received word that the sultan had declared both him and Ibrahim to be outlaws and had proclaimed a blockade of the coasts of Syria and Egypt. Moreover, the sultan also dispatched an army under Husain Pasha to challenge the Egyptians on land. Ibrahim decisively defeated this latter force in the pass of Beylan between Antioch and Alexandretta in northern Syria on July 29. As a result, Syria was now completely open to Muhammad Ali.

There were two options open to the Egyptian leader. The first, which was the more prudent and was favored by him, was to occupy all of Syria and to establish defensive lines north of Aleppo against an attack by the sultan. The second and far more risky course, which was preferred by Ibrahim, was to cross into Anatolia and march on Istanbul, overthrow Mahmud and install his son Abdul Mejid as sultan in his place. Since Abd al- Mejid would owe his throne to Muhammad Ali, the latter would have a free hand in the empire. Ibrahim tried desperately to convince Muhammad Ali of the wisdom of marching on Istanbul, but his father, who was particularly concerned about the British reaction to such a move, would not hear of it. Ibrahim did manage to get him to agree in October 1832 that his forces should advance into Anatolia as far as Konya, in order to seize control of the Taurus passes, and thereby reduce the threat of a Turkish strike into Syria. By December, Muhammad Ali changed his mind and ordered Ibrahim to withdraw to the Aleppo line. However, it was too late to avoid a collision with the Turkish army under Rashid Muhammad Pasha that was advancing on Konya. The battle, which took place near Konya on December 21, was brief. The Turkish forces were routed and Rashid was captured. Once again, Ibrahim appealed to Muhammad Ali from Konya to allow him to take advantage of the open road to Istanbul:

We can march on Constantinople and depose the sultan at once and without difficulty. But I must know as soon as possible if you really want this done . . . propaganda will get us nowhere. It is necessary to threaten Constantinople and force the sultan to agree to our conditions. We cannot do that by staying at Konya which is a long way from Constantinople. They will only make peace with us when we are approaching Constantinople, just as they made peace with the Russians only when they were in the suburbs of Constantinople. This is why we must advance at least as far as Brusa, occupy the Asiatic coast of the Marmora and make arrangements to supply the army by sea. From there . . . we can at least make peace on our own terms. If you hadn't kept me back I would already have been in Constantinople. Why all this delay? Is it because of a fear of the Powers, or something else?[2]

In fact, there was something else that caused Muhammad Ali to temporize, and it marked the differences between father and son in terms of their geopolitical outlooks. Ibrahim was little concerned about the possible breakup of the Ottoman Empire. He was, as John Marlowe described him, "more of an Arab than a Turk. He had no feeling for the Ottoman Empire and would like to have seen it replaced in the leadership of the Moslem world by an Arab Empire based on Egypt and ruled over by his father and his descendants."[3] Muhammad Ali, on the other hand, was entirely Ottoman in outlook and orientation. He did not want to see the Ottoman Empire torn apart, much of it taken over by the European powers. He preferred to see it intact, but acting under his influence. He did not aspire to be the sultan, but rather the power behind the throne. Accordingly, he was unwilling to take those steps that could bring the empire down by effectively inviting the European powers to intervene directly.

As it turned out, the European powers were quite divided in their policies with regard to the conflict between the sultan and the viceroy. The British cabinet itself was split on the question. One faction saw the defeat of the sultan as further eroding the stability of the Ottoman Empire that they wished to preserve for longer-term British interests. A second faction reflected the opposing sentiments of the business community, which benefited significantly from investments and commerce with Egypt and was therefore very supportive of Muhammad Ali. The French were generally in favor of seeing Egypt and Syria made effectively independent of Istanbul, while maintaining a nominal tributary relationship to the sultan, a proposal that was rejected by the Porte in July 1832. Austria and Prussia took their stand with the sultan and ordered their nationals to boycott any trade or commerce with Egypt.

The most significant response, however, came from Russia. In fact, on December 21, 1832, only a few days before the battle at Konya, the Russian envoy to Istanbul made a formal offer of Russian military assistance against Egypt. Moreover, General N. N. Muraviev arrived from St. Petersburg the following day, on his way to Egypt with a message from the tsar demanding that Muhammad Ali submit to the sultan. This apparent solicitousness on the part of the tsar aroused serious concerns about Russia's intentions, making the Porte fearful of becoming too reliant on Russian involvement in the crisis. As a result, the Porte reluctantly turned to the French, indicating its readiness to proceed along the lines that it had rejected only a half year earlier.

On January 7, 1833, Rifaat Khalil Pasha was sent to Cairo to negotiate an accommodation directly with Muhammad Ali, who had already informed General Muraviev of his willingness to instruct Ibrahim to remain in Konya pending conclusion of the negotiations with Khalil Pasha. Ibrahim, however, had already left Konya, ostensibly because he was not adequately provisioned to spend the winter there, and was at Kutahya, about 150 miles from Istanbul, before his father's instructions reached him. In a message to Muhammad Ali sent from Konya, Ibrahim indicated his lack of confidence that the negotiations with Khalil Pasha could produce anything more than a temporary truce. He suggested that it would prove far more advantageous to resolve matters with Istanbul once and for all by getting rid of the sultan and putting a friendly government into power there. "If you tell me," he wrote, "that Europe would not approve, I say that we not give Europe any time to intervene. We will present Europe with a *fait accompli*. If they choose to take advantage of it by partitioning what is left of the Ottoman Empire among themselves, what is that to us? In any case, it is better for both of us to bring matters to a head now."[4] But, once he received his father's instructions, Ibrahim recognized that the moment of opportunity had already passed; Muhammad Ali's indecisiveness had effectively saved the Ottoman Empire from coming under Egyptian control. The possibility of this happening was so strong that, out of concern about Ibrahim's march through Anatolia, on February 2, 1833, the Porte formally requested Russian military and naval assistance, and a Russian naval squadron arrived in the Bosphorus two weeks later.

In the meantime, a messenger from Cairo brought Muhammad Ali's proposals for a settlement as well as the counterproposals offered by Khalil Pasha. The viceroy wanted the four Syrian *pashaliks* plus the *pashalik* of Adana. Ibrahim had argued forcefully that Adana, which included the districts of Antalya, Alaya, and Cilicia, would serve as a primary source of the lumber that was essential for the Egyptian fleet. The Ottoman envoy, on the other hand, offered him only the four *sanjaks* of Acre, Jerusalem, Nablus, and Tripoli. Out of concern that the Russians were gaining too strong a hand in Ottoman affairs, the French ambassador, Admiral Roussin, agreed on behalf of his government to compel Muhammad Ali to accept the terms offered by Khalil Pasha. In return for this intervention, the Porte promised to request a withdrawal of the Russian fleet from the Bosphorus. Roussin followed up by dispatching an emissary to Cairo with what was in effect a French ultimatum. Muhammad Ali, infuriated by what he saw as French perfidy, formally rejected it on March 9, 1833. The viceroy had no intention of withdrawing from territories that were under his complete control, and sent a message to that effect to the Porte. He also sent word to Ibrahim advising him to continue to march on Istanbul if the Porte did not accept his territorial demands within five days.

When the Porte learned of Muhammad Ali's instructions to Ibrahim, it turned to the Russians once again, asking them to expedite the dispatch of forces to render assistance in turning back the Egyptian threat. Recognizing that he had unwittingly precipitated a crisis that he could not control, Roussin abruptly reversed himself on March 26 and urged the Porte to accept Muhammad Ali's terms "rather than expose the country to a conflict between the Russian army and the people."[5] The British echoed this position the following day. Pressed on all sides, the Porte agreed to offer Muhammad Ali the four Syrian *pashaliks* he had requested, but not Adana. The Turks refused to concede Adana for the same strategic reasons that Muhammad Ali wanted it. Control of Adana not only meant lumber for the Egyptian fleet, but also control of the Cilician Gates, through which the main route for an invasion force between Anatolia and Syria passed.

Evidently unaware of or misunderstanding the Turkish position on control of Adana, the emissary sent from Istanbul to negotiate with Ibrahim mistakenly included Adana within the Porte's offer, information that Ibrahim promptly forwarded to Cairo. Immediately upon receiving this word on April 16, 1833, Muhammad Ali publicly announced that a peace accord had been reached. But when he received formal notification at the end of the month confirming him as viceroy of Egypt and Syria, Adana was conspicuously absent from the list of *pashaliks* placed under his jurisdiction. At the same time a message arrived from Ibrahim indicating that the status of Adana was still under negotiation, and that his army would remain in place at Kutahya until the matter was resolved. With the threat of a renewal of the war by Ibrahim considered to be imminent, a threat that would surely bring further intervention by Russia, both the British and the French brought pressure to bear on the Porte to concede Adana in return for an Egyptian withdrawal behind the Taurus. The latter would meet the basic demands of the Russians and undercut their rationale for a military presence in Ottoman territory. The Porte gave in and made the necessary concession. Ibrahim subsequently withdrew behind the Taurus Mountains on June 25, and the Russians completed their evacuation of Ottoman territory on July 9, 1833.

Notwithstanding the settlement of the conflict that was reached at Kutahya, it was evident to all the parties concerned that the agreement was actually nothing more than a truce that would be broken by the sultan or the viceroy as soon as it served either party's interest to do so. Because of this, and before they withdrew their forces from Ottoman territory, the Russians had little difficulty in getting the Porte to agree to a mutual defense treaty. Faced by the possibility of a renewal of the struggle, the Porte did not have any practical alternative to accepting the Russian proposal. After all, it was the Russians and not the other European powers that had come to its aid. By contrast, it was Britain and France that had been instrumental in forcing the Porte to concede Adana to Muhammad Ali.

The Russo-Ottoman Treaty of Defensive Alliance (Hunkar Iskelesi) of July 8, 1833, which was an eight-year mutual defense pact, provided that the Russians would come to the Porte's assistance once again if so requested. This stipulation seemed innocuous enough and apparently did not involve any significant reciprocal obligation on the part of the Ottoman government other than to respond in like manner to an unlikely Russian call for military assistance. However, there was also a secret article to the treaty that was far more important and ominous as far as the other European powers were concerned, once they learned of its contents, which did not take very long. The secret article contained a stipulation that the tsar could absolve the Porte of the need to go to the expense and inconvenience of supplying substantial military assistance when required by the treaty. The condition was that "the Sublime Ottoman Porte, in place of the aid which it is bound to furnish in case of need . . . shall confine its action in favour of the Imperial Court of Russia to closing the strait of the Dardanelles, that is to say, to not allow any foreign vessels of war to enter therein under any pretext whatsoever."[6]

In the capitals of Europe, the treaty was perceived as virtually establishing Russian suzerainty over the Ottoman Empire, something that was widely considered unacceptable. Particularly troubling was the secret clause, which seemed deliberately obscure. Since Russia was clearly seeking advantages over the other powers with respect to the Porte, was it reasonable to conclude that the tsar intended that, in the event of war, Russian warships as well as those of other belligerent nations should equally be denied access to the Turkish Straits? Or was it the purpose of the treaty to provide a distinct strategic advantage to Russia? It was evident that little faith was placed in Russian assurances that there was nothing exceptional or devious about the wording and intent of the treaty. The British secretary of state, Lord Palmerston, registered a formal protest of the treaty that was delivered to the Ottoman government on August 26, 1833, which was followed shortly thereafter by a similar note from France. Reflecting his consistent distrust of the Russians, Palmerston stated that the treaty appeared

to produce a change in the relations between Turkey and Russia, to which other European States are entitled to object. . . . If the stipulations of that Treaty should hereafter lead to the armed interference of Russia in the internal affairs of Turkey, the British Government will hold itself at liberty to act upon such an occasion, in any manner which the circumstances of the moment may appear to require, equally as if the Treaty above-mentioned were not in existence.[7]

In other words, Palmerston was advising the Porte, in effect, that it had no right to enter into such an agreement without Britain's prior approval, and that as a result, the treaty was invalid as far as Britain was concerned.

One significant consequence of the Russo-Ottoman treaty, that surely was not what the Porte intended or desired, was that Britain now moved perceptibly closer to Muhammad Ali, viewing him as a major regional asset in the event that Turkey was drawn completely into the Russian orbit. The expectation was raised that the viceroy would soon have an army of some 125,000 men available to respond to a call for assistance by the British government. Nonetheless, Palmerston continued to maintain the official longstanding British policy of opposition to the dismemberment of the Ottoman Empire. Following the withdrawal of Russian forces from Turkey, British diplomacy shifted to trying to convince the Porte that the power of the British fleet was a better guarantor of Turkey's security against Muhammad Ali than were the Russians. Palmerston also warned the Porte of the "dangers and inconveniences" of the Russian alliance which were avoidable should the Porte look to Britain, "which power has the means and also the disposition effectively to control Mohamed Ali so long as Turkey should continue really independent." Moreover, he threatened, "if the option between the establishment of Mohamed Ali at Constantinople and the subjection of that capital to the power of Russia were to be forced on England, it would be impossible for HM's Government not to prefer the former alternative."[8]

At the same time, Nicholas I was concerned that the revolt of Muhammad Ali against the authority of the sultan was encouraging republicanism in Europe, something that was quite unacceptable to him. Accordingly, he sought an understanding with the equally conservative Austrian chancellor Metternich regarding a common policy with respect to the possible collapse of the Ottoman Empire. As a result of his initiative, a secret Russian-Austrian Convention of Common Action on the Eastern Question was concluded at Munchengratz on September 18, 1833. The key secret article of the agreement called for the parties to take the actions necessary "to prevent the authority of the Pasha of Egypt from extending, directly or in-directly, to the European provinces of the Ottoman Empire."[9]

Over the next several years, the European powers engaged in attempt-ing to improve their political positions in the region by playing the sultan and the viceroy against each other. Muhammad Ali had initially sought to freeze the geopolitical situation as it stood and to focus on obtaining recog-nition of his dynastic line as the hereditary rulers of Egypt and Syria. How-ever, he began to come around to the view that his own security dictated forcing a change in the regime in Istanbul. For his part, Mahmud II seemed determined to find a means of undoing the Treaty of Kutahya and forcing the Egyptians out of Syria. To enable him to achieve this goal, he turned first to the Russians and then to the British for military assistance.

At the time, Metternich, who distrusted the French and therefore sought to bring Russia and Britain closer, was coaxing the Russians into taking a reasonable position with regard to broader European interests. As a result, the tsar refused to assist the sultan on the basis that the Russian-Ottoman treaty only called for Russian aid in the event of an attack on Turkey, but not in an instance where Turkey was itself the aggressor. The British and the French took the same line, advising the Porte that a renewal of the war would endanger the sultan's throne, and that reliance on Britain and France was the Porte's best guarantee of protection against any aggression by Muhammad Ali.

However, despite the best efforts of the European powers to preserve the peace, repeated provocation by both the Turks and the Egyptians promised an outbreak of open hostilities before long. This prospect was ev-idently given greater likelihood by the perceptible deterioration in rela-tions between Muhammad Ali and Lord Palmerston, who increasingly viewed the viceroy with suspicion as a result of actions taken and planned by him, both real and imagined. Perhaps the most serious of these was Palmerston's conviction that Muhammad Ali had serious designs on the Ottoman *pashalik* of Baghdad.

The reassertion of Egyptian control over the tribes of Asir and the occu-pation of the entire Nejd, including those districts adjacent to the Persian Gulf, seemed to have no purpose other than Egyptian expansionism. This assessment was based on the fact that Muhammad Ali already controlled the trade of the Yemen and the Hejaz, and the tribes of the Arabian interior seriously threatened neither. Moreover, the Egyptian forces in Syria were well positioned for an assault on Mesopotamia from the north. An Egyp-tian drive through Nejd to the Persian Gulf coast would place Muhammad Ali in a position to seize control of the mouths of both the Euphrates and Tigris, and therefore of Baghdad, from the south. Palmerston viewed this as clear evidence of Muhammad Ali's ambitions for expansion in a direc-tion that posed a threat to British interests in the Persian Gulf region, partic-ularly in Muscat and Bahrain. Palmerston so advised the British consul at

Alexandria toward the end of 1837. He observed that the movements of Muhammad Ali's troops in Syria and Arabia "seem to indicate intentions on his part to extend his authority towards the Persian Gulf and the Pashalik of Baghdad . . . . You will state frankly to the Pasha that the British Govt. could not see with indifference the execution of such intentions."[10]

Matters began to approach the boiling point when Muhammad Ali made it known on May 25, 1838, that he intended to work to achieve complete independence from the sultan, withdrawing Egypt and Syria from the Ottoman Empire. Palmerston was determined to prevent this from happening. On June 8, he advised the British ambassador in Paris:

The Cabinet yesterday agreed that it would not do to let Mohamed Ali declare himself independent and separate Egypt and Syria from the Turkish Empire. They see that the consequence of such a declaration on his part must be, either immediately or at no distant time, conflict between him and the Sultan, that in such conflict the Turkish troops would probably be defeated, that the Russians would fly to the aid of the Sultan, and that a Russian garrison would occupy Constantinople and the Dardanelles. Once in possession of these points the Russians would never quit them. We are therefore prepared to give naval aid to the Sultan against Mohamed Ali if necessary and demanded.[11]

The political implications of an Egyptian-Ottoman war soon became a serious concern in all the capitals of Europe. Of particular note was the reaction of Metternich. He was equally opposed to a Russian or an Anglo-French intervention and therefore recommended that if an intervention were to prove necessary, it should be carried out by a Concert of Powers that would also include Austria and Prussia. Palmerston soon came to accept the logic of this proposal as a means of effectively scrapping the worrisome Treaty of Hunkar Iskelesi. Bringing Russia into such a collective security arrangement would effectively deny the tsar the freedom of independent action with regard to the Porte that he had under the treaty, since Turkey would become a virtual protectorate of the five powers rather than that of Russia alone. He wrote to Paris on July 6, 1838:

The short of the case appears to be this; if Mohamed Ali finds the least disunion between the Great Powers of Europe, he will endeavor to make himself independent and take advantage of a split which subsequent events may produce among us. But if he does declare himself independent and war ensues between him and the Sultan and the Russians interfere, the chances are that some serious quarrel will ensue between France and England on the one hand and Russia on the other; or else that England and France will be forced to remain passive spectators of things being done by Russia which could not be acquiesced in without discredit to the governments of England and France. The question then is, which is the best way to prevent the evil consequences which that step might produce? Our opinion is . . . that a previous Concert between the five Powers would be most desirable. We think, first, that if we could announce to Mohamed Ali that such a Concert is established and

that we are all prepared conjointly to help the Sultan against him, he would abandon his intentions and remain quiet. But next, we think that if, in spite of this warning, he was to move, such a Concert would afford the best security for bringing the
matter to an end without any disturbance of the peace of Europe.[12]

Notwithstanding Palmerston's support, Muhammad Ali effectively undermined Metternich's proposal. In reaction to the threat of joint action
against him, he declared that he would commit no aggression against the
Porte. Moreover, he expressed hope that he could reach an amicable settlement with the sultan on the basis of the latter's acknowledgment of the hereditary succession of Muhammad Ali's line to the throne of Egypt and
Sudan. Given his declared position of nonbelligerence, Russia, clearly reluctant to concede its preeminent position with the Porte, seized upon it as
a basis for arguing that the proposed Concert of Powers was not necessary.

Amidst this flurry of diplomatic activity designed to prevent a war, the
Porte was busily engaged in preparations for an attack on Syria. Despite
warnings from a number of the European powers, an Ottoman army under
Hafiz Pasha crossed the Euphrates into Syria on April 27, 1839, and the British and French began the movement of naval forces to the Syrian coast for
the purpose of intervening between the belligerents. The Ottoman and
Egyptian armies clashed in battle on June 26 at Nezib, north of Aleppo, and
once again the Turkish forces were defeated. Four days later Mahmud II
died and was succeeded as sultan by Abd al-Mejid I (1839–1861). This transition was followed shortly by the defection of the Turkish fleet to Muhammad Ali, leaving the Porte almost entirely dependent on the European
powers for naval support in the conflict. At this point, the Porte offered Muhammad Ali recognition of his hereditary right to Egypt, an offer that the
viceroy rejected. He countered by insisting on such recognition with regard
to all the territories under his control.

With an impending disaster now facing the Ottoman Empire, a political
initiative was promoted by Metternich to have its affairs completely taken
out of the Porte's hands. The crisis was to be resolved by the European
powers on the sultan's behalf. Metternich resurrected his Concert of
Powers proposal, suggesting that the five powers first agree on the terms of
a settlement and then impose them on Muhammad Ali. By the end of 1839,
four of the five powers were close to agreement on the terms of a settlement. The essence of the plan was to give Muhammad Ali hereditary rule
of Egypt only, and to compel him to return all other Ottoman territories to
the sultan. This time, however, it was France that was reluctant to join ranks
with the others. The French view was that Muhammad Ali would not agree
to the terms and, although he might be dissuaded from attacking Istanbul,
that he would probably move into Mesopotamia, thereby precipitating the
need for a Russian intervention with land forces. Accordingly, it was argued, Metternich's proposal was not based on a realistic appraisal of the
relative strengths of the combatants. France thus tended to side with Mu-

hammad Ali. M. Thiers, who became French prime minister in March 1840, wrote to his representative in Cairo:

Tell the viceroy to prepare himself for any reasonable sacrifice and to put his trust in France. If he is offered Egypt and Syria in hereditary succession, and is ordered to give up Adana, Candia [Crete] and the Holy Cities, he should accept. If he is offered Egypt in hereditary succession and Syria, Adana and Candia for life, he also should accept. If we can get either of these alternatives for him, we shall have done all that can be expected of us. If he refuses to make reasonable concessions we cannot go on supporting him; we are not going to risk our alliance with England in order to uphold unreasonable pretensions. So long as he understands that, he can regard us as faithful, sure and disinterested friends. We will not abandon him so long as he understands his position and adapts his conduct to it.[13]

The European powers, excluding France, finally agreed on a common position, which was set forth in the London Convention of July 15, 1840. It essentially offered Muhammad Ali the *pashalik* of Egypt in perpetuity, and the *pashalik* of Acre, which included all of Cis-Jordanian Palestine, for life. In return, Muhammad Ali was to withdraw his forces from all other Ottoman territories under his control. In fact, by the end of February, Egyptian forces had already been withdrawn from Arabia and Yemen to bolster the defenses of Alexandria.

On September 9, 1840, within days of Muhammad Ali's refusal of the offer, a Turkish force of five thousand men, along with a detachment of fifteen hundred British marines and two hundred Austrians landed unopposed in Junieh Bay, north of Beirut. At about the same time a squadron of nine British warships arrived in the area and placed the city under blockade. From that moment on, the conflict was an unmitigated disaster for the Egyptians. Beirut surrendered on October 9. The next day, the British-led combined forces in the heights above Junieh defeated an Egyptian force commanded by Ibrahim personally. On November 2, after a heavy bombardment by a British naval squadron, the Egyptian commander evacuated Acre. Commodore Sir Charles Napier took command of the British squadron off Alexandria on November 21 and immediately began negotiations with Muhammad Ali to bring an end to the hopeless conflict. Acting on his own initiative, Napier concluded an agreement with the Egyptians on November 27 that effectively gave Muhammad Ali hereditary possession of Egypt in return for the immediate evacuation of Syria. After some wrangling over the fact that Napier had exceeded his authority in concluding an agreement with Muhammad Ali that ran counter to some of the stipulations made in the original four powers offer, the agreement was accepted in principle by the Porte on December 27. It took another five months of haggling before the final terms were concluded. Then, on June 10, 1841, Muhammad Ali accepted the documents confirming his hereditary possession of Egypt and related matters from the sultan's emissaries and put on the decoration presented to him by his suzerain as a reward for his loyal services.

The era of Muhammad Ali in the Middle East had come to an end, and the era of virtually complete European dominance of Middle Eastern affairs had begun.

NOTES

1. Barker to Codrington, December 26, 1827. FO 78/160.

2. Quoted by M. Sabry, *L'Empire Egyptien sous Mehemet Ali et la Question de l'Orient, 1811–1849*, pp. 218–219.

3. John Marlowe, *Perfidious Albion*, p. 199.

4. Sabry, op. cit., pp. 224–225.

5. FO 78/472.

6. See J. C. Hurewitz, ed., *The Middle East and North Africa in World Politics: A Documentary Record*, p. 253.

7. Ibid., p. 254.

8. Palmerston to Ponsonby, December 23, 1833. FO 78/472.

9. See Hurewitz, ed., *The Middle East and North Africa*, p. 255.

10. FO 78/318.

11. William Henry Lytton Bulwer, *The Life of Palmerston*, vol. 2, pp. 267–268.

12. Ibid., pp. 270–71.

13. F. Charles-Roux, *Thiers et Mehemet Ali*, pp. 49–50.

13

The Crimean War

British and Russian policies toward the Ottoman Empire were predicated on two divergent perceptions of national interest. From the British stand-point, the preservation of the integrity of the empire served to help maintain the balance of power in Europe. It also afforded significant opportunities for the marketing of British manufactured goods because of the preferential customs duties provided for under the Capitulations agreement. Accordingly, the British were eager to support the internal Turkish reform movement headed by Mustafa Reshid Pasha, the former Ottoman ambassador to England.

The tsar, also, was not opposed in principle to the preservation of the Ottoman Empire intact, as he had clearly demonstrated in the recent crisis between the Porte and Muhammad Ali. He was, however, quite convinced that the Ottoman Empire was so inherently corrupt that it was beyond salvation. Since it was bound to collapse sooner or later, he wanted to be sure that Russia would be in a position to maximize its share of the spoils. In the meantime, it was in Russia's interest to maintain Turkey as a weak buffer state, which at a minimum helped provide for security of access to the Turkish Straits and the Black Sea. But his approach to dealing with the overall "Eastern Question" was obviously ambivalent, primarily as a result of his basic distrust of France. In the tsar's view, France continued to represent the embodiment of social revolutionary ideas and he therefore sought to align Russia with Britain, Austria, and Prussia in a conservative entente directed against the threat he saw emanating from and inspired by Paris.

Given this perspective, the tsar attempted to find common ground with Britain for dealing with whatever issues arose in the Middle East on a strictly bilateral basis, hoping to exclude France from any role whatever in the region. The timing for such a move seemed ripe in view of the series of Anglo-French political confrontations that were occurring around the world as their respective imperial interests collided in places as remote as Tahiti. Nicholas took the opportunity during a visit to the English Court in the summer of 1844 to amplify his views on the Eastern Question in a memorandum. According to the Duke of Argyll, this document contained the following propositions:

That the maintenance of Turkey in its existing territory and degree of independence is a great object of European policy. That in order to preserve that maintenance the Powers of Europe should abstain from making on the Porte demands conceived in a selfish interest, or from assuming towards it an attitude of exclusive dictation. That, in the event of the Porte giving to any one of the Powers just cause of complaint, that Power should be aided by the rest in its endeavours to have that cause removed. That all the Powers should urge on the Porte the duty of conciliating its Christian subjects, and should use all their influence, on the other hand, to keep those subjects to their allegiance. That, in the event of any unforeseen calamity befalling the Turkish Empire, Russia and England should agree together as to the course that should be pursued.[1]

The British foreign secretary, Lord Aberdeen, warmly received these ideas, and for a moment it appeared that a gentlemen's agreement had been reached between the primary European rivals for dominance in the Ottoman sphere. The consensus view was that Britain and Russia, at the appropriate time, should settle their most difficult common problem through the partition of Turkey between them. This position was seen as a simple recognition of the fact that "by land, Russia exercises over Turkey a preponderant position; by sea, England occupies the same position. Isolated, the action of these two Powers might do a great deal of harm; combined, it may do much good."[2] However, this apparent congruence in British and Russian policy was soon shattered as a consequence of the tsar's actions in response to the revolutions that erupted throughout Europe in 1848.

As a leading conservative power, Russia readily used its troops to intervene as it saw fit to prevent the emergence of revolutionary regimes in the continent. Of particular relevance here was the eruption that took place when the Chamber of Deputies in Budapest declared Hungary to be virtually independent of the Habsburg Empire. Franz Joseph I (1848–1916) reasserted control over Budapest in January 1849, but the Hungarian diet fled the city and declared an independent republic under Louis Kossuth. This move was more than the tsar could tolerate and, at the request of Franz Joseph, he dispatched an army of one hundred thousand troops under General I. F. Paskevich, who suppressed the rebellion on August 9, 1849. In the meanwhile, the revolutionary ferment in nearby Hungary quickly spilled over into the Ottoman principalities of Moldavia and Wallachia. The uprising appeared to be on the verge of success in Wallachia, where the ruling prince, George Bibescu, was forced to accept a revolutionary constitution, which led to the proclamation of the unity and independence of Rumania on June 21, 1848. With the agreement of the sultan, Russian troops suppressed the rebellion in Wallachia while they were on their way to intervene in Hungary.

The extent and success of the Russian suppression of the liberal revolutionary movements eventually struck a discordant note in Britain. When large numbers of the revolutionary leaders fled to safety in Ottoman territory, the Russians demanded that they be turned over to them. Reshid Pasha rejected this demand, leading the Russians to sever relations with the Porte on September 17, 1849. In the light of these developments, and the history of their support for the reform efforts of Reshid Pasha, the British concluded that their interests in the Middle East, in the last analysis, were closer to those of France than Russia. The brief era of British-Russian cooperation had come to an end.

With the threat of a new war between Russia and Turkey now looming on the horizon, both France and Britain dispatched their fleets to the Dardanelles to be in a position to lend support to the sultan in the event of a Russian attack. The immediate crisis was defused when the tsar backed down after evidently reconsidering the implications of an open conflict with the Western powers. However, the relations between the powers failed to improve, and in fact remained particularly volatile, requiring only a spark to ignite a conflict between them. That spark was to be provided by what appeared to be a rather minor sectarian clerical question, far removed from the principal issues of international affairs, but which actually symbolized the great power struggle for dominance in the Middle East.

The inflammatory issue arose as a consequence of the privileged position accorded to France in perpetuity by the Porte in accordance with the Capitulation agreement of May 28, 1740. This grant was made in recognition of the services of the French ambassador to the sultan in connection with the conclusion of the recent war between the Ottoman and Hapsburg empires. One of the privileges granted to the French was the designation of the Latin Catholic monks in Palestine as custodians of the holy places in the country. While this was considered an important concession in the eighteenth century, it was hardly viewed as such a century later. In the wake of the secularism that characterized French governments after the revolution of 1789, the significance of the privilege had become a matter of official indifference. Thus, when it became apparent that the Latin monks were neglecting their responsibilities with regard to the upkeep of the several holy sites, their chores were soon assumed by Greek Orthodox monks with the tacit approval of France, which displayed little interest in the matter at the time.

Over the years, a sort of balance of power had emerged among the various Christian denominations and sects with regard to their parochial rights of access and ritual at the various holy sites. These were established by custom and tradition, and were sanctioned by the Porte as a means of maintaining communal harmony within the non-Muslim population. In general, France assumed the role of primary sponsor of the Latins in the Holy Land, while Russia became the patron of the Orthodox. However, the prevailing equilibrium between the major Christian denominations started to break down after 1829, when the Russians began to actively champion the rights of the Orthodox priests against the Catholics supported by France. The balance was further upset in 1841, when the tsar refurbished two old Orthodox monasteries to accommodate a large number of Russian pilgrims. Then, in 1843, with Russian encouragement and support, the Orthodox patriarch of Jerusalem obtained official approval of his separation from the patriarchate of Constantinople and began to build an independent sectarian power base in Palestine that threatened to diminish the relative importance of the Latins.

Matters began to come to a head in 1847 with the sudden removal of a silver star that marked the location of the Nativity in the church at Bethlehem. Since the inscription on the star was in Latin, it was automatically assumed that the Greeks had removed it. A clamor now arose not only for restoration of the star but also for the assignment to France of certain exclusive rights in the holy places in Bethlehem and Jerusalem. As it turned out, this rather minor sectarian issue soon became an important factor in the domestic politics of France.

Seeking to gain additional domestic prestige by appealing to the religious instincts of the French people at a time when he was planning to transform the Second Republic into a hereditary monarchy, Louis Napoleon became the ardent champion of the cause of the Latin monks of Palestine. In 1852 he instructed the French ambassador to the Porte, General Jacques Aupick, to support their claims to the right of guardianship of the holy places. The basis for this intervention was the original Capitulation agreement of 1740. This meant the exclusion of the Greek Orthodox monks who had administered the sites since 1812.

There was, however, more to this heightened French interest in the holy sites in Palestine than just domestic considerations. This was made clear in a passage that Louis Napoleon's foreign minister wrote to Aupick that was later deleted. "Finally, there is another consideration of great weight in our eyes because it is connected with still higher interests yet, that is . . . the utility that there is for the Porte itself that our influence in the Orient be adequate to counter-balance the always growing [influence] of Russia."[3] It was evidently Louis Napoleon's idea to try to exploit the issue of the holy places to weaken the Holy Alliance by creating a split between Orthodox Russia and Roman Catholic Austria. And, as he correctly anticipated, France's insistence on the return of the regime of the holy places to Latin control received the support of the other Catholic states of Europe, including Austria, Belgium, Naples, Portugal, Sardinia, and Spain, thus transforming the issue into a matter of international importance.

The sultan, who had little interest or stake in the outcome of this sectarian squabble, but wanted to lessen intercommunal strife in the empire, suggested a compromise that was subsequently incorporated into an edict issued on February 9, 1852. The matter was to be resolved by awarding three of the keys to the Church of the Nativity in Bethlehem to the Latin monks, and by also granting them the right to say mass at the tomb of the Virgin. This compromise was quite acceptable to Louis Napoleon, who was primarily interested in its domestic political value as an example of his successful pursuit of Catholic interests abroad. Nonetheless, there was also a negative aspect to France's diplomatic victory in the affair since it involved setting a new and potentially troublesome precedent, albeit inadvertently, that would create some significant political problems later on.

Until this time, although functioning within the traditional Ottoman *millet* or communal system under which the non-Muslim communities were effectively ruled by their own religious authorities, the organizational status of the relatively small Latin community in the Ottoman Empire was fluid as compared with the much larger Greek Orthodox community. A patriarch headed the latter, whereas the Latins had no central local authority. Accordingly, the interests of the multinational Latins were usually represented by the consular missions of the various European states. But, once the French government assumed that oversight role, any issue arising with regards to the rights of Roman Catholics within the Ottoman Empire was routinely negotiated between the Porte and the resident French minister. This gave the French a position of influence at the Porte that was particularly disturbing to the tsar, who could not make a similar claim to represent the Orthodox community. Historically, the Greek Orthodox Church in the Ottoman Empire was considered as equal in standing to the Russian Orthodox Church. Indeed, technically speaking, the patriarch in Istanbul was superior to the authorities of the Russian Church even in Russia. The tsar became jealous of the advantage that France had reaped from its position relative to the Latin community, and it would not be long before he would attempt to achieve identical status within the Ottoman Empire with respect to the Orthodox communities. This effort would have not inconsequential political and strategic significance.

Nicholas's reaction to the sultan's *firman* regarding joint administration of the holy places was completely negative, and he immediately demanded and received a secret edict from the sultan, dated March 12, 1852, that annulled the concessions previously awarded to France and the Latins. Thus, while Louis Napoleon's envoy was receiving the congratulations of the pope on his signal achievement, the tsar had already reversed the reality.

Once what had happened became public in September of that year, the whole issue of the holy places was opened again, with the Porte caught between the competing pressures of the Latins and the Greeks, each of which was backed by its patron state. However, when the Turkish commissioner in Jerusalem, Alif Bey, refused to block access to the holy places by Latin monks and pilgrims regardless of the secret edict, the tsar was made to look ridiculous.

Once Louis Bonaparte overthrew the French Republic on November 2, 1852, and declared himself Emperor Napoleon III, he lost interest entirely in the holy places issue. It had served his purposes and was no longer useful. Indeed, to ease tensions with Russia over the affair, he was prepared to negotiate a new compromise on control of the holy sites with the tsar. Nicholas, however, had been embarrassed by the blow to his prestige and felt the need to obtain some new concessions to save face. At a minimum he wanted an agreement with the Porte that would put the Greek Orthodox on an equal legal footing with the Latins and that would recognize the tsar as the protector of the Orthodox *millet*, a counterpart to the French role with regard to the Latins. What had started as a minor sectarian squabble had now grown into the more serious and dangerous question of the future relations between the Russian and Ottoman Empires.

Before undertaking his effort to get the Porte to comply with his wishes, Nicholas attempted to resurrect the bilateral cooperation with Britain that existed immediately prior to 1848. With Lord Aberdeen now the British prime minister, Nicholas sought to reach agreement early in 1853 on the disposition of the territorial assets of the Ottoman Empire in the event of its dissolution. His concept, as conveyed in a series of conversations with the British ambassador, George H. Seymour, was that no outside power would be permitted to control Istanbul. Bulgaria, Serbia, and the Principalities would become independent within a Russian sphere of influence, and as compensation, Britain might take Crete and Egypt for itself. France, of course, was to get nothing. No agreement to such effect was ever formally concluded. But the fact that the proposal was not explicitly rejected led Nicholas to conclude that the British were giving it serious consideration, and that they would support the new demands he was about to make on the sultan with regard to the holy places in Palestine.

In March 1853, Nicholas sent Prince Alexander Menshikov to the Porte not only to insist on a reversion of control of the holy places to the Orthodox clerics. He also wanted what amounted to a formal acknowledgment by the sultan, to be reflected in a document equivalent to a treaty, of the tsar's role as protector of all the Orthodox Christian subjects of the Ottoman Empire. The essence of the Russian proposal was contained in the following draft treaty article submitted to the Porte:

The Imperial Court of Russia and the Ottoman Sublime Porte, desiring to prevent and to remove forever any reason for disagreement, for doubt, or for misunderstanding on the subject of the immunities, rights, and liberties accorded and assured *ab antiquo* by the Ottoman emperors in their states to the Greek-Russian-Orthodox religion, professed by all Russia, as by all inhabitants of the principalities of Moldavia, Wallachia, and Serbia and by various other Christian populations of Turkey of different provinces, agree and stipulate by the present convention that the Christian Orthodox religion will be constantly protected in all its churches, and that the ministers of the Imperial Court of Russia will have, as in the past, the right to make representations on behalf of the churches of Constantinople and of other places and cities, as also on behalf of the clergy, and that these remonstrances will be received as coming in the name of a neighboring and sincerely friendly power.[4]

What the tsar was asking the sultan to agree to was, in effect, a perpetual right to interfere in internal Ottoman affairs. As a practical matter, this proposed convention meant that since everyone who professed Orthodoxy would look to the tsar as his protector, some twelve million Ottoman subjects would owe their primary allegiance to the tsar rather than the sultan. The tsar's demands placed the Porte squarely between the opposing interests of France and Russia. The sultan tried to wheedle his way out of this awkward situation by diplomatic sleight of hand, telling each party what he wanted to hear. But the tsar was not satisfied and would not let the matter rest. Indeed, he began pressing for implementation of his plan to attack and seize Istanbul, a plan that was opposed as impracticable by his closest advisors.

The British encouraged the Porte to respond favorably to the tsar's demand concerning the administration of the holy sites. However, the second demand, which called for formal recognition of the tsar as the protector of all Orthodox persons in the Ottoman Empire, was deemed so insupportable that the British effectively urged the Porte to reject it completely, which it did in the latter part of May. Menshikov left Istanbul on May 22, taking the entire staff of the Russian embassy with him, a clear indication of what was likely to follow.

On May 31, 1853, the tsar, agreeing to a less dramatic course of action than his original idea of attempting to seize Istanbul, issued an ultimatum to the sultan warning that unless his demands were met, Russian forces would occupy the Danubian Principalities. Moreover, the tsar insisted that such action was not to be considered as an act of war, but merely as a guarantee of Ottoman good faith during subsequent negotiations. At this point, on June 2, Britain ordered its fleet to Besika Bay, near the Dardanelles, where it was joined a few days later by a French squadron, and gave authority to its ambassador to the Porte to order the fleet to Istanbul in the event of a Russian attack. With Britain evidently willing to back it, the Porte rejected the Russian ultimatum. This put the tsar into a corner, forcing him either to make good on his threat or to look foolish before the world. There could be little doubt about which alternative he would choose. On July 21, 1853, a large Russian army under Prince Gorchakov crossed the Pruth and began the occupation of Moldavia and Wallachia.

The tsar evidently hoped to avoid a general war, which he was sure Britain did not want, by announcing to the powers that the occupation was not intended as an act of war, but rather as an expedient to compel Ottoman compliance with Russia's just demands. In an effort to diffuse the situation, Britain encouraged the Porte to make a unilateral compromise statement confirming the traditional privileges enjoyed by the Orthodox Church, but this failed to satisfy the tsar. Nicholas had come to believe that he held the upper hand in the developing crisis. He expected Austria and Prussia, because of their concerns about Louis Napoleon's ambitions, to align with Russia rather than with an Anglo-French entente, thereby pressuring the British to back down from their aggressive posture in support of Turkey. Nicholas probably also believed that Austria was obligated to Russia for its intervention in 1848 to assist in suppressing the Hungarian uprising. However, as the Austrian Minister Schwartzenberg stated at the time: "Austria will surprise the world with her ingratitude."[5]

The tsar also attempted to place additional pressures on the Porte by enlisting Persia as an ally. To get Persia to join in an attack on Turkey in the increasingly likely event of war, Nicholas apparently offered to forgive that portion of the outstanding indemnity still due to Russia under the Treaty of Turkmanchai. Moreover, he was prepared to offer the shah a cash payment of twice the amount of the outstanding debt, in addition to providing supplies for the Persian army. In addition, Russia proposed that Persia could annex any Ottoman territory it might conquer during the conflict. The shah, however, was not prepared to enter into a conflict that would place him directly in opposition to Britain. Given the prospect of a major conflict in the region that would involve the major powers, the shah proposed instead that Persia join with the entente against Russia on the basis of the same terms offered by the latter. The only exception was that instead of Turkish territory it would seek territorial compensation in the Persian provinces lost to Russia in the war of 1826–1828. However, by the time that the Persian counterproposals were relayed to London, the Russo-Turkish conflict had already widened into a general conflict among the major powers, and little attention was given to the Persian offer of assistance.

Representatives of Austria, Britain, France, and Prussia convened in Vienna in July 1853 to attempt to find a diplomatic solution to the crisis. They finally agreed on the text of a diplomatic note that was worded in a manner that they, apparently naively, believed would satisfy the requirements of both sides in the dispute, without accommodating the tsar's demand for a protectorate. The note, which the Porte was to send to the tsar, would reaffirm Ottoman adherence to "the letter and spirit of the Treaties of Kainardji and Adrianople relative to the protection of the Christian religion." Since the Russians claimed that the Treaty of Kuchuk Kaynarja awarded them a protectorate over the Greek Orthodox community, the text of the proposed note was quite acceptable to them. Nicholas sent a telegram on August 3 indicating his acceptance on the condition that no changes were subsequently to be made to the proposed note. However, the Porte was unwilling to go along with the ploy as proposed. It took umbrage that it had not even been consulted about the composition of the note, that the note was submitted in draft to the tsar before a copy was even sent to the sultan, and that it did not adequately address Ottoman concerns. The Porte made its acceptance conditional on a modification of the key clause of the document to refer "to the stipulations of the Treaty of Kainardji, confirmed by that of Adrianople, relative to the protection by the Sublime Porte of the Christian religion."[6]

This proposed revision of the note was acceptable in principle to the powers. However, it soon became clear that the original wording of the clause was accepted by the Russians only because it permitted them to interpret it as satisfying their claim to being the protectors of the Christian religion and, by extension, of the sultan's Christian subjects as well. However, by insisting upon the modification it proposed, apparently with the direct encouragement of the British ambassador, Lord Stratford, and contrary to the policy of his government, the Porte made it clear that the sultan and not the tsar would protect the Christians of the empire. For the Ottomans it was not merely a matter of pride but one of political survival. As was to be expected, this rewording of the note was completely unacceptable to the Russians and the prospect of war loomed once again as the powers were unable to get the Porte to back down from its position in favor of Russia. Further complicating matters was a strong upsurge of anti-Russian demonstrations in Istanbul which assured the Porte of strong public support for a confrontation with Russia. The British tried to pressure the Porte to be more accommodating by withdrawing their fleet from the Dardanelles, but this gesture came too late to have any practical effect. It was now evident that if the Russians did not withdraw from the Principalities, the sultan would declare war.

On October 4, 1853, the Ottoman commander at Shumla, Omer Pasha, presented an ultimatum to Prince Gorchakov, the Russian commander in the Principalities, demanding the evacuation of Russian forces within fifteen days. During this period, Reshid Pasha sought to obtain unequivocal and extensive commitments of support from the Western powers. He made it clear that Ottoman war aims would be to establish a series of buffer regions across the entire stretch of the Russian-Ottoman frontier to separate the empires. Although the Principalities in the west already presumably served this purpose, he also urged a rollback of the Russians from Circassia and Daghestan in the Caucasus, a proposal that struck the British as rather fanciful. It seems that the war fever had led the Ottoman leaders to believe that they were in a better military position than was the actual case.

When there was no Russian reply to the Ottoman ultimatum within the specified time limit, the Porte initiated hostilities on October 23 and launched a major assault across the Danube four days later. At the same time, the Ottoman provincial army that was based in Erzerum and Kars, in eastern Anatolia, crossed the frontier into the southern Caucasus. An Ottoman naval squadron sailed into the Black Sea in anticipation of a Russian naval assault through the Bosphorus. Not finding the enemy, it anchored in the Bay of Sinope for the winter, where it was attacked and completely destroyed by the Russian Black Sea fleet on November 30.

It seems that the Russians had hoped that a decisive naval victory over the Ottomans would have a cooling effect on Anglo-French support for the Porte in the conflict. The effect, however, was quite the opposite. This naval action had serious repercussions in both England and France where, coupled with the news of a significant Russian advance on the eastern front near Kars, Russian military superiority was clearly acknowledged. Moreover, the fact that it was a naval victory caused acute embarrassment to both Britain and France, whose fleets had been dispatched to the region precisely for the purpose of protecting the Turks. This development placed the European powers in the uncomfortable position of having to choose between coming to the sultan's assistance or allowing the Russians to dismember the Ottoman Empire, a prospect rife with possible unanticipated consequences. Support for a decision in favor of compelling a Russian retreat now became irrepressible.

Ironically, just as the Porte was about to gain the direct Anglo-French support that it had been seeking for months, Reshid Pasha suddenly had a change of heart and became anxious to find a negotiated solution to the conflict. One of the principal factors causing this reversal of positions was the news from Persia. A report from the French resident at Baghdad, dated November 30, revealed that a mission dispatched by Nicholas had apparently convinced Nasir ad-din Shah to lend military support to the Russians in the east, raising the prospect of a much wider conflict on that vulnerable front. It appears that the Russians presented the shah with an ultimatum that placed him in a particularly difficult position. In exchange for Persian military support, Russia was prepared to wipe out the large indemnity that was still owed by Teheran and to offer aid against any British retaliation by a Russian occupation of Afghanistan, deflecting British concern to the security of India. However, if the shah were to refuse to cooperate with the tsar, then Nicholas threatened to invade Azerbaijan and the Caspian region. Feeling more immediate pressure from the Russians than the British, the shah ordered the mobilization of some seventy-five thousand men. As a result, the British resident at Baghdad, Henry Rawlinson, anticipated an immediate Persian attack on Ottoman Iraq. He wrote to the government of

India in late November: "The Shah has openly adopted the side of Russia in her quarrel with the Porte and Baghdad is threatened with invasion. Under such circumstances, unless assistance be rendered from India, the Turks will almost certainly be driven out of these countries, and the shock occasioned thereby will place in jeopardy the whole fabric of [the] Ottoman Empire in Asia."[7]

The crisis, however, was short-lived. The British made it clear to the shah that the only prudent course for Persia was one of neutrality, and that if it succumbed to adventurism in support of Russia, it would suffer penalties in southern Persia, which was completely open to British intervention. To give credibility to this threat, relations with Persia were temporarily severed in November 1853, ostensibly because of a relatively trivial incident concerning the servants of the British resident. The Bombay government was instructed to prepare to seize Kharg Island in the Gulf, an action that became unnecessary, and plans were laid for a British landing at Bushire and a possible march on Shiraz, or an augmentation of the Turkish defenses of Baghdad or Basra.

The British concern about the events taking place in the region evidently went beyond the question of maintaining the integrity of the Ottoman Empire in Asia. They did not believe that Persia could successfully compete with Russia for control of the Caspian region. Accordingly, it was expected that Persia would come under Russian domination, making British influence in the Ottoman Empire and Afghanistan more important than ever for the protection of India. Since Afghanistan was quite unstable, this meant that the only potentially useful regional ally for its Asian policy was the Ottoman Empire, which therefore had to be maintained intact in Asia at all costs. As a result, the British also became anxious to find a negotiated settlement to the conflict before a major irruption with unpredictable consequences took place in western Asia.

Notwithstanding their renewed interest in a negotiated settlement, events drew the British and French ever more into direct confrontation with Russia. A general war became highly probable by December 23, when the British ordered their fleet to protect the Ottoman flag and territory. It became a virtual certainty on January 4, 1854, when it was announced that the British and French fleet commanders had been issued instructions to compel all Russian vessels in the Black Sea to return to their harbors. Russia refused to back down and severed diplomatic relations with both Britain and France on February 6. Even so, the powers were not yet at war, and a last attempt to prevent one was made at the initiative of Austria, which intimated that it would align with Britain and France if the latter would present an ultimatum to the Russians demanding their withdrawal from the Principalities. The allies agreed and issued an ultimatum on February 27 calling for the evacuation of Moldavia and Wallachia by April 30. The Russians rejected this demand on March 19, leading to declarations of war by

Britain and France on March 27 and 28 respectively. Once war was declared, Austria let it be known that its promised support was intended to be diplomatic only, and Prussia similarly held aloof from direct involvement, splitting the Concert of Powers and turning the conflict into one between Russia on one side and an Anglo-French-Ottoman alliance on the other.

The allies rushed armies to Turkey and prepared them for an invasion of the Principalities. However, before they could even begin to force the Russians out of Moldavia and Wallachia, the Russians launched a major offensive across the Danube, driving the Ottoman army back to its main defense line that linked Shumla, Varna, and Silistria, the last falling to them on June 23. In the meanwhile, Austria concluded a separate treaty with the Porte on June 14 that granted it the right of occupation of the Principalities for the duration of the war in exchange for its support against the Russians. At the same time, Austria and Prussia were still pressuring the tsar to prevent a general European war by withdrawing from the Principalities. Faced by the prospect of a possible war with Austria, it became impracticable for the Russians to continue fighting on the Danube front since it would become necessary to redeploy their troops to defend the Russian frontier.

Although the tsar was not at all pleased about the idea of the Austrians replacing his forces in the Principalities, he did concur with the idea that permitting them to do so would certainly be more acceptable than turning the territories back to the Ottomans. By acceding to this proposal, he would be able to withdraw his forces and thereby eliminate the justification for the war that he faced with Britain and France. Accordingly, Russian forces evacuated Moldavia and Wallachia in mid-June 1854 on the express condition that the Austrians who replaced them would not permit any Ottoman, British, or French troops to enter the territories.

However, instead of bringing the war to an end, the Russian withdrawal from the Principalities merely brought about a significant change in its course. On July 22, Lord Clarendon made it quite clear that the allies would no longer accept a reversion to the situation that had prevailed before the Russians crossed the Pruth. Among other things, the question of freedom of navigation on the Danube was raised. Moreover, the allies now insisted that the perpetual threat of attack on Istanbul by the Russian navy in the Black Sea be eliminated. Indeed, the allies had already reached the major decision to "strike at the very heart of Russian power in the East—and that heart is at Sebastopol."[8] The focus of the allied effort thus shifted from the liberation of the Principalities to the destruction of Russia's naval capabilities in the Black Sea by an assault on its principal bases in the Crimea.

The siege of Sevastapol began in the autumn of 1854 and lasted until September 8, 1855. The fall of the city was not in itself decisive for the course of the war from a strictly military perspective. The garrison had been defended by some 130,000 troops, which represented only a small fraction of the two million men in the Russian army. In fact, the taking of Sevastopol left the allies with a major dilemma—what to do next. To carry the war into the interior of Russia would have required a massive land invasion, which was not really feasible unless Austria and Prussia both agreed to commit their armies for the purpose. Since neither was willing to do so, the Anglo-French alliance was left with only two plausible options. One was to move the naval war from the Black Sea to the Baltic and seek to destroy the Russian fleet there and perhaps to capture Saint Petersburg. The second was to attempt to force Russia into submission by an extended naval blockade of all its coasts. As the allies contemplated these possibilities, developments in Asia had an unanticipated impact on the subsequent course of events.

Although the war on the Crimean front had been a disaster for them, the Russians were more successful against the sultan's forces in the Caucasus region. After a five-month siege, the Turks were compelled to surrender Kars on November 26, 1855. Strategically, this was a dramatic loss for the Turks because Kars was the eastern gateway into Anatolia. Moreover, there were no longer any regular Turkish troops to stand in the way of the Russian siege army of fifty thousand men, to stop them from marching across the peninsula along the military road to Erzerum and into the Asian underbelly of Istanbul itself. It was also an acute embarrassment to the allies since they were sitting in the Crimea with some two hundred thousand troops and had done nothing to prevent the Russian victory. In fact, after the fall of Kars, the Russians were in control of more captured territory than was the Anglo-French alliance.

Although France evinced little interest in southwest Asia, it was of vital importance to Britain especially since such a Russian advance posed a potential threat to the security of India. Accordingly, Britain began developing plans for opening a special theater of war in Asia Minor and the Caucasus in 1856, even without French participation if necessary. A decision on this was deferred, however, until the scheduled meeting of the allied war council in mid-January 1856. At the same time, the conquest of Kars seemed to compensate Russia in a sense for the loss of the Crimea, and therefore appears to have made it easier for the new tsar, Alexander II (1855–1881), to accept a settlement from a position of relative strength. It also seems that the prospect of a wider war, stretching from the Baltic to the Caucasus, would have imposed military requirements that exceeded Russia's mobilization potential without first instituting major internal reforms. Accordingly, by the time the allied war council convened, Russia had already indicated its readiness to negotiate peace.

Formal peace negotiations were initiated in early 1856 and soon resulted in the Treaty of Paris (March 30, 1856). On the whole, the terms of the treaty, which had actually been under negotiation for nearly two years, constituted a significant setback for Russia and the tsar. For a century and a half, Russian foreign policy in the region had been focused on three objectives:

establishing its naval supremacy in the Black Sea, obtaining freedom of passage through the Turkish Straits to the Mediterranean, and achieving acknowledgment as the protector of all Christians in the Ottoman Empire. The Treaty of Paris effectively negated each of these goals.

Although Russia received Sevastopol back in return for its withdrawal from Kars, it lost the right to maintain its Black Sea fleet, which was neutralized. This mandate was clearly given at the insistence of Britain, which wanted to prevent the tsar from using the security afforded by a closing of the straits to build a naval capability that might ultimately rival its own. At the same time, a new regime was imposed over the Turkish Straits that closed them to all foreign naval vessels. This provision also affected Russia far more than Britain, which, as the preeminent naval power of the age, could position a fleet just outside the Dardanelles and send it through the straits in the event of a renewal of hostilities. Indeed, one of the main thrusts of Russian policy during the next decade and a half concerned finding a means for undoing the Black Sea clauses of the treaty. The pact also provided that the southern part of Bessarabia was to be annexed to Moldavia, thereby depriving Russia of any direct control of the Danube. Finally, Russia had to abandon its claim as exclusive protector of the Orthodox Christians in the sultan's domains. Instead, all the Christians in the Ottoman Empire were henceforth placed under the protection of the Great Powers, which also undertook to respect and guarantee the independence and territorial integrity of the Ottoman Empire. Britain, France and Austria subsequently reaffirmed this assurance in a Treaty of Guarantee (April 15, 1856).

As one writer observed: "It is ironic that the Crimean War, a British victory, hurt Britain in the long run, since the attenuation of Russian influence in the Balkans and in Europe encouraged the Russians to drive for expansion in Asia and thus provided the occasion for the growth of new tensions between the two European fringe powers."[9]

NOTES

1. See John A. R. Marriott, *The Eastern Question: An Historical Study in European Diplomacy*, p. 247.

2. Vernon John Puryear, "New Light on the Origins of the Crimean War," in Brison D. Gooch, ed., *The Origins of the Crimean War*, p. 7.

3. Ann Pottinger Saab, *The Origins of the Crimean Alliance*, p. 10.

4. Ibid., p. 27.

5. George Vernadsky, *A History of Russia*, p. 154.

6. Marriott, *The Eastern Question*, p. 262.

7. John B. Kelly, *Britain and the Persian Gulf, 1795–1880*, p. 455.

8. *The Times*, June 24, 1854.

9. Winfried Baumgart, *The Peace of Paris 1856*, p. 6.

14

Britain and Russia in Persia and Central Asia

It was noted earlier that Russia had attempted to pressure Persia into the Crimean War on its side in 1853 but was successfully offset by British counterpressures that kept Persia neutral in the conflict. But being forced into such a position ran directly counter to the ambitions of Nasir ad-din Shah (1848–1896), who wanted very much to reap some tangible benefits from the discomfiture of both of Persia's long-standing enemies. Blocked from attempting to recover any former Persian lands from either the Ottoman or Russian Empires, the shah, most probably with Russian encouragement, once again began eyeing Afghanistan, his neighbor to the east.

Persian ambitions in this direction, however, were anathema to Britain, which saw them as eventually leading to further Russian penetration of a region uncomfortably close to India. As early as March 1854, Lord Dalhousie, the governor-general of India, wrote that it behooved the British government to leave nothing undone "which would tend to make Afghanistan an effectual barrier against Russian aggression, or which would encourage the Afghan tribes to make common cause with us against an enemy whose success would be fatal to the common interests of both Afghan and British power."[1] What this meant, as a practical matter, was that the British were interested in enlisting the powerful Afghan chief and former adversary Dost Muhammad as an ally, and a treaty to this effect was signed on his behalf by his son Ghulam Haider on March 30, 1855. Moreover, the British envoy at Teheran was specifically instructed to make it clear to the Persian government that Britain would not tolerate any attempt by the Persians to extend their influence into Afghanistan in any manner that might lead to a loss of Afghan independence.

It had been British policy for at least a decade to keep the states of Herat, Kabul, and Qandahar separate and independent, and the British were not prepared to see this arrangement disturbed by Persia. Nonetheless, rumors abounded in the summer of 1855 that Dost Muhammad was preparing to march against his half-brothers at Qandahar and to attempt to weld Kabul, Herat, and Qandahar into a single Afghan state. The shah became determined not to allow this to happen, since, at a minimum, he wanted Herat for Persia. The opportunity for the shah to realize this ambition seemed to be at hand in October 1855, when there was a successful palace coup in Herat that brought Shahzadeh Muhammad Yusuf, a former Persian pensioner, to power, probably with Persian connivance. To give himself greater freedom of action with regard to his intention to annex Herat, the shah was anxious to get rid of the watchful British envoy in Teheran and contrived a dispute over protocol that soon escalated to a break in relations with Britain on November 19.

The news of the rupture was still being assessed by the British when Dost Muhammad captured Qandahar in December 1855 and prepared to march on Herat. Muhammad Yusuf promptly appealed to the shah for assistance, and Nasir ad-din Shah eagerly agreed to the request. A Persian army under Sultan Murad Mirza was dispatched into Khorasan in February 1856 and promptly laid siege to and captured Ghorian, a fortress that dominated the approach to Herat from the west. The shah next demanded the placement of a Persian garrison in Herat. At this point, when the Heratis recognized that instead of defending them against Dost Muhammad the Persians intended to seize the city for themselves, they overthrew Muhammad Yusuf and sent an appeal for help to the government of India. The British, however, were ambivalent about how to deal with the problem and procrastinated, discouraging Dost Muhammad from taking any action against the Persians on behalf of Herat because they were unsure of the shah's intentions. When it became clear in May that the shah intended to take Herat, Lord Palmerston raised a storm with the British government, convinced that the Russians were behind the move. He advised Lord Clarendon: "It is of great and essential importance that Persia should not possess Herat. Persia was for many years deemed our barrier of defence for India against Russia. . . . We must now look upon Persia as the advanced guard of Russia."[2]

On July 10, 1856, instructions were sent to India to encourage and support Dost Muhammad in forcing a Persian withdrawal from Herat. The following day an ultimatum was issued to the Persian government demanding withdrawal. The Persian response, which came on July 16, suggested that the British were getting upset over nothing, that Persia had only moved to relieve Herat from a threat by Dost Muhammad, and that the Persian forces would retire when Dost Muhammad's troops returned to Kabul. It seemed clear that the Persians were not going to back down in the absence of an unambiguous display of British force. Further instructions were issued to the government of India on July 22 to prepare for the seizure of Kharg Island in the Gulf as well as the area around Bushire on the mainland.

Presumably, the purpose of a British attack on Persia from the southwest was to force the shah to fight a two-front campaign, something he could ill afford and could not possibly win given his actual circumstances. The Persians could, in fact, only place some twenty thousand men in the field to block such a British move. But Palmerston evidently had something else in mind as well as he pressed the cabinet to send orders for the campaign to the government in Bombay. He wrote to Clarendon, with regard to Kharg, "That island might become important to us if the Road to India should end by being through Asia Minor instead of through Egypt."[3]

The government of India, however, was very reluctant to undertake the campaign against Persia, primarily because it involved too many uncertainties. It remained unconvinced that the seizure of Kharg Island and Bushire would force a capitulation, as it had in 1838. If it did not, the British would be committed to a major land campaign in an area that had not seen a European army since the days of Alexander the Great. But Palmerston was unrelenting and succeeded in getting the cabinet to authorize the invasion. War was declared on November 1, 1856, citing the Persian attack on Herat, which fell on October 26, as the principal justification.

British forces made a successful landing south of Bushire on December 7 and established a strong foothold in the country. The Persians were almost immediately prepared to negotiate a withdrawal on the basis of their own withdrawal from Herat. However, the shah, apparently with Russian encouragement, insisted on a British guarantee that Dost Muhammad would not extend his power westward and that Qandahar would be returned to its former rulers as a condition of a Persian retreat from Herat. For their part, the British demanded the dismissal of the shah's principal minister, Mirza Agha Khan, a condition that Nasir ad-din Shah deemed unacceptable. In the meantime, the campaign ground to a temporary halt as the British awaited the arrival of Major-General Sir James Outram from England and reinforcements from India. If, upon the latter's arrival at Bushire, he found that the shah had still not withdrawn from Herat, he was to transfer the bulk of the British expeditionary force to the Shatt al-Arab, seize Muhammarah, proceed up the Karun River into Khuzistan and then to move on to take Isfahan.

During this lull period, the shah issued a proclamation of holy war on January 8, 1857, that was evidently intended to inflame the Muslim population of India against the British. It began to become increasingly evident that Nasir ad-din Shah was being encouraged by the Russians to continue to challenge the British. This would explain why, notwithstanding the

presence of a large Russian force in the Caucasus, he felt free to move virtually all his troops from Azerbaijan to the south.

With General Outram's arrival at Bushire on January 27, the campaign
got under way, but soon proved to be inconclusive and the negotiations for
a settlement began once again, this time in Paris. Once more, the sticking
point was the Persian insistence on a British guarantee against the future
unification of Afghanistan. The shah wanted to be free to attempt to reclaim
former Persian territory at some later date without having to confront a
united Afghan front. The British approach to the question of Afghan unification, however, was quite different. From their perspective, if the three
Afghan states had little chance of retaining their independence within a
Russo-Persian sphere of influence, it would better serve British policy to
encourage their unification into a more potent political entity that presumably would be aligned with Britain. In view of Britain's refusal to go along
with the shah's wishes, the Persian negotiator Farrukh Khan sought Russian backing for breaking off the negotiations. Since none was forthcoming,
the Russians apparently having concluded that the situation might even be
worse for their interests if fighting resumed and the British marched into
northern Persia, Farrukh had no practical alternative but to agree to the
modified British terms for peace. The net result of the subsequent Treaty of
Paris (March 4, 1857) was that the shah was required to withdraw his forces
from Herat and to relinquish all claims of suzerainty in Afghanistan generally, and Herat in particular. Moreover, he was required to submit any Per-
sian-Afghan disputes to resolution through the good offices of the British.

In short, the shah emerged from his Afghan adventure significantly
weaker than he was when he started. Ironically, the principal engagement
of the entire war was fought three weeks after the peace treaty was signed,
a consequence of the difficulty of communications in the remote region,
when General Outram finally launched his attack on Muhammarah on
March 25, ten days before he learned of the peace treaty. Persian troops
were eventually withdrawn from Herat in September 1857 and were completely out of Afghanistan by March 1858, the British completing their
withdrawal from Persia a month earlier.

Despite their refusal to give the shah the guarantee he desired, as a matter of practical policy the British prevailed upon Dost Muhammad to respect the independence of Herat as long as the Heratis caused no trouble to
any of his possessions. The situation in Afghanistan remained relatively
stable for the next five years until the ruler of Herat, Sultan Ahmed Khan,
attacked the disputed town of Farrah, which had been under Dost Muhammad's control since 1856. This provided the latter with the justification for
seizing Herat, which he annexed on May 27, 1863. Moreover, when Dost
Muhammad moved aggressively in 1861–1863 to assert his claims in Sistan,
the shah appealed to the British repeatedly to intervene in accordance with
the terms of the Treaty of Paris. However, the British government found it

inconvenient to do so. Instead, it advised the shah: "Her Majesty's Government, being informed that the title to the territory of Sistan is disputed between Persia and Afghanistan, must decline in the matter, and must leave it to both parties to make good their possession by force of arms."[4]

Presumably, Sistan was then considered to fall outside the potential Russian sphere of influence, and Britain would not act to restrain its loyal Afghan ally, Dost Muhammad, from seizing the province if he could. The situation was viewed differently in 1870, however, when Shir Ali Khan (1867–1879, 2nd reign) again threatened war with Persia over Sistan. This time the British did intervene. What had changed over the decade was the British perception of the Russian threat to India, which loomed larger in 1870 as a result of the significant advances that the Russians had made into central Asia.

RUSSIAN EXPANSION IN CENTRAL ASIA

Finding itself effectively excluded from the Ottoman Empire as a consequence of the Crimean War, Russia under Alexander II refocused its expansionist efforts further east, in the Caucasus, Transcaspia, and central Asia. Because of British sensitivity to anything that could be interpreted as a potentially significant threat to their interests in India, the Russians had to proceed with caution if they were to avoid another collision with Britain. This policy guided their expansionism in Asia during the rest of the nineteenth century.

In 1856 Prince A. I. Bariatinsky, the viceroy of the Caucasus, mounted a systematic campaign to wipe out the longstanding resistance to the Russian advance in the hills of Daghestan. The resistance was completely crushed two years later, and the Russians conquered the entire eastern Caucasus from the Georgian military road to the Caspian Sea. From there, Bariatinsky turned west and completed the subjugation of Circassia, forcing some two hundred thousand tribesmen who refused to move from the hills into the valleys, where they could be more easily controlled, to relocate to Turkey. Further east, a Russian army had already reached the Syr-Darya, near its mouth in the Aral Sea, in 1847. The construction of a fortress, Aralsk, at the site marked a major milestone for Russian expansion in the region. Although it became necessary to move further upriver to Ak-Mechet (renamed Perovsk in 1853) because of incursions from the khanates to the south, the Russian frontier had moved southwards from Orenburg to the boundaries of Turkestan, and the Russians looked covetously at the fabled provinces of Bukhara and Samarkand.

At the beginning of the nineteenth century, those provinces had come under the domination of one of the local Uzbeg princes who established the relatively powerful Khanate of Khokand, which was centered in the Ferghana Valley. The Khokands attempted to conquer the Khirghiz, who had long ago submitted to Russian rule, and tribal war raged along the frontier. The Russians were soon to intervene, expanding further southward in the process, incorporating the territories they conquered into the newly formed province of Turkestan. Their expansionist efforts were accelerated considerably in the early 1860s because of the special economic implications of events that took place halfway around the globe. The outbreak of the Civil War in the United States had a tremendous impact on the world cotton market, and Turkestan produced large quantities of the commodity. Indeed, between 1861 and 1864, the price of Turkestan cotton rose more than 500 percent, and the Russians wanted to reap their share of the seller's market that emerged.

The persistent southward drive of the Russians raised British concerns, initiating a period of highly duplicitous diplomacy that was designed to assuage the British while facilitating continued Russian territorial expansion. Thus, when the capital of Khokand, Tashkent, came under Russian attack, the tsar's chancellor, Prince A. M. Gorchakov, assured the British that the Russians would not hold on to the city. When it fell on June 17, 1865, the British foreign secretary, Lord John Russell, sought a formal exchange of notes between the two powers. He wanted both to "declare that they had no intention of extending their territories in such a manner that their frontiers would approach each other more than they then did."[5] The Russians, however, avoided any such formal undertaking. They also reneged on their promise not to retain Tashkent. It seems that a principal reason for the Russian determination to dominate Khokand was its role in the facilitation of trade with China. Anticipating that a similar fate awaited him, the emir of Bukhara attempted to render assistance to Khokand, but it was too late. In May 1866, Russian troops attacked Bukhara which, along with Samarkand, finally fell in 1868. Under the peace imposed by the Russians, Samarkand and adjacent areas were annexed in 1876, while Bokhara became a protectorate, a status it retained until 1917.

The tsar's advances in this part of Asia continued to raise British concerns that the Russians were approaching dangerously close to India, but there was a strong division of views as to what to do about it. The viceroy of India, Sir John Lawrence, was opposed to taking any military action to stop the Russian advance and was even prepared to accept a Russian occupation of Afghanistan. Indeed, in a note dated October 3, 1867, he argued: "I am not myself at all certain that Russia might not prove a safer ally, a better neighbour, than the Mahomedan races of Central Asia and Kabul. She would introduce civilization, she would abate the fanaticism and ferocity of Mahomedanism, which still exercises so powerful an influence in India."[6] The British commander-in-chief in India, W. R. Mansfield, also shared this view. In general, the policy consensus in the British government was for a diplomatic solution, and a new attempt was made to reach an accommodation with the tsar to stabilize the situation. Accordingly, in 1869

Britain proposed that a neutral zone be established between Russian and British possessions in the Middle East. Under this scheme, Afghanistan would have been included within the British sphere of influence, while the Russian sphere would extend to the Amu-Darya and the frontier of Persia.

The Russians, however, delayed responding to this initiative for some time, presumably seeking some additional compensation in the Black Sea as an inducement to sign on to the British plan. The Russian position unexpectedly became stronger in this regard as a result of France's total preoccupation the following year in the Franco-Prussian War of 1870. With the threat of a renewal of hostilities with an Anglo-French alliance no longer a matter of imminent concern, the tsar became quite convinced that Britain would not attack alone. On October 31, 1870, Alexander II announced his intention to repudiate the Black Sea clauses of the Treaty of Paris. He quickly received the backing of Prussia, which wished to further isolate France. As anticipated, without the French alliance, Britain did nothing. Indeed, the Russian position was soon given the sanction of an international Black Sea Conference that resulted in the Treaty of London (March 13, 1871), which effectively scrapped the naval restrictions imposed by the Treaty of Paris. Having achieved a major diplomatic victory that allowed Russia to refortify its harbors and to rebuild its Black Sea fleet, the tsar was now ready to reach the accommodation offered earlier by the British with respect to the establishment of a neutral zone in Asia.

Gorchakov declared Russia's willingness to keep its hands off Khiva, the last and least accessible of the central Asian khanates. Indeed, Count Shuvalov assured Lord Granville in London in January 1873: "Not only was it far from the intention of the Emperor to take possession of Khiva, but positive orders had been prepared to prevent it."[7] Nonetheless, this commitment was soon put aside, ostensibly because of continuing raids against Russian territory coming from there. War soon broke out and the khanate fell to the Russians in May 1873. Under the treaty concluded with Russia, all Khivan territory on the north bank of the Amu-Darya River was annexed by the tsar, while Khiva itself became a protectorate, remaining in that status until 1917. With the establishment of its southern territorial limits in Central Asia on the Amu-Darya, where it now shared an approximately six-hundred-mile-long frontier with Persia, Russia once again became directly involved in the volatile politics of the Middle East.

This latest Russian advance naturally aroused British suspicions about the tsar's intentions once again. However, Gorchakov was able to convince them once more that the extension of Russian control over Khiva posed no threat to British interests in the subcontinent. This was, of course, a highly dubious proposition since the Russian moves in central Asia seemed designed precisely to threaten British interests in India. In this regard, it is particularly interesting to take note of the rationale provided for the Russian advance by General Leonid Sobolev several years later.

Sobolev represented the school of Russian strategists who argued that the principal goal of Russian foreign policy was ultimately to expel the Ottomans from Europe and to seize control of the Turkish Straits, providing the necessary unhindered egress from the Black Sea into the Mediterranean. The British, however, were successfully frustrating the realization of this goal. Accordingly, he held that it was necessary to draw British attention away from Turkey and the Near East by posing a more serious immediate threat to their interests in Afghanistan and northern India. He wrote:

It has now become perfectly clear that England and Russia have entered the lists as . . . rivals on the Asiatic continent. England gave the first provocation when she threw down the gauntlet under the walls of Sebastopol. We boldly, though sorrowfully, accepted the challenge, and if Russian standards are displayed on the banks of the Syr-Darya and the Oxus, and at Merv, and if the points of Russian bayonets glisten in the neighbourhood of Herat and the Hindu-Kush it is to the English themselves that this is due. It is the British who have impelled us into Asia.[8]

NOTES

1. W. K. Fraser-Tytler, *Afghanistan*, pp. 122–123.
2. John B. Kelly, *Britain and the Persian Gulf, 1795–1880*, p. 464.
3. Ibid., p. 471.
4. Rouhollah K. Ramazani, *The Foreign Policy of Iran 1500–1941*, p. 59.
5. FO 65/1202.
6. Ibid.
7. FO 65/1150.
8. Firuz Kazemzadeh, "Russia and the Middle East," in Ivo J. Lederer, ed., *Russian Foreign Policy*, pp. 495–496.

15

The Russo-Turkish War of 1877

The combined effect of the elimination of the restrictive Black Sea clauses of the Treaty of London of 1871 and Russian advances in the Caucasus and central Asia, was to promote a new and even more volatile relationship between the expanding Russian and the stagnating Ottoman Empires. Regional stability was further tested by the breakdown of the security arrangements established in Europe by the Peace of Paris of 1856. The Concert of Europe was shaken by the Franco-Austrian conflict of 1859 over Italy and soon came apart at the seams with the Prussian-Austrian War of 1866 and the Franco-Prussian War of 1870. In the wake of the unification of the German states under the "Iron Chancellor" Otto von Bismarck, Germany emerged as the dominant power in central Europe and now sought to impose a freeze on political developments in order to protect its recent gains. One aspect of this policy was to prevent the sudden dissolution of the Ottoman Empire. It was feared that such a development, if uncontrolled, could draw Europe into another general war. This concern provided an opportunity for the tsar to work out a new security arrangement between Russia, Germany, and Austria, known as the League of the Three Emperors.

France, whom the three emperors wished to keep isolated, was deliberately excluded from the League. The French retaliated by supporting self-determination movements in the territories of the three emperors as well as in the Ottoman Empire, which threatened to destabilize the entire region. To offset French troublemaking, the Russians began promoting Pan-Slavism, the idea that all Slavs should be united under the leadership of Russia. Since, in fact, most of the Slavs outside Russia were under either Hapsburg or Ottoman rule, this Russian initiative could only be realized at the expense of the Austrians and Turks. As it turned out, the challenge was principally to the latter, its initial focus being in the Balkan tinderbox.

The Peace of Paris terminated the right of the sultan to station Ottoman garrisons in autonomous Serbia, which had remained neutral during the Crimean War. The Serbian Prince Michael (1860–1868, 2nd reign) skillfully exploited the troubled relations between the Serbian population and the remaining Ottoman forces and residents in the country to get Sultan Abd al-Aziz (1861–1876) to agree to their complete withdrawal on April 18, 1867. In return, Michael agreed to permit the Ottoman flag to fly beside the Serbian over the citadel at Belgrade as a sign of continued but merely nominal Ottoman suzerainty. In effect, Serbia had already become independent.

Michael, however, had imperial ambitions of his own and sought to create an anti-Ottoman alliance of all the newly independent and autonomous Balkan states. Moreover, he willingly cooperated in the Russian Pan-Slavic scheme to free the southern Slavs from both the Hapsburgs and the Ottomans. In this regard, Michael initiated a system of alliances, with Rumania in 1865, Montenegro in 1866, and with Bulgarian opponents of Ottoman rule in 1867. He also concluded an agreement with Greece in 1867, under which the latter was to receive Epirus and Thessaly in exchange for permitting Serbia to annex Bosnia and Herzegovina. While these several coalitions were not to bear any significant fruit for another half century, the climate they engendered made the Balkan region a tinderbox, ready to ignite at any moment. This was especially true in Montenegro and Bosnia and Herzegovina, in which the population was divided roughly evenly between Christians and Muslims, although both groups were primarily ethnic Slavs.

Further compounding the problem, the reassertion of Russian power in the Black Sea effectively convinced the sultan that it was necessary to shift from the traditional Ottoman reliance on Britain and France as an offset to Russia. He began to seek an accommodation with the powerful neighbor to the north. As a practical matter, this shift in orientation had the effect of giving the Russian envoy at Istanbul, Count Nicholas Ignatiev, who was a strong advocate of Pan-Slavism, the opportunity to influence Ottoman policy to an unprecedented extent while meddling interminably in the Ottoman European borderlands.

Pan-Slavic agitation had its first noteworthy results in volatile Bosnia and Herzegovina, where the Christian peasants were induced to revolt against the landowners and tax farmers in 1874, leading to violence and ultimately to a major international crisis. As developments unfolded, there was a split in Russia's government over the matter, the Pan-Slavs urging major support for Ignatiev's efforts to exacerbate the crisis, and a more cautious approach being advocated by Gorchakov, who was concerned about upsetting the balance of power in Europe. Gorchakov's view prevailed for the moment, and the League of the Three Emperors held a conference in

Berlin where they decided to demand certain reforms by the Ottomans in Bosnia and Herzegovina in order to mitigate the looming crisis (December 30, 1875). Surprisingly, as a result of Ignatiev's influence, the Porte was willing to accept the foreign political intervention and agreed to institute the stipulated reforms on February 13, 1876. At the same time, however, Ignatiev undertook unilaterally to prevent the crisis from being resolved peacefully, quietly encouraging the rebels to reject the proposed reforms.

As the situation worsened, the Slavs of the affected regions began to clamor for open Russian and Austrian intervention, raising the specter of another European war. To forestall this, the League of the Three Emperors met in Berlin once again on May 13, 1876, and drew up a new set of reform proposals to be demanded of the Porte. The conference also agreed that, in the event of the disintegration of the Ottoman Empire in Europe, Austria would absorb part of Bosnia, while Russia would help itself to southern Bessarabia.

By the time that the revised Berlin proposals were sent to Istanbul, a new crisis emerged in Bulgaria, where a Pan-Slavic revolt had broken out on May 2, 1876. Ignatiev single-handedly poured oil on the flames of the revolt by urging the Porte to suppress the insurrection harshly and at the same time encouraging the appointment of incompetent Ottoman officials to carry out the decision. The bungled attempts at suppression of the revolt led to the death of some four thousand Christians and considerably more Muslims. To make matters worse, the death toll of Christians was imaginatively exaggerated by American missionaries to around fifteen thousand, which was further embellished by the Bulgars themselves to as many as one hundred thousand fatalities. The whole affair was blown completely beyond the bounds of reality.

One significant international political consequence of this was that Gladstone and the opposition, on the basis of its unconscionable support for the repressive Ottoman regime, effectively immobilized the pro-Ottoman British government of Disraeli. Popular sentiment in Britain became such that it was no longer possible to make a case for British intervention to prevent a dismantling of the Ottoman Empire in Europe by Russia.

Sensing the favorable change in the international climate for intervention, Russia proceeded to further compound the crisis. Under Russian pressure, Prince Milan of Serbia (1868–1889) formed an alliance with Montenegro on May 26, 1876, and then secretly declared war on the Ottoman Empire four days later. As it turned out, the Bulgarian revolt had been virtually completely suppressed by June 9 and things were beginning to return to normal. Milan, however, now sent an ultimatum to the Porte, demanding that he be appointed governor of Bosnia and Herzegovina so that he might occupy the province with Serbian troops to restore order there. Moreover, he insisted that Herzegovina be turned over to Montenegro. Not surprisingly, the Porte rejected the ultimatum, and on June 30 and July 1 respectively, Serbia and Montenegro formally declared war on Turkey.

Although Russia and Austria agreed to stay out of the conflict, at least for the moment, their decision to abstain was predicated on the presumption that the Ottomans would not decisively defeat the Serbs and Montenegrins. If such a defeat were to appear likely, they were determined to intervene to assure the continued independence of Montenegro. Moreover, if such intervention were to become necessary, the ultimate disposition of the territories of Bosnia and Herzegovina would be in accordance with their earlier agreements.

To facilitate the eventual disintegration of the Ottoman regime in the Balkans, a stream of Russian volunteers went to Serbia and a Russian general, M. Chernayev, was appointed commander of the Serbian army. But, despite the nationalist fervor that led to the conflict in the first place, Serbia was not really prepared to take on the Turks, and the Serbian army under Chernayev was effectively demolished by the Ottoman forces in the battle of Alexinatz (August 19–24, 1876). Serbia was compelled to sue for peace, and for a moment it seemed as though the crisis was finally over. However, the Pan-Slavs in Belgrade, backed by the remnants of the Russian-led Serbian army, forced Prince Milan to renege on his own proposals. At the same time, Ignatiev threatened a direct Russian intervention if the Serbs were not left alone. The Sultan Abd al-Hamid II (1876–1909) caved in and ordered the withdrawal of Ottoman forces from Serbia on November 3, 1876. Ironically, the threat of Russian intervention raised the possibility of a war with Austria, which had ideas of its own about the disposition of the western Balkans.

To resolve the budding crisis among the European powers, Bismarck proposed a division of the Ottoman Empire that would satisfy all the interested parties entirely at the sultan's expense. Under his scheme, Austria would get Bosnia and Herzegovina, while Russia would receive southern Bessarabia and control of Rumania and Bulgaria. France would take Syria, and Britain could have Egypt. Britain, however, was opposed to the scheme because it did not wish to see any further increase in Russian and Austrian power in Europe.

To resolve the problem of the threat of unilateral Russian intervention in the Balkans, an international conference was convened in Istanbul in December 1876 at which it was generally agreed to confirm the boundaries of Serbia and Montenegro as they stood at the time. Bosnia was to be united with Herzegovina in a single province that would be ruled by a governor appointed by and responsible to the sultan. The gubernatorial appointment was to be made with the advice and consent of the European powers. With regard to Bulgaria, a special regime would be established that provided for a Christian governor. Muslim soldiers were only to be permitted to be garrisoned in the principal cities and forts. All other internal security functions would be carried out by Christian and Muslim militias respectively in those areas where their coreligionists predominated.

Lord Salisbury made it clear that unless the sultan agreed to these terms, Russia would probably attack and Britain would do nothing to prevent it. The Porte, however, was faced by another bleak reality as well. Capitulation to such blatant foreign intervention in Ottoman affairs effectively meant the end of Ottoman independence. Given the choice of political survival or a risky war against superior forces, the Porte chose the latter. It therefore rejected these new demands and asserted that it would only to carry out the reforms to which it had previously agreed. The Porte's adamant position led to an impasse, and the Istanbul conference adjourned on January 20, 1877, without having resolved the crisis.

Nonetheless, the Porte understood that it was unacceptable to the Great Powers for it to simply adopt a position of intransigence. It therefore proceeded to carry out its own diplomatic campaign to ameliorate the situation. Separate peace negotiations were undertaken directly with Serbia and Montenegro, and an agreement with the former was concluded on February 28, 1877, that effectively restored the earlier arrangements that had prevailed in the province. That is, Serbia would really be autonomous although it would formally be under nominal Ottoman suzerainty. However, it proved impossible to reach a similar agreement with Montenegro, which was more directly under Russian influence. It was clear that the tsar wanted Montenegro to continue the conflict with Turkey in order to provide a justification for direct Russian intervention on behalf of its Slavic population. Consequently, no matter what arrangements the Porte tried to reach with its European vassals, an eventual Russian attack remained a virtual certainty.

The failure of the Istanbul conference finally provided the tsar with the leverage he needed to get Austrian agreement to allow the passage of Russian troops through Rumania, which had been occupied by Austria in 1854, to facilitate an attack on the Ottomans in the Balkans. By a secret Russo-Austrian agreement concluded at Budapest on January 15, 1877, Austria promised to remain neutral in the event of a Russo-Ottoman war in return for a free hand in Bosnia and Herzegovina. There was also a further understanding that Russia would stay out of Serbia and Montenegro but would be free to annex Bessarabia. Finally, in the event that the Ottoman Empire was dissolved or that it withdrew from the Balkan region, Bulgaria, Albania, and Rumelia were to become independent; Crete, Thessaly, and part of Epirus were to be annexed by Greece; and Istanbul and its environs were to be declared a free city. The cabal was put into effect on April 24, when Tsar Alexander II declared war and the Russian army crossed the Pruth.

The Russian war plan contemplated a two-front attack on the Ottoman heartland. In the west, there was to be a drive southward through the Balkans towards Istanbul and the Straits, while a second assault was to be mounted through the Caucasus that would seize Kars, Ardahan, and Erzerum, and then drive through Anatolia to invest Istanbul from the south. Once having secured control of northern Anatolia, Russian forces would then continue the drive southward toward Alexandretta and the Mediterranean, providing Russia with free access to the sea for the first time.

Anticipating the Russian plan of attack, the Turks established their main line of defense in the west along the Danube, heavily fortifying the region between Varna and Vidin, and placing heavy reinforcements at key positions in the area. The secondary line of defense was strung through the Balkans, linking Varna, Shumlah, and Sofia. In addition, the Dardanelles was fortified to prevent any attempt by the Russians to use their Baltic fleet to break through the Straits. Since there had not been sufficient time for the Russians to rebuild their Black Sea fleet, no significant threat was expected from that direction. Finally, the garrisons at Kars and Erzerum were heavily reinforced.

The Russians struck in June 1877 with a two-pronged attack across the Danube, one directed at the Dobruja while the second broke through the Turkish lines near Nicopolis and, bypassing the strong point, began driving toward the Balkan passes and Sofia and Edirne early in July. After these initial setbacks, which sent a shock through the Porte, the situation began to improve under the leadership of Suleiman Pasha, the former commander of the Military Academy, who was shifted from Montenegro to take over the defense of the Balkan passes. He brought his forces by sea to Alexandroupolis and then marched overland into northern Bulgaria, quickly driving the advanced Russian forces back through the Shipka Pass. At the same time, another Russian force that had taken Vidin was now blocked at Plevna. As a result, the expected rapid thrust through to Istanbul soon ground to a halt in the Balkans. Events in the east followed a similar pattern. The initial Russian advances from the Caucasus that swept up Ardahan on May 18 and Dogu Bayezid on June 20 soon ground to a halt before Kars.

To the surprise of everyone, the Turks had successfully withstood the initial Russian onslaught, and the shoe now appeared to be on the other foot. With their armies bogged down in the Balkans and in eastern Anatolia, the Russians became concerned about their own vulnerability to European intervention. They therefore began to explore the possibility of terminating the conflict on the basis of a restoration of the situation as it existed prior to the outbreak of hostilities. To make matters worse, by this time Disraeli had been able to swing public opinion in Britain in favor of supporting the Ottomans. The British cabinet was considering sending the fleet to assure that the Russians were kept out of Istanbul and the Straits. Consideration was also being given to a possible expedition into eastern

Anatolia to drive the Russians out of the Middle East, thereby reducing the emerging threat to India.

But, as the war ground on, the Ottoman defenses began to crumble. By mid-November 1877, Kars was abandoned, and the main defense line in the east was established at Erzerum, leaving all of eastern Anatolia to the Russians. Similar developments took place in the Balkans. The Turkish forces that had blocked the Russian advances at Shipka and Plevna were ultimately forced to surrender on January 9 and 10, 1878, respectively. Sofia fell soon thereafter, as did Edirne on January 20. With the western front in a state of collapse, Montenegro declared war, as did King Milan of Serbia, who now felt free to proclaim his independence on January 24, entering the war four days later.

Although both Britain and Austria belatedly became concerned about the Russian advances into Bulgaria and the possible impact on the balance of power in southeastern Europe, they were ineffectual in getting the Russians to relent. In the face of impending disaster, the Porte had no alternative but to seek an armistice, which was agreed to at Edirne on January 31. But, before the subsequent peace conference at San Stefano even took place, the Ottomans had in effect agreed to a virtually unconditional surrender to the Russians. They assented to full autonomy for both Bosnia and Herzegovina and Bulgaria, also agreeing that the Europeans would supervise the reforms that were to take place there. Finally, the Porte agreed to pay a substantial war indemnity and Russian ships were to have unrestricted freedom of passage through the Straits.

In the meantime, as Russian troops advanced to the suburbs of Istanbul, the British fleet finally arrived in the Straits, anchoring just outside the city. The possibility of an extension of the conflict, now including the British, had a stabilizing effect on the situation. It facilitated the conclusion of the peace negotiations at San Stefano, with the Russians and Turks in agreement that they would both reject any protest raised by outside powers about the pact concluded between them. Under the terms of the Treaty of San Stefano (March 3, 1878), Montenegro and Serbia were granted independence, as was Rumania, to which the Porte agreed to pay a war indemnity. Russia annexed southern Bessarabia, and Rumania received compensation for this loss with parts of the Dobruja region. Bulgaria, while remaining under nominal Ottoman suzerainty, was to be autonomous, with its territories stretching from the Danube to the Aegean, including the provinces of Salonica and Monatsir, but excluding the ports of Dedeagach and Salonica, which were primarily Muslim and Jewish in population. In the east, Russia was to receive the Anatolian districts of Kars, Ardahan, Batum, and Dogu Bayezid.

Although the Armenian Patriarch Nerses Varjabedian made a strong appeal to the Russian Grand Duke Nicholas at San Stefano to create an independent Armenian state, as compensation for assistance rendered against the Turks during the course of the war, the Russians refused to go along with the idea. Instead, an article was inserted into the San Stefano treaty, against Ottoman objections, that acknowledged some of the concerns of the Armenians and effectively placed them under Russian protection. It called for appropriate administrative reforms to be carried out by the Porte, as well as measures to ensure the security of the Armenians from depredations by Kurds and Circassians. However, the treaty provisions ignored any consideration of Armenian autonomy or self-determination. As a practical matter, the Russians preferred to have a large number of discontented Armenians within the Ottoman Empire rather than an independent Armenian state on their Caucasian frontier that might encourage the Armenians of Russia, as well as other ethnic minorities, to similarly demand independence or autonomy. This laid the basis for the troublesome "Armenian Question" that the Russians were later to exploit to serve their regional interests.

Ironically, the terms agreed to by the Porte were found to be quite unacceptable to the other European powers, which reacted with vehemence to the enhancement of Russia's power position as a result of the treaty. Indeed, it soon became apparent that unless there was a European conference to review and reconsider the results of the Treaty of San Stefano, there was a serious likelihood of a major European war at least between Russia and Austria, and possibly one involving Britain as well. Accordingly, to prevent a breakup of the League of the Three Emperors, Bismarck prevailed upon the Russians to agree to a conference in Berlin to review the terms of the treaty. The key objections raised by the European powers that are of particular relevance to the subject of this work included a British demand for a compromise that would limit the territory of the new state of Bulgaria to the area north of the Balkans. This was apparently intended to keep the Russian sphere of influence as far from the Straits and the Mediterranean as possible. The rest of the region assigned to Bulgaria by the treaty was to be returned to Turkey in the form of an autonomous province to be known as East Rumelia.

Although Britain agreed to the annexation by Russia of Kars and Batum, it insisted on the return of the rest of eastern Anatolia to Turkey. Even so, the British were still unhappy about the potential for Russian troublemaking from their new position in eastern Anatolia, which might include a subsequent attempt to break through to the Mediterranean or the Persian Gulf. Accordingly, the British undertook to guarantee the integrity of the Ottoman Empire in Asia and insisted on a British occupation of Cyprus to provide a regional base from which to intervene promptly in the event of a crisis triggered by Russian expansionism in the region. Disraeli wrote to Queen Victoria on May 5, 1878: "If Cyprus is conceded to your Majesty by the Porte and England at the same time enters into a defensive alliance with Turkey, guaranteeing Asiatic Turkey from Russian invasion, the power of

England in the Mediterranean will be absolutely increased in that region, and your Majesty's Indian empire immensely strengthened."[1]

Although the Porte was not enthusiastic about the idea, it saw it as clearly preferable to leaving the Russians with a completely free hand to create trouble. Accordingly, the Porte went along with the Cyprus Convention of June 4, 1878, under which Britain was to administer the island in the name of the sultan. In return, Britain committed itself to the defense of eastern Anatolia against a Russian attack.

The Congress of Berlin, which convened on June 13, 1878, ultimately confirmed most of the understandings reached earlier at San Stefano, with some significant changes that primarily affected Russia rather than the Turks. The Porte did cede Kars, Ardahan, and Batum to Russia, with the stipulation that Batum would become a free port that was not to be fortified. On the other hand, the Eleshkirt valley and Dogu Bayezid, which were previously ceded to the Russians at San Stefano, were to be returned to Turkey. The net outcome of the Russo-Turkish War of 1877–78 and the Congress of Berlin was the loss of about 40 percent of the territory of the Ottoman Empire and about 20 percent of its population, that is, some five and a half million people. For all practical purposes, except for its vital foothold in Thrace that gave it continued control of the Straits, the Turks had been driven out of Europe.

NOTE

1. Joan Haslip, *The Sultan: The Life of Abdul Hamid*, p. 142.

16

Confrontations in the Persian Gulf and Egypt

Once the tsar repudiated the Black Sea clauses of the Peace of Paris in October 1870 and it became clear that the European powers would go along with it, it also became quite evident to the Porte that its days as a European power were numbered, as indeed they were. Accordingly, there was a growing sense in Istanbul that, while it was necessary to hold on in Europe for as long as possible, if there was any future for the Ottoman Empire it lay in Asia, and it was there that the Porte should concentrate its energies.

This reorientation toward consolidation of its position in the Islamic world was probably also influenced by the fact that communications to its remoter regions had been just made considerably easier by the opening of the Suez Canal in late 1869. This new route now made it relatively easy for Turkish forces to be dispatched south to the Arabian peninsula and its surrounding waters and coastal areas. Thus, at the same time that the fuses that would ignite the Balkans were being lit, the Porte elected to attempt to consolidate its control over the Arab lands nominally under its imperial jurisdiction.

The immediate focus of Ottoman concern was the state of Nejd, in central Arabia, where a violent contest for supremacy was taking place between the Amir Abdallah ibn Faisal and his brother Saud. This struggle, which had been going on since Abdallah's succession to the emirate, came to a decisive stage during the winter of 1870–1871. Abdallah was supported primarily by the settled population of the region, and Saud mostly by the Bedouin, who had now become strong enough, for the first time, to pose a major direct threat to Abdallah's continued rule. In the latter part of 1870, Saud made his bid for power in Hasa, where he found support from his maternal tribe, the Bani Khalid. He soon captured Qatif and then the Hasa oasis. Gathering momentum, he challenged Abdallah's forces in the heart of Nejd and conquered Riyadh early in 1871, where the majority of the tribes proclaimed him as amir. Abdallah fled north to Taiyib Ism on the eastern edge of the Jabal Shammar, from where he appealed to the Ottoman governor of Baghdad, Midhat Pasha, for assistance in ousting his brother from Riyadh. Since this appeal for help coincided well with its interest in refocusing its orientation to Asia, the Porte responded affirmatively, perhaps even eagerly, to his request. At the same time, the Porte completed its final preparations for a simultaneous campaign to reassert its control over Asir and the Yemen, the latter having effectively been independent since the first half of the seventeenth century. A steady stream of propaganda poured from Istanbul emphasizing the sultan's role as the caliph of Islam and which asserted his traditional right to all of Arabia. One could hardly avoid concluding that it was the sultan's intention to challenge the established British position of dominance in the region stretching from Aden to Bahrain.

Needless to say, any reassertion of Ottoman power in a region where British interests were rapidly expanding quickly became a matter of substantial concern. Although forewarned of the pending Ottoman intervention in Arabia by Khedive Ismail of Egypt in December 1870, the British did not themselves become aware of what was happening until March 1871. At that time, Midhat Pasha advised the British consul-general at Baghdad that the Ottoman government had no alternative but to take action to restore Abdallah to his legitimate position as an Ottoman vassal. Accordingly, he planned to send several regiments of troops, supported by artillery and tribal levies, by steamer from Basra to Arabia. The British representative, however, understood what had actually motivated the decision to intervene. "There can be no doubt," he wrote,

that there is a great wish on the part of Midhat Pasha, and probably on that of the Ottoman Government, to obtain command of Bahrein and Kateef, and to establish the supremacy of the Porte over the whole of Central and Southern Arabia, and this desire, together with a growing jealousy of British influence in the Persian Gulf, appears to be the motive of the present action.[1]

Had the Ottoman plan been one for a strictly overland military assault, while the British may not have liked the idea, there would hardly have been any significant reaction to it. However, the fact that it was intended to be a sea-borne attack raised far more sensitive issues. Thus, the British government of India took a rather dim view of the proposed naval intervention, which it saw as a potential challenge to its preeminent position in the Gulf and a direct threat to Bahrain. Subsequent reassurances by the Porte that it had no designs on Bahrain, and that it had no intentions of engaging in naval operations in the Gulf were not considered adequate, and the Bombay government tried unsuccessfully to derail the Ottoman initiative. It was difficult to see how naval operations in the region could be avoided, since the maritime Arab principalities and sheikdoms were increasingly being drawn into the conflict on one side or the other. Thus, the sheik of Kuwait had aligned himself with the Turks and Abdallah, while the sheik of Bahrain had offered his support to Saud. The British were concerned that such local participation in the conflict could upset the arrangements between Britain and the Trucial Sheikdoms and Bahrain, which it was committed to defend and might draw it into taking sides in a local tribal affair in which it had no real interest. C. U. Aitchison, the Indian foreign secretary, expressed the British concerns in a note of May 3, 1871:

We cannot make our policy at sea depend on Arab politics ashore . . . . To do so would involve us in the intimate domestic relations of the Arab tribes, which we neither know or are capable of understanding . . . . If the Turks send their troops by sea, the Wahabis and the Arab chiefs who support Saud have clearly a right to attack them by sea. If the Arabs are defeated, we cannot prevent the Turks from exercising over them all the rights of successful war, and establishing their supremacy over the Arab country. There is an end to our policy in the Gulf; or if the Arab Chiefs, remaining quiet now, wish hereafter to fit out some naval force, how are we to prevent them when we have permitted the Turks to do so, or how are we to make the prohibition intelligible?[2]

The British proceeded to apply pressure on the Porte to stop the intervention, something that the latter steadfastly refused to do. It was one thing for the British to interfere in Russo-Turkish affairs that affected the balance of power in Europe and quite another for it to attempt to dictate Ottoman policy with respect to its hinterland in Asia. The Porte would not hear of it.

The Turkish expeditionary force ultimately departed Basra by sea as planned and landed at Ras Tanura on May 26, 1871, marching from there to Qatif, which fell on June 3 after a three-hour bombardment by Turkish artillery and Kuwaiti naval guns. The Turkish strategy was quite straightforward. Once having secured a beachhead on the coast, the Turks would first target the Hasa oasis, from which they would march on Riyadh. Interestingly, this coincided precisely with Saud's strategy, which was to draw the Turks away from the coast and into the interior as fast and as far as possible, where they would be forced to fight in unfamiliar desert terrain, subject to continual harassment by the Bedouin cavalry and camel-troops. Thus, when the Turks marched south from Qatif to Dammam, which was supposed to be defended by Abd al-Aziz ibn Saud, they found that he had unexpectedly abandoned the town without a fight on June 5, effectively beckoning them to follow him into the desert. The Turks began their march on the Hasa oasis in early July, arriving there unopposed some two weeks later, with their forces in very poor shape from lack of food and suffering heavy losses to cholera. In fact, the state of the Turkish expeditionary force was such that it could not really advance beyond the oasis, while at the same time Saud was not strong enough to drive them out of Hasa. In effect, there was a stalemate in the desert, and the campaign ground to a stop by late summer 1871.

The situation changed somewhat in early fall as a result of the growing disenchantment of the people of Riyadh with Saud and his turbulent and somewhat impious Bedouins. Rallying behind his uncle, Abdallah ibn Turki, they soon forced Saud out of the capital, causing him to seek refuge in Qatar. From there Saud attempted to continue the campaign against the Turks, trying to trap them in the Hasa oasis by cutting their communications to Qatif and the coast, but he suffered a setback in this as well. By this time, near the middle of November, Midhat Pasha arrived at Qatif with reinforcements and announced that henceforth the Porte was assuming direct administration of both Nejd and Hasa. This raised the prospect of a three-way struggle in the desert, since Abdallah now felt betrayed by the Turks, who ostensibly were intervening to restore his authority. At the same time, the Porte was rapidly growing weary of the unproductive campaign which was costing far more than it was worth, and Midhat Pasha was soon replaced by Rauf Pasha, who was given clear instructions to bring the intervention to a successful conclusion one way or another.

Since Abdallah ibn Faisal was still holding out for a change in Turkish policy, Rauf Pasha turned to Saud in midsummer 1872, offering to confirm him as amir of Nejd in return for his submission to the sultan. Saud had few other realistic options and was amenable although he wished to involve the British as intermediaries and appealed to them to act as such. Once again, Aitchison saw the long-term strategic implications of British involvement, which are reflected in his note of July 1872:

It is generally understood that, since we threw the Turks over in the Black Sea affair, they are on far better terms with Russia than they ever were before. Whatever may be their ultimate objective, it is beyond dispute that the Turks have, within the last two years, shown every disposition to extend their authority in Arabia and the Persian Gulf both by sea and by land . . . . I think the opening of the Suez Canal has made it ten times more our interest to be on good terms and intimate terms with Turkey than it ever was before . . . . Turkey is a far more valuable ally than Persia, who is, and will continue to be, under the thumb of Russia.[3]

Accordingly, Aitchison strongly recommended British mediation in the affair. However, his recommendation was rejected by the acting viceroy of India on the legalistic ground that there was no formal basis for such a British role since Nejd was not a party to the maritime truce that governed British policy in the region. As a result, the negotiations between Saud and Rauf Pasha soon broke down and the former, having recovered his strength, returned to Riyadh and drove Abdallah out of the city a second time. Once again Saud attempted to enlist Britain as a mediator between him and the Turks, this time offering to submit to the sultan's suzerainty in return for control over Hasa, but, as was the case earlier, the effort came to nothing. At this point the Turks became determined to break off all further negotiations with Saud and simply continued to hold Hasa as a directly administered Ottoman territory.

The situation in Arabia remained essentially unchanged until the beginning of 1875 and the death of Saud from smallpox at Riyadh on January 25, followed by the succession of his brother Abd ar-Rahman ibn Faisal to his role as leading contender for the emirate. This apparently had an unsettling effect on the tribes of Hasa, and to tighten their grip on the province, the Turks subsequently incorporated it into a newly formed vilayet of Basra and southern Iraq. Then, in August of the same year, Abd ar-Rahman was overthrown by his brother Abdallah ibn Faisal, who was finally prepared to come to terms with the Turks, thereby effectively bringing an end to the entire episode, at least for the next few years. However, once it was clear that the Turks were almost totally preoccupied with the Russo-Turkish War of 1877, the sons of Saud ibn Faisal exploited the opportunity to trigger a rebellion against the Turks by the tribes of Hasa in the summer of 1878. This soon brought the entire coastal region into a state of chaos that persisted for years, forcing the Turks to cooperate with the British in restoring order in the Gulf region.

THE BRITISH OCCUPATION OF EGYPT

The situation in Egypt was more politically complex and of the greatest importance for the subsequent history of the Middle East. Following the death of Muhammad Ali in 1849, his heirs Abbas I (1849–1854) and Said Pasha (1854–1863) recognized that the European powers would not permit Egypt either to withdraw from the Ottoman Empire, or to take it over. They therefore resolved to assume the role of loyal vassals of the sultan, abandoning the territorial ambitions of their grandfather. At the same time, the khedives were determined to resist attempts by the Porte to subjugate Egypt completely, and toward this end were happy to involve the British and French directly in the country's political relations with Istanbul. The construction of a railroad between Alexandria and Cairo with British assistance became a test case of Abbas's independence of the sultan. The latter, presumably at the suggestion of the French who were not sanguine about the growing British influence in Egypt, insisted that his permission was required for such a project. Lord Palmerston objected to such a demand. He argued that the sultan's authorization should reasonably be required only with regard to matters that had "an important political bearing on the condition of Egypt as part of the Ottoman Empire, and can scarcely be construed as applying to so simple a domestic improvement as the construction of a railway."

He suggested, however, that such a requirement for Ottoman authorization should certainly apply to the French plan for a ship canal from the Mediterranean to the Red Sea. In his view, the latter "would be a different thing, as such a work, changing as it would the relative position of some of the maritime Powers of Europe towards each other, would involve the possibility of political consequences of great importance and might seriously affect the foreign relations of the Ottoman Empire."[4] As a result of British pressure on the Porte, the sultan's authorization for the enterprise was received rather promptly, avoiding a test of wills over the issue.

The British and French had found it expedient to play down their conflicting interests in Egypt, particularly with respect to the proposed construction of the Suez Canal, because of their need for each other during the Crimean War period. Nonetheless, it was clear that Palmerston, who became the British prime minister in 1855, was strongly opposed to British support of the French project on primarily strategic grounds. For one thing, in the event of any future conflict between Britain and France in the region, the latter would have a distinct advantage in being able to send ships and troops through the canal to the Indian Ocean. Moreover, Palmerston argued:

It is quite clear that the scheme is founded on intentions hostile to British views and interests, and the secret intention no doubt is to lay a foundation for the future severance of Egypt from Turkey and for placing it under French protection . . . . A deep and wide canal interposed between Egypt and Syria studded with fortifications would be a military defensive line which, with the desert in front of it, would render the task of a Turkish army very difficult. . . . If land is to be conceded to the French company, a French colony on French territory would be interposed between Turkey and Egypt and any attempt by Turkish troops to cross that line would be held to be an invasion of France. From the moment the enterprise was completed Egypt would be completely cut off from Turkey and would be placed under the protection of France.[5]

Accordingly, for the next decade, until Palmerston's demise, Britain remained opposed to the canal project as long as France was the principal backer and potential political beneficiary of the project.

In the meanwhile, the economic situation in Egypt deteriorated sharply from what it had been at the time of Muhammad Ali. Maladministration was endemic, and by the time of Khedive Said's death at the beginning of 1863, the Egyptian treasury was empty and the country was deeply in debt. Egypt's economic problems soon reached crisis dimensions under Ismail (1863–1879) who, with British encouragement, became determined to assert his independence of the Porte. He resorted to enormous extravagances and financially disastrous schemes to gain European support in his struggle with Istanbul. Particularly noteworthy in this regard was Ismail's plan for an Egyptian empire in Africa, to replace that which Muhammad Ali had lost two decades earlier.

Although Ismail's imperial ambitions far exceeded his ability to realize them, his aims, to the extent that they can be known with any confidence, appear to have been geopolitically quite sound, at least from an Egyptian perspective. Given that the basic economy of Egypt had always been critically dependent on the regular annual flooding of the Nile, it seems that Ismail was committed to including the source of the Blue Nile in Lake Tana within Egyptian territory. He also wanted to push as far south in the direction of the sources of the White Nile as was feasible. At the same time he would attempt to secure the western flank of the Nile by taking control of the Sudanese districts of Darfur and Bahr al Ghazal. He also appears to have wished to establish a more favorably situated frontier with historically troublesome Ethiopia, which was pursuing an aggressive foreign policy of its own under Emperor Theodore II (1855–1868) in eastern Sudan by occupying the foothills between the Sobat River in the Sudd and the Red Sea. Moreover, he wished to capture Ethiopia's overseas trade by seizing the Ethiopian coast between Massawa and Cape Guardafui, denying the Ethiopians access either to the Red Sea or the Gulf of Aden.

Ismail had good reason to be concerned about the potential impact of the Europeans on the region once the Suez Canal was completed. The French had already been seeking ports of call and coaling stations along the periphery of the Indian Ocean, hoping to offset the preferential position in the area obtained by Britain through its occupation of Aden. At the same time, the British sought to insure their continued control of access to the Red Sea by occupying the island of Perim in the Bab al-Mandeb Straits in 1857. Ismail correctly assumed that once the canal became operational, which it did on November 17, 1869, France and Britain would divert the trade of the region through their own entrepots, and might even use their influence in Christian Ethiopia to apply pressure on Egypt whenever it served their purposes.

Under Ismail's leadership, Egypt increasingly asserted its independence of the Porte and, with British assistance, attempts were made to extend Egyptian rule into the Sudan and Ethiopia, with considerable success in the former, and to a far more limited degree in the latter. However, Ismail's pursuit of his ambitions cost a great deal of money and he contracted some very large international loans, saddling Egypt with a crushing debt in just a few years. In November 1875, he was forced to sell his shares in the Suez Canal Company to the British government, giving the latter a tangible stake in the canal for the first time. Over the next several years, particularly as a result of their new efforts at mutual cooperation that were engendered by the events surrounding the convening of the 1878 Congress of Berlin, the British and French took over control of the finances of the bankrupt country. Ismail was ultimately forced to abdicate in July 1879.

By this time, neither France nor Britain was any longer interested in maintaining effective Ottoman sovereignty over Egypt. On the contrary, they were now determined to prevent any such reassertion of the sultan's power in a country where they had such vital interests at stake. Accordingly, they applied sufficient pressure on the Porte to force it to drop the idea of installing Prince Halim, the sultan's candidate, as khedive. Instead, they settled on Tewfik Pasha (1879–1892), whom they believed would be easier to control. In fact, they succeeded in getting the new khedive to agree to the appointment of both British and French comptrollers with the autonomous power to manage the finances of the country.

Popular resentment at such blatant foreign interference in Egyptian internal affairs precipitated an attempted military coup in September 1881 by a group of army officers led by Ahmed Arabi Pasha. They took over the government, dismissed the foreign comptrollers, and sent troops to Alexandria to prevent any intervention by the European powers. This created a political problem for Britain, which was obligated under the Cyprus Convention to serve as protector of the Ottoman Empire. Prime Minister Gladstone was reluctant to intervene militarily in Egypt unless specifically requested to do so by Sultan Abd al-Hamid II (1876–1909) and even then was inclined to do so only in conjunction with an Ottoman force. France, on the other hand, was more than eager to move into Egypt regardless of the wishes of the sultan because such a move would probably cause a split between Britain and the Porte. This would restore France to a major role in Egypt that it had not experienced since the days of Napoleon.

To forestall this, the sultan urged both Tewfik Pasha and Arabi to restore the foreign financial control system in Egypt as a means of mitigating the immediate threat of foreign intervention while the Porte attempted to resolve the remainder of the country's problems. Nonetheless, while negotiations were in progress, both British and French naval squadrons appeared off Alexandria, provoking riots in the city that cost the lives of several foreigners. This, plus the continued construction of fortifications in the harbor, soon led to an ultimatum from the British commander Admiral Seymour demanding the restoration of order in the city and the cessation of construction in the harbor. When his demands were ignored, Seymour bombarded the undefended city on July 13, 1882.

Although the Porte tried desperately to prevent any further foreign interference, it was already too late. With Gladstone about to retire from office, the mood shifted decisively in favor of those demanding further intervention. British troops were sent ashore at Alexandria and inflicted a decisive defeat on the Egyptian forces at Tell al-Kebir on September 13. Cairo was occupied four days later. Although the Porte vigorously protested the British action, in fact there was little it could do to reverse it. When the British were finally prepared to relinquish direct control of the country to the sultan in 1885, the Porte was no longer in any position to assume either the financial or military burdens of its rule. Accordingly, the sultan had to be satisfied with the agreement ultimately reached on October 24, 1885, which confirmed his suzerainty over Egypt and assured him regular payments of tribute, while the British remained in virtually complete control of the country.

Viewed from a geostrategic perspective, the significance of the opening of the Suez Canal on British imperial policy can hardly be overstated. For decades, the only practical policy for offsetting the Russian advance into central Asia, and the threat that this posed for the security of India, was to assure continued Ottoman control of the Turkish Straits. With Britain as the sultan's protector, it was positioned to pose the threat of a naval attack on Russia in the Black Sea, which was the most effective way that Britain could counter Russian superiority in ground troops in Asia, and thereby force the tsar to act with restraint. However, as the Suez Canal started to become the principal communications artery from Europe to India and the Far East, the focus of British foreign policy in the Middle East began to shift from Istanbul and the Straits to Egypt and Suez. Indeed, as the head of the India Office, Lord Kimberly, wrote in March 1885: "Does any one really suppose that if we did not possess an Indian Empire we should have interfered in Egypt!"[6]

NOTES

1. See John B. Kelly, *Britain and the Persian Gulf, 1795–1880*, p. 719.
2. Ibid., p. 722.
3. Ibid., p. 740.
4. Palmerston—S. Canning, July 24, 1851, FO 97/411.
5. Palmerston minute, May 26, 1855, FO 78/1156.
6. Rose Louise Greaves, *Persia and the Defence of India, 1884–1892*, p. 64.

17

Resurgence of Anglo-Russian Rivalry

In addition to their advances into the Caucasus and central Asia in the second half of the eighteenth century, the Russians had also been pressing forward in the vicinity of the Caspian Sea, where they occupied Krasnovodsk in 1869 and Mikhailovsk the following year. By 1874 the area seized by them as far south as the Atrek River was sufficiently large to justify having been organized under a separate Transcaspian administrative authority. Although expansionist activity in the region came to a virtual halt during the period of the Russo-Turkish War of 1877–1878, it was resumed in 1879, taking advantage of Britain's apparent preoccupation at the time with their own problems in Afghanistan.

The appointment of Lord Lytton as viceroy of India in 1876 marked the beginning of a more activist British policy with respect to Afghanistan. A treaty with the khan of Kalat made possible the occupation of Quetta that same year, and Lytton hoped to get a British mission established at Kabul. This was viewed as an initial step to taking control of Afghanistan's foreign relations and to assuring the exclusion of Russians from any positions of influence in the Afghan capital. When diplomatic efforts to achieve this goal failed in 1877, Lytton made it clear that he fully intended to establish the outer perimeter of the Indian frontier at the Hindu Kush and that he was prepared to do so by force if that should become necessary.

When a British mission was turned back at the Khyber Pass in September of the following year, Lytton proved as good as his word. He immediately sent his available forces to invade Afghanistan, quickly occupied Qandahar and Jalalabad, and forced Shir Ali to seek refuge with the Russians. By the subsequent Treaty of Gandamak (May 1879), which was concluded with Shir Ali's son, Afghan foreign policy was to be coordinated with the British, who were to have a permanent representative in Kabul. In addition, the British were to be responsible for the security and control of the Khyber Pass and other strategically important frontier areas in return for an annual subsidy to the Afghan ruler. However, the terms of the treaty were never fully carried out. The British mission to Kabul was massacred, and the liberal government that had taken office in London was more prepared to reach a new compromise with the Afghans, in the hope of averting a war that Gladstone had little interest in prosecuting.

In the meantime, the task of completing the Russian conquest of the Transcaspia region fell to General Mikhail Skobolev, the success of which was contingent upon the decisive defeat of the Turkomans. Skobolev demonstrated strategic foresight by his insistence, as a condition of his assuming the responsibility of command, on the construction of the first section of the Transcaspian railway from Mikhailovsk across the desert to Kizil Arvat, along a route running parallel to the Persian frontier for nearly three hundred miles. It became, as George Curzon characterized it, "a sword of Damocles perpetually suspended above his [the shah's] head."[1] It also became a strategic thorn in the side of the British because it gave the Russians the capacity to reinforce their position in Transcaspia by drawing troops virtually at will from those stationed throughout the Caucasus. As a result, the strategic equation in the region had changed dramatically by 1883. Twenty years earlier, the Russians were separated by nearly seventeen hundred miles of desert and mountains from the most advanced outposts of British India. Now, the zone of separation was effectively cut in half.

With a rail line at its disposal, a Russian army no longer had to face the prospect of struggling across the formidable barrier presented by the Hindu Kush, or the deserts of Bukhara and Merv, in order to approach India. It could now proceed far more easily from its base at Ashkabad through Turkoman territory, obtaining necessary supplies from the rich, nearby Persian province of Khorasan. Indeed, General Frederick S. Roberts, in examining the question of the feasibility of a Russian invasion of India in 1883, concluded that the strategic advantages offered by the railroad were quite worrisome. He observed:

So late as 1878, troops would have taken some six months to reach Samarkand from Orenberg, the terminal point of the Russian railway; while now, reinforcements could be marched in six days to Askabad from Kizil-Arvat, which is in direct rail and steamboat communication with St. Petersberg, via Michaelovsk, Baku and Batoum. We may shortly expect to hear of the extension of the trans-Caspian railway from Kizil-Arvat to Askabad, 146 miles, and Sarakhs, 186 miles, leaving a distance of 202 miles only to Herat.[2]

With the decisive defeat of the Turkomans at Geok Tepe in January 1881, there was nothing to stand in the way of a Russian assault on the Merv oasis, perhaps the most strategically important position in the entire region and the traditional route of invasions from the north into India. One can perhaps gain some sense of the significance of such a possibility by considering how it was viewed by those primarily responsible for the security of British India. Thus, in a dispatch dated July 2, 1877, the viceroy of India, Lord Lytton, wrote:

Russia may establish herself at Merv almost without Europe being aware of it. And yet Merv is undoubtedly the most important spot in Central Asia. Situated in a country of almost fabulous fertility, it commands equally Turkistan, Afghanistan, and Khorassan. All the lines of communication for military and commercial purposes between Meshed and Bokhara, Khiva and Herat, necessarily converge upon Merv. In every respect, and especially with respect to Russia, the position of Merv is infinitely superior to that of Herat; and the very fact that this celebrated capital of Khorassan is in ruins testifies to that superiority of position which, placing it in the pathway of all our conquerors, has marked it out as the bloodstained stage on which the barbarous hordes of Asia contend.[3]

Accordingly, there was considerable concern that a Russian advance to Merv might well trigger an Anglo-Russian war on the Afghan frontier. To allay British concerns, between 1874 and 1884 the Russians repeatedly disavowed any intentions to further expand the territories under their rule in central Asia. Nonetheless, it seemed quite clear to all concerned that these assurances were no more to be relied upon than the comparable commitments made by the Russians with regard to Khiva. The Russians continued to expand the territory under their control, albeit cautiously, seeking to achieve their goals while minimizing the risk of a direct confrontation with Britain. In effect, they tied their timetable for expansion to the pace of the deepening British involvement in Egypt. Unexpectedly, Egypt and central Asia became related elements in a common geopolitical environment. Thus, just as Britain began to encounter serious problems in the Sudan with an indigenous uprising under the leadership of the Mahdi, in February 1884 the Russians announced that the tsar had decided to accept the allegiance of the Merv Turkomans. It was difficult to avoid the conclusion that the timing of the Russian annexation of Merv was both deliberate and well calculated.

The British reaction to the Russian initiative was muted, there being little desire in London to engage in a war in central Asia as long as the threat to India did not appear to be imminent. Nonetheless, there was agreement in the government that there had to be some visible demonstration that the British were not prepared to continue to accept such Russian penetration of the Indian hinterland indefinitely. Accordingly, a decision was made to continue construction of the British railway to Quetta, which was intended to demonstrate Britain's firm commitment to the defense of Afghanistan.

The principal Russian threat, however, was not one of a direct thrust into India. Such would have been much too costly an approach for the tsar to pursue, since it probably would have resulted in the eruption of a major European war, something the tsar surely did not wish to precipitate. After all, the primary purpose of placing Russian pressure on India was to facilitate British acceptance of the tsar's interests in southeastern Europe. Accordingly, the threat to India, as understood by Lord Salisbury, was of a far more subtle character. What was to be expected, he wrote,

would not be a direct attack of the Russian Army coming through the Khyber and Bolan Passes. It would be the undermining of his [the viceroy's] strength in India by the production of intrigues and rebellions among the Natives of India, the gradual weakening of respect for the English arms . . . and the gradual crumbling away of our resources before Russia has struck a blow against our frontier. That is the real danger we have to fear; that is why it is a matter of life and death to us that Afghanistan should be kept clear not only of Russian soldiers, but of Russian influence and intrigue.[4]

The principal British reaction, however, was limited to pressing for a joint British and Russian delimitation of the Russo-Afghan frontier, hoping thereby to deter any further Russian expansion southward. There was simply no support in London for taking a stand that could lead to a conflict in a remote corner of the world. For their part, the Russians were amenable since such boundary delimitation gave them the opportunity to gain international recognition of their encroachments on Persian territory, without effecting the real nature of the threat they posed to the British position in India. Moreover, although they agreed in May 1884 to a joint boundary commission, they refused to countenance British participation in the ongoing Russo-Persian negotiations over Khorasan.

The agreement to demarcate the boundary, however, failed to have the anticipated deterrent effect on further Russian expansionism. While the negotiations were under way, Russian forces continued to press southward into Afghanistan, overrunning the Penjdeh oasis on March 30, 1885, after a bloody battle with the defending Afghan forces. Gladstone, the British prime minister, as disinclined as he was to do anything that might lead to a wider conflict in central Asia, nonetheless felt compelled to admit that the Russian actions constituted unprovoked aggression against a state that Britain had committed itself to defend. There was particular outrage over the fact that, only two weeks earlier, the Russian foreign minister, N. K. Giers, assured the British ambassador that there would be no movement of Russian troops into the disputed area. Accordingly, Gladstone asked for a substantial fund for war preparations, and Britain began to gear itself for a broad-based conflict with Russia. Instructions were sent to the commander of the British forces in China to occupy Port Hamilton as a base for operations against Vladivostok. In India, the viceroy made ready to advance some twenty-five thousand troops to Quetta.

It seems clear that the principal issue, notwithstanding the pronouncements about British responsibility for the security of the Afghan frontier, was the potential threat to Herat, which was long considered as a major gateway to India. It will be recalled that the question of control of Herat was the cause of two earlier wars between Britain and Persia. General Sir Peter Lumsden, the Indian government's secretary of state for war, described the strategic significance of Herat on July 24, 1885: "The Herat valley has in past times subsisted very large bodies of men for considerable periods, and there can be no question that under favorable circumstances the resources of the valley will again in the future be capable of producing all the food and forage required for a large army." Historically, he pointed out, "Herat has afforded a resting place, base, and depot of supply, whilst from its position it covers Turkestan, overawes Khorassan, and threatens Afghanistan and India." He considered its value to an invader of India always to have been considerable, since "in it concentrate the highways from Persia, the Caspian, Merve, Bokhara, and Afghan Turkestan; and from it, roads lead by Hazara to Kabul, and by Furrah to Kandahar and Seistan."[5] The security of Herat was thus viewed as critical to the defense of India. Consequently, Lord Kimberly reflected the gravity with which a Russian threat to Herat was perceived in the unequivocal statement on March 25: "An attack on Herat will mean war with Russia everywhere."[6] Indeed, the British envoy informed the Russian foreign minister that any attempt to occupy Herat would in itself be considered as equivalent to a declaration of war.

Recognizing that they had pushed as far as they might without risking a major conflagration, the British threat of worldwide war finally brought the Russian advance to a halt in the Kushk valley. It was evident that Russia was in no financial position to precipitate a major conflict, and the tsar was convinced by his advisors of the wisdom of accepting arbitration of his outstanding territorial claims. Moreover, it was becoming clear that the tsar's allies in the Three Emperors League were willing to back Russia against Britain as long as the contest was confined to Asia. However, they were unwilling to throw their support behind the tsar unequivocally in the event of the conflict spilling over into Europe where their immediate interests would be affected. Although there were a number of sensitive moments in the ensuing Anglo-Russian negotiations, as a practical matter the threat of major war soon dissipated. This did not mean, however, that Russian expansionism in the region had come to an end. It merely shifted its immediate focus from Afghanistan to Persia.

With a string of Russian bases strewn along his frontier in Khorasan, the government of Shah Nasir ad-Din desperately sought to reach some kind of mutual security agreement with Britain, the only power that could block what was perceived as an inevitable Russian advance into Persia. With the conservatives coming back into power in London in mid-1885, the shah's concerns struck a sympathetic chord with Lord Salisbury, who took the position that "the integrity of Persia is a matter of serious importance to this country."[7] Indeed, Salisbury conveyed to the Persians his opinion that it would be strategically desirable to relocate the capital of the country from Teheran to Isfahan, three hundred miles to the south. The reason he gave was that Teheran was located "uncomfortably near to the Russian strongholds on the Caspian, and dangerously distant from the more friendly shore of the Indian Ocean."[8]

The fundamental problem facing the British in any attempt to guarantee the territorial integrity of Persia, obviously for the purpose of securing the routes into India, was the fact that they were at a distinct logistical disadvantage compared to Russia. The tsar not only had large land forces in the region at his immediate disposal, but also had constructed a railway system that gave the Russian military great strategic flexibility. It seemed that the only way that Britain could impose any significant constraints on Russia's pursuit of imperialist aims in central Asia was through generating a countervailing threat to Russian interests in Europe and the Mediterranean. However, it was becoming increasingly difficult for Britain to do this unilaterally, and it was therefore decided to attempt to enlist the support of Germany, which was committed at the time to preventing the eruption of a war in Europe, in such an effort.

Sir Phillip Currie, Salisbury's unofficial envoy, told Count Herbert Bismarck on August 3, 1885: "The position is critical and, if a settlement is not arrived at within the next few months, is very likely to lead to war." He cautioned that the outbreak of a conflict in central Asia between Britain and Russia would not be confined to that region, but would be prosecuted "in every part of the world where England could deal a blow at her antagonist." More specifically, Currie advised that if war broke out, Britain would move to sever Russia's lines of communication with its provinces in Transcaspia. And, ominously from a European perspective, this would be done only after Britain had achieved free access through the Turkish Straits into the Black Sea, something Britain "should unquestionably do by some means or other, whatever view Europe might hold as to the localisation of the war."[9]

By January 1886, it had become quite clear that Germany was unwilling to enter into an anti-Russian alliance with Britain. This left the British government no practical alternative other than to attempt to reach an accommodation with Russia with regard to the territorial integrity of Persia, an effort that engaged the British for the next two decades. At the same time, in return for certain economic concessions in his country, the British gave the shah the guarantee that he had long sought. It was presented to the Persian government by Sir Henry Wolff on October 24, 1888, in a written statement. "In the event of any power making an attack without just cause or provocation on Persia, or attempting to take possession of Persian territory against the will of the Persian Government, Her Majesty's Government engage to make earnest representations against such proceedings, and to take such steps as may in their judgement be best calculated to prevent any infringement of the integrity of Persia."[10]

Notwithstanding the British guarantee, the Russians persisted in pressuring the shah for concessions that would permit them to build a railroad from central Asia through Khorasan, as well as a line from the Caspian to the Persian Gulf. Although justified by the Russians as legitimate commercial ventures important to enhancing Transcaspian trade, the British War Office considered the potential military implications worrisome if not unacceptable. The director of military intelligence, General Sir Henry Brackenbury wrote on March 7, 1889, that it was in Britain's interest to prevent or at least delay for as long as possible the Russian railway construction plans for a line through Khorasan. That province, he argued, "is not only the base from which serious operations against India will be undertaken, if ever they should be attempted, but its possession is essential to Russia for sustained operations in Western Afghanistan." Moreover, the War Office noted a week later, the construction of a Caspian-Persian Gulf line would effectively give Russia "control of the whole Persian Kingdom, and gain a position on the Indian Ocean that would necessitate an increase of British naval forces in the Indian waters, and add to our already heavy burdens."[11]

Caught between the competing demands of the Russians and the British, the Persian prime minister, Amin os-Soltan, managed to maneuver into a position where he was able in 1890 to defer a decision on railroad concessions in Persia for at least another decade. Although this had the unintended consequence of impeding internal development in the country, it was deemed a political necessity if Persia was to retain its independence.

NOTES

1. George N. Curzon, *Russia in Central Asia*, pp. 275–276.
2. Rose Louise Greaves, *Persia and the Defence of India, 1884–1892*, pp. 60–61.
3. FO 65/992.
4. Greaves, *Persia and the Defence of India*, p. 67.
5. FO 65/1248.
6. Greaves, *Persia and the Defence of India*, p. 76.
7. FO 65/1246, July 17, 1885.
8. FO 60/471, August 12, 1885.
9. Greaves, *Persia and the Defence of India*, p. 93.
10. Cited in India Office Memorandum on Persian Railways, June 20, 1911; FO 371/1186.
11. Ibid.

18

The Close of the Ottoman Era

On its western flank, the disintegrating Ottoman Empire was confronted by the growing assertiveness of Greece. The attainment of Greek independence in the early part of the century had been accompanied by a lingering irredentism that was being nourished with the popular idea of a restored Graeco-Byzantine Empire in many of the territories still under Turkish rule. As a practical matter, however, neither the government of Greece nor the large numbers of Greeks residing in the Ottoman Empire were in a position to do much about it. Nonetheless, Greek politicians publicly vied with one another over plans and predictions for gradual Greek expansion north into Thessaly, Epirus, and Macedonia, and south into the Aegean Islands and Crete. Although the European powers would award to Greece a good part of both Thessaly and Epirus within three years, it already was clear in 1878 that Greek ambitions with regard to Macedonia would be thwarted because of the competing interests in the territory, which Serbia and Bulgaria also coveted.

Blocked from further advances in the north, and frustrated by what they considered shabby treatment of Hellenic interests in the region in the Treaty of San Stefano (March 1878), Greek politicians increasingly directed their attention to Crete, which became the focus of Greek nationalist agitation. The island had a long history of Ottoman maladministration of its overwhelmingly Greek population, although there had been some recent improvements in this regard as a result of the Ottoman administration's Organic Regulation of 1868.

With the covert support of the Greek government, it was not long before widespread revolts erupted against Ottoman authority in the island. To alleviate the crisis, the indigenous Cretan leaders invited British mediation, something the Ottomans, exhausted by the continuing struggle with Russia, felt compelled to accept. Accordingly, in October 1878, an agreement (the Halepa Pact) was concluded under the auspices of Adossides Pasha and the British consul Sandwith that provided for the creation of a representative assembly that was to have a Greek majority.

These positive political developments had no effect, however, on the Greek nationalists who continued to infiltrate agents into the island for the purpose of promoting insurrection. As a result of their efforts, another major rebellion erupted in 1889 that produced anarchy and a good deal of intercommunal bloodshed between the island's Christians and Muslims. The sultan intervened to restore order and used the occasion to impose martial law on the populace. Both the Organic Regulation and the Halepa Pact were suspended, effectively nullifying these hard-won reforms in order to reestablish direct Ottoman control of the island. These extreme steps proved counterproductive as intercommunal clashes continued over the next several years, precipitating further interventions by the European powers into Cretan affairs. For example, in 1894, the sultan was pressured into nominating a Christian, Karatodori Pasha, to be governor of the island, in addition to declaring a general amnesty. But these concessions had little effect on reducing the extent of the violence between Muslims and Christians, which flared again after the recall of Karatodori in 1895.

While the Greek government had been cooperating with the European powers in trying to establish calm in the island, its foreign policy was coming increasingly under the control of a secret nationalist organization known as the *Ethnike Hetaireia*. The group was committed to precipitating a war with Turkey in the hope that Greece would then be able to seize Macedonia as its reasonable share of the spoils of the disintegrating Ottoman Empire, and it found ready allies in the Christians of Crete. In January 1897, groups of indigenous rebels augmented by mainland Greeks mounted an open insurrection, proclaiming the political union of Crete and Greece. This was followed in February with the arrival of a Greek military force of some ten thousand men that occupied the island in the name of King George, triggering widespread massacres of the Muslim population. At this point, on March 20, the European powers intervened militarily, blockading the coast and bombarding the insurgents' positions at Malaxa, and placing the island under European protection. At the same time, the powers unilaterally declared that Crete was to become autonomous under Ottoman suzerainty and voiced their opposition to any immediate union of the island with Greece.

In the meanwhile, the *Ethnike Hetaireia* pushed King George toward war with the sultan, and Greek irregulars began crossing the frontiers of Thessaly. The sultan responded with a declaration of war on April 17, 1897, and the Thirty Days' War began. The Greeks began withdrawing their forces from Crete on May 9. Russia, anxious to see the Greeks put in their place, made it clear that it wanted no intervention by the Balkan states in the conflict, and without outside help the Greeks were quickly pushed back across the frontier. However, when the Ottoman army under Edhem Pasha won two decisive victories at Pharsalos and Domokos and threatened to march on Athens itself, the European powers imposed an armistice on the belligerents on May 20, bringing the conflict to an end.

In Crete, matters took a turn for the better for the Greeks as the president of the insurgent assembly, Sphakianakis, took over responsibility for maintaining order in the island in cooperation with the commanders of the international force. The European powers, except for Germany and Austria, which had withdrawn from the Concert of Europe in April 1898, subsequently divided the island into four departments which they administered. The last Ottoman troops departed on November 14, 1898, never to return. Two weeks later, the powers invited Prince George of Greece to act as high commissioner in Crete on their behalf, a step that was ultimately to lead to the union of Crete with Greece.

GERMANY ENTERS THE MIDDLE EAST

In 1889 German Kaiser Wilhelm II undertook his first state visit to Istanbul to see the sultan, Abd al-Hamid. The visit, undertaken at the urging of Count Hatzfeld, who had served as ambassador to the Porte several years earlier, marked a radical departure in Hohenzollern policy with regard to the Middle East. For decades, German policy in the region had been set by the "Iron Chancellor," Otto von Bismarck, for whom the Middle East had little intrinsic interest; he viewed it simply as a backdrop to German diplomacy in southeastern Europe and the Balkans. Now the German emperor was taking an extraordinary step to bring the Ottomans within the ambit of German foreign policy.

Since the sixteenth century, at least one of the major European powers had always played a significant role at the Porte, influencing developments and events in the Middle East. Until the time of Napoleon, France had filled that coveted position almost exclusively. Throughout most of the nineteenth century, however, Great Britain had contended more or less successfully for the role. But Britain's popularity at the Porte declined significantly following the conclusion of the Cyprus Convention of 1878 and ended completely after the British occupation of Egypt in 1882. This displacement left a diplomatic vacuum in Istanbul that Germany hoped to fill.

The German diplomatic campaign for political preferment began with the dispatch of a military mission under the soldier-scholar Baron von der Goltz, who spent a dozen years reorganizing the Ottoman army. The ease with which the latter pushed back the Greeks in the Thirty Days' War in 1897 was a tribute to his efforts and clearly established the credibility of Germany as a valued ally. A veritable army of traders and financiers that soon spread throughout the Ottoman Empire followed the German military mission. As noted by a French journalist of the period, in the commercial war that was taking place in the Ottoman arena, Germany was on the offensive, England was in a defensive position, and France had already begun to capitulate. In the meantime, a festering problem within the Ottoman Empire had risen to the surface with such vehemence that the sultan desperately needed the face-saving support of a major power. The kaiser was only too willing to fulfill this role as a means of furthering German interests in the region. The vexing problem with which Abd al-Hamid had to deal was the complex and highly charged "Armenian question."

It will be recalled that at the conclusion of the Russo-Turkish War of 1878, Russia had occupied a substantial slice of Armenia, including Kars, Ardahan, Erzerum, and the upper Euphrates valley. Under pressure from Britain, which insisted that Russian occupation of Erzerum posed an unacceptable threat to the security of the overland route to India, the Russians reluctantly agreed to withdraw from Erzerum and the upper Euphrates. But as a price for this strategic retreat, they demanded the incorporation of a provision in the Treaty of San Stefano that obligated the Porte to carry out local reforms in the Armenian provinces as well as to guarantee their security against depredations by the Circassians and Kurds. Britain saw this as providing too ready a basis for later Russian intervention in Armenia and took steps to close this loophole. Accordingly, at British insistence, Article 52 of the Treaty of Berlin effectively transferred oversight of the Porte's guarantee of Armenian security from Russia to the six signatory powers, which for all practical purposes meant to Great Britain.

There can be little question that the Anglo-Russian rivalry over the Armenians, which as far as Abd al-Hamid was concerned was purely an internal Ottoman concern, and the resulting intervention of the Great Powers contributed significantly to making the loyalty of the Armenians highly suspect in the sultan's eyes. Given the recent Ottoman experience with the troubles caused by nationalist movements in Bosnia, Serbia, and Bulgaria, the prospect of an emergent Armenian nationalism, possibly nurtured by interfering foreign governments, raised an alarm at the Porte. For a time, then, the Armenians found themselves in the comfortable position of having their security guaranteed by the major European powers, while the sultan fretted over the prospect of their direct intervention in internal Ottoman affairs.

In the meanwhile, however, Russia's attitude toward the Armenians changed from one of support of their national aspirations to one of opposition to their aims and interests. The reasons for this were strictly geopolitical. Bulgaria, to the dismay of the tsar, insisted on demonstrating its independence by effectively blocking Russia's direct land access to the Ottoman capital. With the way to Istanbul closed to it, Russia placed a higher premium on retaining freedom of movement in the area between

Baghdad and Tehran and along the road to India. But that freedom of movement might be impaired by a successful Armenian bid for national autonomy, since the Armenians were perceived by the Russians to be clients of the British.

Notwithstanding their guarantee of Armenian security, the capacity of the European powers to take effective action in such regard soon diminished considerably. Russia was no longer interested in backing the Armenians. Germany was primarily interested in building its relationship with the Porte at the expense of the other major powers. And with Britain and France at odds over Egypt, it soon appeared safe for the sultan to deal with the perceived threat to the internal political integrity of the empire posed by the resurgence of Armenian nationalism. By 1894 the sultan felt that the time was ripe to deal decisively with the Armenian question.

In response to a reappearance of Armenian revolutionary propaganda, an irregular force of Kurds, acting as tax collectors for the Ottoman government, were encouraged to increase their extortion of taxes from the Armenian villagers. When some resisted, the Kurds, supported by regular army troops, carried out a massacre of between three and nine hundred Armenians (the exact number being a matter of some dispute) in the mountainous district of Sasun in August 1894. The news of the massacre, which was wildly exaggerated in the world press, forced the European powers to take some action to honor their pledge to the Armenians. Accordingly, at British insistence, and with the lukewarm support of Russia and France, an international Commission of Inquiry was established to review the situation and to propose reforms that would alleviate the problem. Under British pressure, the sultan was forced to agree to a proposed set of reforms in October 1895. At the same time, however, Abd al-Hamid also gave the signal to accelerate the massacres of Armenians, resulting in the slaughter of between fifty thousand to eighty thousand people in the countryside and another six thousand in Istanbul itself in August 1896.

Abd al-Hamid was now viewed as a bloodthirsty pariah by the European powers, none of which would have any further contact with him, with the notable exception of Germany. For the kaiser, the sultan's isolation offered a unique opportunity to advance Germany's new interest in the Middle East, and he was determined to exploit it to the fullest. Following the Ottoman victory in the Graeco-Turkish War of 1897, in which the military mission headed by Baron von der Goltz played a significant preparatory role, the kaiser took advantage of the opportunity to make a second congratulatory visit to the sultan. The latter was expected to appreciate and lavishly reward such a public gesture. Accordingly, it was no mere coincidence that during the kaiser's visit to Istanbul the Porte granted the port of Haidar-Pasha as a concession to the German Company of Anatolian Railways. With the port concession, the German scheme for a railroad linking Hamburg, Vienna, Budapest, Belgrade, and Nis to Istanbul, ultimately connecting to Baghdad, Basra, and the Persian Gulf, seemed to take a giant step toward realization. It was, in effect, a scheme to outflank the British in the Middle East by constructing a modern land route from Europe to the Gulf, while Britain concentrated on control of the sea route. Its significance was noted by a British diplomatic historian writing in 1917, during the First World War: "Should it materialize it will turn the flank of the great Sea-Empire, just as, in the fifteenth century, Portugal, by the discovery of the Cape route to India, turned the flank of the Ottoman Turks."[1]

Germany's "railway diplomacy" was an integral part of its approach to imperial expansion in the Middle East. As early as 1848, German economists and orientalists suggested that Asia Minor should become Germany's share of the disintegrating Ottoman Empire, a region offering significant opportunities for future colonization. As one of these wrote in 1886:

The East is the only territory in the world which has not passed under the control of one of the ambitious nations of the globe. Yet it offers the most magnificent field for colonization, and if Germany does not allow this opportunity to escape her, if she seizes this domain before the Cossacks lay hands upon it, she will have secured the best share in the partition of the earth. The German Emperor would have the destinies of Nearer Asia in his power if some hundreds of thousands of armed colonists were cultivating these splendid plains; he might and would be the guardian of peace for all Asia.[2]

A decade later, the Pan-German League published a brochure that stated: "As soon as events shall have brought about the dissolution of Turkey, no power will make any serious objections if the German Empire claims her share of it. This is her right as a World-Power."[3]

By the turn of the century, the kaiser's political strategy for gaining a preferential position in the disintegrating Ottoman Empire clearly seemed to be working, Germany's stock rising in Istanbul as Britain's fell. Perhaps nowhere in the Middle East was this development of more concern to Britain than in the Persian Gulf region. In January 1909, a subcommittee of the Committee of Imperial Defence reported that "British claims to political dominance in the Gulf are based mainly upon the fact of our commercial interests having hitherto been predominant, and should our trade, as a result of a German forward policy, be impaired, our political influence would proportionately diminish."[4] The Germans and Ottomans, however, saw the problem in more geopolitical terms, as indicated in an October 1909 dispatch to the German Foreign Office from Baron von Marschall: "The Grand Vizir, in particular, now sees the reason for the British opposition to our Baghdad railway is that a rail connection between the Capital and the vilayet of Baghdad would strengthen the authority of the Turkish state in the south and disturb the British aim of expansion northwards from the Persian Gulf."[5] Two years later, Lord Curzon clearly pointed out the negative political and strategic implications of any possible diminution of British influence in the Gulf region. He insisted that "the Gulf is part of the maritime frontier of India." As such, it was essential that the British position there be maintained. "It is a foundation principle of British policy that we cannot allow the growth of any rival or predominant political interest in the waters of the Gulf, not because it would affect our local prestige alone, but because it would have influence that would extend for many thousands of miles beyond."[6]

THE ANGLO-RUSSIAN CONVENTION

While these events were transpiring in the western part of the region, Anglo-Russian rivalry over influence in Persia continued unabated. George Curzon, a major figure in the formulation of Britain's Middle Eastern policy, was convinced that Russian imperial ambitions in the region ran counter to Britain's interests and had to be stopped or, at the least, contained. In 1892, he warned his countrymen:

Russia regards Persia as a power that may temporarily be tolerated, that may even require sometimes to be humoured or caressed, but that in the long run is irretrievably doomed. She regards the future partition of Persia as a project scarcely less certain of fulfillment than the achieved partition of Poland; and she has already clearly made up her mind as to the share which she will require in the division of the spoils. It would be safe to assert that no Russian statesman or officer of the General Staff would pen a report upon Russian policy towards Persia and the future of that country that did not involve as a major premise the Russian annexation of the provinces of Azerbaijan, Gilan, Mazanderan and Khorasan—in other words, or the whole of North Persia, from west to east . . . . Russia's appetite for territorial aggrandizement does not stop here. Not content with a spoil that would rob Persia at one sweep of the entire northern half of her dominions, she turns a longing eye southwards, and yearns for an outlet upon the Persian Gulf and the Indian Ocean.[7]

Curzon's concerns were by no means without a foundation in fact. The Russians had undertaken a major program of railroad construction to facilitate the consolidation of their territorial acquisitions in central Asia and were actively considering the feasibility of building a line through Persia to the Gulf that would give them direct access to the Indian Ocean. Indeed, a Russian-Persian agreement of 1899 obligated Persia not to grant any railroad concessions to any other power without Russian consent. Moreover, in early 1890 the Russian Foreign Ministry was suggesting that the security needs for such a railroad line might justify the establishment of a Russian naval station on the Gulf.

Nonetheless, the growing concern over the new German penetration into the region made it increasingly important for Britain to reach some accommodation with Russia to stop the kaiser's poaching on territory that had already been staked out for its own imperial expansion. Thus, as early as 1893, a British India Office memorandum suggested that a basis for an Anglo-Russian accommodation with regard to Persia "might be found in the direction of claiming for ourselves the right of exercising in the South of Persia any privileges which may be conceded to Russia in the North."[8] By the end of the decade, even Curzon was interested in a deal with Russia as a check on German expansion in the Gulf region.

The Russians, however, were not particularly interested in such an arrangement with Britain, since they believed that the tide of events in the region was moving in a manner that was to their advantage. Indeed, with the British preoccupied with the Boer War in South Africa, which broke out in 1899, the moment seemed ripe for a Russian thrust toward the Persian Gulf. Representatives of the Russian government began visiting sites in the region, seeking appropriate locations for a coaling station and port and, on February 14, 1900, a Russian gunboat entered the harbor at Bandar Abbas for refueling. The visit was followed by negotiations with the Persian government for a facility at the port.

The British viewed these developments as inimical to their interests, and they began to formulate a harder line toward Russian expansionism in the region. On January 6, 1902, Foreign Secretary Lord Lansdowne restated the British position, which contained an unequivocal warning to the Persians. He made it clear that it would be unacceptable that any Russian commercial facilities in the Persian Gulf provide a "pretext for the occupation by Russia of points possessing strategical importance or for the establishment of such an ascendancy in the south as she already enjoys in the north." Britain could not consent to the existence of a Russian military or naval station in the Gulf, and would regard such as "a challenge to Great Britain and a menace to her Indian Empire." Finally, he warned Persia that Britain would take whatever measures it deemed necessary to secure its interests in the region.[9] Two weeks later, Britain entered into an Anglo-Japanese alliance designed to contain Russian expansionism in Asia. Although ostensibly negotiated to deal with problems in the Far East, it clearly served British interests in the Middle East by diverting Russia's attention to the war with Japan that broke out in February 1904, a conflict that was facilitated by the alliance with Britain.

It was not until after the Russian defeat in the Russo-Japanese War in 1905 that the tsarist government's attitude towards the British proposal to establish spheres of interest in Persia changed significantly. Russia now desperately needed a period of stability in its foreign affairs that would allow it to direct its attention fully to the domestic crisis precipitated by the military debacle.

Negotiations on an Anglo-Russian agreement began in October 1905. Britain was quite forthcoming in meeting some of the Russian concerns. It was prepared to go so far as to allow Russia to have a port in the Persian

Gulf, but not on the Indian Ocean coast, where it might serve to support a potential naval threat to the security of India. The British were now willing to allow a Russian port and facilities at Bandar Abbas, as long as the British navy had the capacity to seal the Gulf by blockading the Strait of Hormuz in the event of a crisis. The negotiations dragged on for two years, principally because of the intense mutual distrust of the parties to the proposed agreement. Finally, they concluded a general agreement on August 31, 1907, that, among other things, effectively partitioned Persia into two spheres of influence.

The Persians, who were not consulted at all, were outraged by what they saw as a British betrayal of their interests. However, there was little that the Persians could do about it. For all practical purposes, Persia remained under the joint control of Britain and Russia until the outbreak of World War I. One of the long-lasting effects of the Anglo-Russian Agreement was a fundamental shift in Persia's political orientation away from Britain towards Germany.

The fact that the Porte was not consulted at all concerning the Anglo-Russian accord infuriated Abd al-Hamid, and he became more determined than ever to enhance the Ottoman position on its eastern flank with Russia and Persia. As a practical matter, the Turks had been encroaching on the Persian frontier since the incident in March 1904 when Persian Kurds, who skipped across the border into Turkey, killed an American missionary. When the Persians dispatched an expeditionary force to bring the culprits to justice, border skirmishes took place with Turkish soldiers. The following autumn, Turkish troops occupied a ten- to fifty-mile-wide strip of land between the border and Lake Urmiye, which Istanbul then claimed as part of its eastern district. The Persians protested the Turkish move, and a bilateral border commission was set up to deal with the problem. Nonetheless, the Turks continued their penetration into Persia, slowly but relentlessly, until Urmiye itself was occupied on August 6, 1907.

The signing of the Anglo-Russian convention that same month, an agreement that did not deal with the northwestern corner of Persia, further encouraged the sultan to push forward to consolidate the Ottoman position in the country. Persia was being divided into two spheres of influence separated by a neutral zone, and the sultan was not anxious to have either Russia or Britain as a neighbor on Turkey's eastern frontier. Accordingly, the time seemed ripe for him to lay claim to the Sunni Muslim and Turkish-speaking province of Azerbaijan, which could serve as a buffer zone between the Ottoman and Russian Empires in the Caucasus.

Turkish advances to some strategic points that potentially challenged the tsar's supremacy in the Caucasus region particularly alarmed the Russians. A demand was made in mid-1908 that the Turkish-Persian boundary commission should be reactivated to resolve the question of the demarcation of the border between the two countries, and the Porte had no alternative but to agree, at least for the moment. The geopolitical situation changed significantly soon thereafter, and the commission was dissolved in September of that same year. When Austria occupied Bosnia, the Turkish interest in expanding eastward became intensified and the boundary commission was seen as an impediment to be removed. It seems that the Porte was convinced that the European powers would compensate Turkey in Asia at the expense of Persia.

The situation in Azerbaijan became very unstable toward the end of 1908, when internal political troubles erupted in violence in Tabriz. As the Turks prepared to move on the provincial capital, the Russians, who arrived there first and increased their garrison in the city to about four thousand troops by the following summer, preempted them. At that point, the Turks flatly refused to consider even a partial withdrawal from northern Persia. Indeed, in March 1909, the Ottoman foreign ministry flatly asserted that the disputed territories were legitimate Turkish possessions. Although the negotiations with Persia continued inconclusively for the next couple of years, it seemed clear that the Turks had no intention of ever withdrawing. Nonetheless, the situation changed dramatically with the outbreak of war in the Balkans, which effectively forced the Turks to withdraw from Persian Azerbaijan in November 1912.

THE FIRST BALKAN WAR

As Ottoman power declined, the disparate peoples that had long squirmed under the sultan's rule, particularly in the Balkan region, began to seek self-determination under the sponsorship of one or another of the great powers. The net effect of this was to further destabilize the empire. A wave of unsuccessful insurrections against Ottoman rule took place in Macedonia between 1893 and 1903, spreading in the latter year to Thrace as well. Russia and Austria-Hungary, which vied for influence and control in the region, joined forces in 1903 for the purpose of imposing a reform regime on the troubled area and pressed their demands on the sultan. In effect, the two powers established a condominium over Macedonia. However, by early 1908, Austria-Hungary concluded that the joint effort with Russia no longer served its national interest. It announced that it was seeking permission to link the Bosnian railway with another line that reached to Salonica, giving it direct access to the Adriatic and the Mediterranean. The Russians interpreted this gambit, quite correctly, as an obvious Austrian bid for control of the western Balkans to secure its unrestricted access to the sea. The temporary alliance between the two imperialist competitors came to an abrupt end.

That same year, a number of other events of great historical significance took place in the region as well. On October 5, 1908, Prince Ferdinand declared the independence of Bulgaria in clear violation of the Treaty of

Berlin, under which Bulgaria was to remain under Ottoman suzerainty. This was followed two days later by the formal annexation of Bosnia and Herzegovina to the Hapsburg Empire. Then, on October 12, the Cretan Assembly voted in favor of union with Greece. However, the event of greatest long-term significance took place somewhat earlier, in the summer of 1908, when a number of junior officers, informally known as the "Young Turks" and formally as the Committee of Union and Progress, took control of the Ottoman government in a bloodless revolution.

The Committee was originally formed in Geneva in 1891 by a group of young Turkish nationalists committed to the modernization and reform of their country. Operating with notable secrecy, the Committee established its headquarters in Salonika in 1906. Its first practical objective, the one that would make or break the movement, was to gain the support of the Ottoman Third Army Corps stationed in Macedonia. In early July 1908, a number of officers known to be supportive of the sultan were assassinated. Then, on July 24, the Committee proclaimed that the Turkish Constitution of 1876 was now in effect, and the Third Army Corps prepared to march on Istanbul to back up that decision. Seeing the handwriting on the wall, Abd al-Hamid moved quickly to coopt the movement by making a similar proclamation regarding the constitution that very same day. The attempt to introduce Western reforms into the empire, however, proved far more difficult than the Young Turks had imagined, and there was great dissatisfaction in the country, particularly among the military forces in Istanbul. As a result, by the spring of the following year, Abd al-Hamid felt strong enough to launch a counterrevolution, which took place on April 13, 1909. But the sultan had made a serious miscalculation regarding the support he expected to get from the Istanbul garrison. Troops of the army in Macedonia, under the control of the Committee, marched on Istanbul unopposed and occupied the city on April 24. Three days later, Abd al-Hamid was formally deposed by the unanimous vote of the Turkish National Assembly. His younger brother was placed on the throne as Mehmed V Rashid (1909–1918), but he was never more than a puppet in the hands of the military officers who took control of the country.

Unfortunately, the change of regime in Istanbul did not have the positive effects that were widely expected by the European powers. It turned out that the Young Turks were first and foremost advocates of Ottoman supremacy, and that their concern with internal political reforms clearly took second place in their order of priorities. This agenda became abundantly evident with the renewed massacres of Armenians that took place in Anatolia at the end of April 1909 and claimed some thirty thousand lives. In Macedonia, where the reform movement originally was launched, the situation of the Christians became increasingly precarious as the Young Turks pursued a relentless policy of "Turkification." Whereas Abd al-Hamid had been principally concerned with the financial exploitation of the predominantly Christian provinces, the Young Turks sought to change their cultural character in an even more tyrannical fashion. The plight of the Macedonians, in particular, was soon to trigger another conflagration involving the Christian states of the Balkans and their common enemy, the Muslim Ottomans.

The idea of a permanent alliance between the several Christian states in the Balkans had been under consideration ever since the Treaty of Berlin. It was prevented from happening, however, by the conflicting ambitions of Bulgaria, Serbia, and Greece with regard to Macedonia. Bulgaria, in anticipation of a future union with Macedonia, with which it had numerous ethnic and cultural affinities, advocated integral autonomy for the province. Both Serbia and Greece, however, which were not in as favorable a position as Bulgaria, wanted the province to be partitioned among them. It is one of the ironies of history that it took the extremist policies of the Young Turks to bring the Christian states together in common cause. Although it took several years of secret negotiations, Bulgaria and Serbia entered into a mutual security pact on March 13, 1912. The pact, among other things, also defined their respective claims in Macedonia, should that province be partitioned subsequent to its prospective liberation from Ottoman control. In April, a similar informal agreement was concluded between Bulgaria and Montenegro, which had its own interests and ambitions in the Adriatic coastal region. Then, on May 10, a comparable although more limited alliance was formed between Bulgaria and Greece. The latter agreement made no stipulations with regard to the future partition of Macedonia, while providing explicitly that in the event of a war between Greece and Turkey over Crete, Bulgaria was merely obligated to maintain benevolent neutrality.

By the summer of 1912, there was a growing sentiment for war among the states of the newly formed Balkan League. For one thing, a major insurgency had broken out in Albania in the spring, which was joined by many of the Turkish troops in the country. This was followed by a mutiny of the Ottoman troops in the vilayet of Monastir, who agitated for the overthrow of the Young Turk regime. As a consequence, the Albanians were now openly calling for the annexation of Monastir and Uskub, which threatened to undermine the positions of both Greece and Serbia in Macedonia. Although these latter events were of relatively minor interest to Bulgaria, the Turkish massacres of Macedonian Bulgars were a rather different matter. In late August, the Balkan League decided to declare war within two months. In the meantime, an appeal was made to the Great Powers to join the League in demanding major reforms in Macedonia and Thrace. The powers, in turn, attempted unsuccessfully to prevent war through diplomatic means. Of course, at this point, neither the Balkan League nor the Porte were really interested in their efforts. King Nicholas of Montenegro declared war first on October 8, 1912, followed by the other three states ten days later.

The war turned out to be an unmitigated disaster for the Ottoman Empire. Within a few weeks, the Turks lost all their possessions in Europe except for a small enclave around Istanbul. The Turkish army, demoralized and poorly organized to fight on three fronts simultaneously, collapsed in the face of the highly motivated forces of the Balkan League. By November 4, the Porte was appealing to the Powers to mediate the conflict. With their assistance, an armistice agreement was signed on December 3. The Treaty of London formally concluded the final dissolution of the Ottoman Empire in Europe (May 30, 1913). Before the First Balkan War, the population of European Turkey was estimated to be about six million and its territory about sixty-five thousand square miles. After the war, it was reduced to a population of less than two million and its territory shrunken to a mere eleven thousand square miles. It was truly the end of an era.

NOTES

1. John A. R. Marriott, *The Eastern Question*, pp. 406–407.

2. A. Sprenger, *Babylonien das reichste Land in der Vorzeit und das lobnendste Kolonisationfeld fur die Gegenwart*. Cited by Charles Andler, *Pan-Germanism*, p. 40.

3. Cited by Andler, p. 38.

4. "Report of the Sub-Committee of the Committee of Imperial Defence on the Baghdad Railway, Southern Persia, and the Persian Gulf," January 26, 1909, Cabinet Office records 16/10.

5. *German Diplomatic Documents, 1871–1914*, vol. 3, p. 368.

6. *Parliamentary Debates, House of Lords*, 5th series, vol. 7 (1911), cols. 587–588.

7. George N. Curzon, *Persia and the Persian Question*, 2, pp. 593–597.

8. Briton Cooper Busch, *Britain and the Persian Gulf, 1894–1914*, p. 118.

9. *British Documents on the Origins of the War, 1898–1914*, 4, no. 321a.

19

The Last Ottoman War

One result of the Turkish defeat in the Balkan War was a *coup d'etat* that brought a more militant group of young officers to power in Istanbul on January 23, 1913. The coup was led by Talaat Pasha who became minister of the interior, Djemal Pasha who became military governor of Istanbul, and Enver Pasha who became minister of war, along with about a dozen others who exercised varying degrees of influence on the course of future events. The fact that Enver had previously served as Ottoman military attaché in Berlin appears to have been an especially significant factor in influencing subsequent political developments in Turkey.

The new military regime soon denounced the armistice, and hostilities with the Balkan states were resumed on February 3, even though as a practical matter the Ottoman armies in Europe were virtually nonexistent. The renewal of the conflict proved disastrous for Turkey. Once again the Turks were forced to retreat, surrendering one strong point after another until Adrianople (Edirne) was forced to capitulate on March 24, bringing the conflict to a close.

Turkey was not a major belligerent in the Second Balkan War that broke out at the end of June 1913 with a Bulgarian attack against both Serbia and Greece. Nonetheless, Enver Pasha found himself in a position to take advantage of Bulgaria's precarious position, and Turkish forces reoccupied Adrianople by the middle of the following month. Enver then proceeded to establish a not very formidable Ottoman defense line along the Maritza River.

Turkey's ignominious defeat in the First Balkan War had a traumatic effect on the leaders of the Committee of Union and Progress (C.U.P.) who had taken control of the Turkish government. They had come within an inch of losing the Ottoman foothold in Europe entirely and became convinced that what remained of the empire could be salvaged only by an alliance with Britain and the Triple Entente.

In June 1913 the C.U.P. raised the question of an Anglo-Turkish alliance but the British rejected the idea. Sir Louis Mallet, who became British ambassador to Istanbul in 1914, observed: "Turkey's way of assuring her independence is by an alliance with us or by an undertaking with the Triple Entente. A less risky method would be by a treaty or declaration binding all the Powers to respect the independence and integrity of the present Turkish dominion, which might go as far as neutralisation, and participation by all the Great Powers in financial control and the application of reform."[1] The British seemed completely oblivious to the fact that the C.U.P. leaders could not possibly accept such a proposal, which would, in essence, have constituted the ultimate humiliation of Turkey from their perspective. Not surprisingly, some of the new Turkish leaders became inclined to turn to Germany and the alliance of Central Powers in search of a better offer.

With the army having made such a poor showing in the Balkan Wars, the C.U.P. became determined to thoroughly modernize the Turkish police and armed forces along western European lines. The reorganization of the police was entrusted to the French General Baumann, while the British Admiral Limpus began restructuring the Turkish navy. For the reorganization of the Turkish army, the principal arm of the Ottoman military, the C.U.P. turned to Germany, a move that would soon prove of some significance in terms of the greater conflagration that was about to engulf the region.

The Germans were only too pleased to accommodate the Turkish request for technical assistance, for at least two reasons. It would certainly enhance Germany's position in the competition among the European powers for influence in Istanbul. It also provided an opportunity for Germany to erase the embarrassment of the fact that the Ottoman army that performed so badly in the Balkan War was a German-trained force that had been under the tutelage of General von der Goltz since the early 1880s.

In late 1913 General Liman von Sanders was dispatched to Istanbul to take the Turkish forces in hand. He was accompanied by an initial mission of some forty officers, many of whom were given important staff positions at the War Ministry and in the various field headquarters. Moreover, Von Sanders was also slated to assume personal command of the First Army Corps stationed at Istanbul. In effect, both the army and the capital were to be placed under German control. The general's arrival in Istanbul precipitated a storm of protest from St. Petersburg, with the Russian foreign minister Sergei Sazanov complaining bitterly about undue German influence in Turkey. The Russians were particularly upset about the possibility of the Straits coming under the control of a foreign power that could pose a threat to their own aspirations in the region.

The furor over the appointment of Liman von Sanders soon threatened to escalate into a full-blown international crisis. As the British ambassador at Istanbul, Sir Louis Mallet, pointed out: "The diplomats accredited to Constantinople would be under the dependence of Germany; the key of the Straits would be in the hands of Germany; a German general could, by his military measures, hold in check the sovereignty of the Sultan. Moreover, the balance of powers, by which even the existence of Turkey is guaranteed, would be broken."[2] The crisis was defused to some extent only when Von Sanders was given a promotion to lieutenant general in the German army, making him the equivalent of a marshal in the Turkish army. Because of this promotion, he now held too high a rank to be in personal command of the troops in Istanbul, thus ostensibly mitigating the issue of greatest immediate concern to the Russians. However, he did become inspector general of the Turkish army, a post that prospectively promised to prove even more important in influencing Turkish policy as the threat of a general European war became a reality following the assassination of Austria's Archduke Franz Ferdinand in Sarajevo, Bosnia, in late June 1914.

Anticipating the outbreak of a general war, Enver Pasha was clearly inclined to cast his lot with the Central Powers. Similarly, Djemal Pasha, who had previously advocated alliance with the Entente Powers, changed his position once fighting broke out in Europe. He wrote later, in retrospect:

Germany, whatever else might be said, was the only Power which desired to see Turkey strong. Germany's interests could be secured by the strengthening of Turkey, and that alone. Germany could not lay hands on Turkey as if she were a colony, for neither the geographical position nor her resources made that possible. The result was that Germany regarded Turkey as a link in the commercial and trading chain, and thus became her stoutest champion against the Entente Governments, which wanted to dismember her, particularly as the elimination of Turkey would mean final 'encirclement' of Germany . . . . Thus we had two groups of Powers before us, the ideal of one of which was to get us in its power, while the aim of the other was to make friendly approaches to us in view of certain prospective advantages, and to conclude an alliance with us based on equal rights and obligations. Could this offer be rejected?[3]

Djemal's account understandably glossed over some of the difficulties that had to be overcome before the German-Turkish alliance actually came into being. On July 22, 1914, Enver proposed to the German ambassador, Wangenheim, that the Ottoman Empire enter into a formal alliance with the Central Powers. Wangenheim was initially cool to the idea, primarily because of Turkey's poor state of military readiness. Only a week earlier, the German secretary of state in the ministry of foreign affairs, Gottlieb von Jagow, wrote: "For the next few years Turkey could only be a liability on account of her poor military state. She would be in no position to take the field against Russia . . . . She would be sure to make demands on us. We could certainly not give her definite protection against, for instance, a Russian attack on Armenia."[4] Wangenheim essentially repeated these arguments in his report to Berlin. Nonetheless, negotiations were opened a few days later on the personal instructions of Kaiser Wilhelm II (1888–1918), who believed that the strategic benefits of such an alliance outweighed the risks about which Von Jagow and Wangenheim expressed such concern.

Following the kaiser's intervention, a formal though still secret treaty was signed in Istanbul on August 2. Among other things, it stipulated that Liman von Sanders and his military mission were to be given effective influence over the general direction of the Ottoman army, a commitment that the Turks ultimately refused to honor. Moreover, instead of immediately attacking Russia as was expected, since Germany had declared war on Russia the previous day, the Porte adopted a position of armed neutrality which it continued to profess for several months notwithstanding the terms of its treaty with Germany.

It seems that some influential Turkish leaders still had lingering concerns about the prospect of going to war with Britain. Indeed, when the Porte learned of Britain's entry into the conflict as an ally of Russia, it promptly reversed itself and, on August 5, Enver Pasha proposed to the Russian military attache, General Leontiev, that Turkey enter into an alliance with the Entente. To gain Russian support for such a treaty, he suggested that Turkey would be willing to withdraw its troops from its border with Russia in the Caucasus as a good will gesture. He assured Leontiev that Turkey was not bound to anyone else and would act in its own interests as it saw fit. Moreover, Leontiev reported that Enver had suggested that "if Russia desired to fix her attention on the Turkish army and use it for her cause, he did not think this combination is impossible."[5]

The Russian foreign minister, Sazanov, however, was reluctant to enter into an arrangement with the Porte that might tie his hands later on. Uncertain of how to respond to the Turkish overture, he temporized. He wrote to the Russian ambassador at Istanbul on August 10:

Keep in mind that in conversations with Enver we must gain time. Remember that possible action on the part of Turkey against us directly gives us no anxiety. At the same time, . . . endeavour to intimate to them that actions on their part which do not receive our sanction will jeopardize the whole of Asia Minor, whose existence we, in alliance with France and England, hold in our hands, while they are not in a position to harm us.[6]

Sazanov evidently was convinced that it was to Russia's advantage to keep Turkey from joining the Central Powers, but only if it could do so without entering into an alliance with the Porte that would prejudice its own freedom of action with regard to the future disposition of the Straits.

It was also clearly in the interests of both Britain and France to keep Turkey out of the war, for a number of reasons. One was that it would eliminate the need to open another front in the Middle East, and thereby divert forces that were sorely needed in Western Europe. A second concern was that Turkish entry into the conflict would necessarily close the Straits to the Russian grain trade, thereby making it difficult to keep the country economically solvent and adequately supplied. There were, however, two other concerns that were of particular importance to Britain. First, there was a fear that a war between Britain and the preeminent Muslim state, nominally headed by a sultan who was also the caliph of Islam, might have serious repercussions among the very large Muslim populations of both India and Egypt, the latter still nominally under Ottoman suzerainty. Moreover, there was serious concern about a possible military threat to the Suez Canal just at a time when its security was critical to the transfer of troops from India to France. Notwithstanding these considerations, neither power did anything of any significance to promote Turkish neutrality. Indeed, it was Britain's heavy-handed treatment of Turkish sensibilities that helped justify the Porte's decision to enter the war on the side of Germany.

When the war first broke out, considerable attention was directed to the naval balance of power in the North Sea. To bolster its position, the British Admiralty impounded two Turkish cruisers that had been under construction in British shipyards and were about to be delivered. Even though the British returned the money paid for the vessels, the seizure itself was an act that embarrassed and infuriated the C.U.P. leadership and influenced public opinion in Turkey. The funds for the project had been raised in part from public contributions for the expressed purpose of altering the balance of military power in the Aegean region to favor Turkey against Greece. Enhancement of the Turkish fleet was considered essential to getting the Greeks to relinquish control of two islands that they occupied during the Balkan War, a goal that had considerable public support.

While the Turks were still fuming over the impounding of their cruisers, the British unintentionally permitted two German cruisers, the *Goeben* and the *Breslau*, that had sailed to the neutral Italian port of Messina in Sicily for refueling, to slip past them and make their way to the Dardanelles. This happened precisely at the time that Sazanov was considering Enver's proposal of a military alliance, against Germany. The entry of the German warships into the Straits raised the prospect of a German-Ottoman alliance, and Sazanov, unaware that such an alliance had already been secretly concluded, was now spurred to act to prevent such from happening. He advised the other members of the Entente on August 16 of a Russian proposal that Turkey be offered border rectification in western Thrace, as well as in the islands of the Aegean, as compensation for remaining neutral in the conflict. But both France and Britain rejected the notion of a pact with Turkey. The French had little confidence that anything would come of the negotiations with Enver, and the British were opposed to the recommended territorial concessions to Turkey. They preferred to see the islands controlling access to the Straits in more accommodating Greek rather than Turkish hands. In Britain's view, if Turkey wanted to remain neutral, it was free to do so. But it rejected the notion that Turkey should be rewarded with territory for adopting a policy that was in its own best interest.

In the meantime, the Porte sought to justify the presence of the two German warships in its nominally neutral territorial waters by claiming to have bought the vessels as replacements for the ships previously confiscated by Britain, even though the cruisers remained under German command. This explanation was rejected by the British, who reacted to the presence of the German warships in the Sea of Marmara by ordering a naval blockade of the Straits and the Aegean coast, effectively treating all Turkish ships as enemy vessels. The import of this development was fully appreciated by the American ambassador, Henry Morgenthau, who wrote on August 17:

The *Goeben* and *Breslau* . . . gave the Ottoman and German naval forces control of the Black Sea. Moreover, these two ships could easily dominate Constantinople and thus they furnished the means by which . . . the German navy . . . could terrorize the Turks. The passage of the Straits by these ships made it inevitable that Turkey should join Germany at the moment that Germany desired her assistance . . . and it likewise sealed the doom of the Turkish Empire.[7]

It was at this point that the British cabinet started giving earnest consideration to revising the long-standing policy of maintaining, as far as possible, the territorial integrity of the Ottoman Empire. Turkey was increasingly characterized as unfit to be an imperial power, and the dissolution of the Ottoman state began to be seriously contemplated as a fit punishment for its long history of excesses, most notably against the peoples it had made subject to its rule. Reflecting this sentiment, Sir Edward Grey stated on August 15, 1914, "If Turkey sided with Germany and Austria, and they were defeated, of course we could not answer for what might be taken from Turkey in Asia Minor."[8]

One of the principal factors influencing the Turkish decision to attempt to legitimize the German naval presence in the Straits was the financial and economic crisis that resulted from the outbreak of the Austro-Serbian War in July. European-controlled businesses in Turkey suspended operations, and shipping companies ceased using Turkish ports, creating panic in Istanbul. The treasury was virtually bankrupt and Ottoman credit was frozen. Only Germany was willing to lend some financial assistance to the Porte, albeit for a high political price—Turkey's entry into the war. Throughout September and early October 1914, the Germans repeatedly placed heavy pressure on the Porte to begin to take military action against Russia and the Entente in accordance with their secret agreement of August 2. However, it was not until German shipments of two million liras in gold arrived in Istanbul on October 16 and 21 that the die was cast. It was to be only a matter of days before Turkey would finally intervene in the conflict.

Apparently acting on his own initiative and without the knowledge or agreement of his colleagues, on October 25 Enver authorized Admiral Wilhelm Souchon, the commander of the German Mediterranean Squadron, to lead the German-Turkish fleet into the Black Sea and to "attack the Russian fleet at a time of your choosing."[9] As British Ambassador Mallet reported two days later, Enver "was determined to have war, whatever his colleagues might desire. Turkish fleet would be sent into Black Sea and he could easily arrange with Admiral Souchon to provoke hostilities."[10]

On October 28, Souchon launched an attack against the Russian ports of Odessa, Theodosia, and Novorossysk, as well as against Russian shipping in the Black Sea. The very next day, at a meeting of the key members of the Turkish Cabinet, most of the ministers declared their opposition to entering the war. They agreed to propose to the Entente powers that an inquiry be made into determining responsibility for the incident, hoping thereby to forestall a violent reaction from Russia.

Sazanov was unwilling to consider the idea of an investigation into the circumstances of the attack. Nonetheless, he indicated to the Ottoman envoy in St. Petersburg that, "if the Sublime Porte decided upon the immediate dismissal of all German military officers and men, it might not be impossible to reach some basis of satisfaction to be given by Turkey for the illegal act of aggression against our coasts and for the damage thereby inflicted."[11] Although most of the members of the Ottoman government were prepared to accede to this demand, Talaat pointed out to them that it was simply unrealistic since Istanbul and the government itself were under the threat of German guns. Unable to receive the assurances he demanded, Sazanov withdrew his ambassador from Istanbul on October 31, the British and French envoys doing likewise immediately thereafter. As far as St. Petersburg was concerned, the point of no return had been crossed. Russia declared war on November 2, its tenth war with the Ottoman empire in two centuries, followed by Britain and France three days later. On November 9, British Prime Minister Asquith observed in his Guildhall speech, "The Turkish Empire has committed suicide, and dug with its own hands its grave."[12]

It is not entirely clear what Turkey expected to gain by joining the war on the side of the Central Powers. It seems that some of the leaders of the C.U.P., especially Enver and Talaat, in addition to their personal fantasies of conquest and glory, saw the war principally as an opportunity to regain some control of their nation's destiny, which seemed to be slipping through their fingers. They were heartened by what they saw happening in the Far East, where Japan exploited the conflict to consolidate its own position on the Asian mainland by compelling Germany to relinquish its holdings in China. It may be assumed that the Turkish leaders believed that their participation in the war would place them in a similar position to exact some significant although still ill-defined benefits from their allies, most probably at Russia's expense.

For Germany, by contrast, the benefits to be gained by Turkey's involvement in the conflict as an ally were quite evident from the first. Turkish participation would result in the interruption of the supply of allied war materiel to Russia and would divert British and Russian forces to the Middle East and away from the European fronts. It therefore became an operating principle of German policy after August 1914 to do or say nothing that might limit Turkish involvement in the conflict. Thus, when the Turks unilaterally abolished the longstanding Capitulations system on September 9, 1914, Berlin remained silent despite its evident annoyance with what it considered an act of effrontery on the part of the Porte.

In November, seeking to derive further benefit from their politically advantageous position with Germany, Istanbul demanded that the treaty with Germany be revised to include more tangible benefits and guarantees for Turkey. The initial German reaction was decidedly negative. As Chancellor von Bethmann Hollweg pointed out, "the exaggeration and spread of the system of alliances," had helped trigger the current war, and that an extension of the treaty was "basically undesirable." He noted that "we decided only with great reluctance to conclude a formal alliance with Turkey."[13] Nonetheless, when the issue of the treaty revision became a factor threatening to split the Turkish regime, Berlin relented and agreed to give the Turks what they wanted.

Although Persia formally declared its neutrality on November 1, 1914, it too was soon drawn into the conflict. Russia and Britain both supported Persian neutrality, principally for strategic reasons. It was to their mutual advantage to have Persia serve as a neutral buffer zone between Turkey and both Russian Central Asia and British India. The German and Ottoman generals quite naturally took the opposite view. For them, Persia provided the primary route for an assault on Russian and British interests in Asia. In any case, once war broke out, the long-standing presence of Russian troops in the country constituted a clear violation of Persian neutrality, and the Turks quickly exploited the opportunity to introduce their own forces into the country, after formally protesting the Russian military presence there. Britain urged the Russians to withdraw from Persia to undercut the justification for a similar Turkish violation of Persian neutrality, but the Russians refused to comply. On December 29, Turkish forces crossed into Persia, seizing Tabriz ten days later. However, they failed to consolidate their position there and were driven out of Persia by the Russians by the end of January 1915.

THE DARDANELLES CAMPAIGN

In November 1914, the Russians moved to set up an active defense against Turkey in the Caucasus by occupying the Alashkirt valley and the key crossing points along the Aras River, which served as the border between the two countries. At the same time, the Turks struck across their northern border taking Artvin and Ardanuch. Then, in December, the Turkish Third Army, under the direct command of Enver Pasha and against the advice of Liman von Sanders, launched a major offensive against the key Russian position at Sarykamysh that was soon to prove a military debacle for the Turks.

Enver had a grandiose plan to encircle the main Russian positions on the Caucasus plateau, capture them, and then march through Afghanistan to the conquest of India. He evidently had little concern over the fact that he did not possess the necessary transport to carry out his plan. Moreover, he had not counted on the severe winter conditions the Turkish troops would have to face without adequate supplies. The heavy snows forced Enver to leave his artillery behind, and what was supposed to be a coordinated attack turned into disaster as the several Turkish corps arrived on the battlefield at different times only to be destroyed piecemeal by the Russian forces. Moreover, the Turkish defeat in the Caucasus permitted Russia to mount an invasion of eastern Anatolia in 1916 and to begin construction of rail lines along the Black Sea in preparation for a westward drive toward Istanbul and the Straits. Had the plans of Grand Duke Nicholas for an offensive not been derailed by the internal turmoil in Russia, it is conceivable that Turkey might have been forced to capitulate by the summer of 1917. As it was, with a revolution in progress at home, the Russians failed to exploit the opportunity they had long awaited to realize their dream of seizing control of the Turkish Straits.

At the time of the Turkish assault in the Caucasus, however, the Russians did not know that Enver was so inept a general, and they were genuinely concerned that the Turkish advance would break through their defenses, opening southern Russia to invasion. Accordingly, on January 2, 1915, Lord Kitchener, the British secretary of state for war, received an appeal from Grand Duke Nicholas for immediate assistance in relieving the Turkish pressure on the Russian army in the Caucasus. Kitchener was unable to divert the necessary forces from the western front for a major assault, and therefore decided to mount a naval assault against the Dardanelles instead. Winston Churchill, heading the Admiralty, proposed to take the matter a step further and exploit the opportunity to force a passage through the Straits by first seizing the Gallipoli peninsula and then moving on Istanbul.

The prospect of a British seizure of Istanbul probably generated as much concern in St. Petersburg as did the Turkish offensive in the Caucasus. The last thing that the Russians wanted as an outcome of the war was to replace

Ottoman control of the Turkish Straits with that of Britain. On March 4, 1915, a secret telegram from the Russian foreign ministry was received in London and Paris conveying a demand by the tsar that Istanbul and the Straits be turned over to Russia in the event of their capture during the Dardanelles campaign.

Russia's territorial claims were received with equanimity in London, where both Grey and Asquith were inclined to accommodate Russia's long-standing aspirations for control of egress from the Black Sea. London therefore responded affirmatively to the Russian demands on March 12. In Paris, however, the Russian demand was viewed with dismay. Control of the Turkish Straits would make Russia a Mediterranean power and a rival of France. The net result of this spurt of diplomatic activity was that it generated the need to begin to consider seriously how the Ottoman Empire was to be carved up among the victorious allies.

As it turned out, the Russian concern over Britain's designs on Istanbul and the Straits was premature, since the Dardanelles campaign did not produce the anticipated results. The British failed to act with sufficient dispatch to catch the Turks off guard. By the time that a British expeditionary force finally made a landing at Gallipoli, the defending Turkish forces had been sufficiently reinforced to be able to prevent the British from advancing much beyond the beachhead they had established. Moreover, Enver turned over command of the Turkish troops defending the Dardanelles to Liman von Sanders, who quickly reorganized them in a manner that made them more effective in dealing with the British assault. The net result was an urgent need to significantly expand the commitment of Allied troops to the effort, which soon included the deployment of two French divisions. By July 1915, what was originally intended to be a naval expedition against light defending forces turned into a massive trench warfare battle that pitted twelve British divisions against a Turkish force that had quickly swelled to fifteen divisions. While the British were able to hold onto the two footholds in the peninsula they had managed to establish, the expedition, which could have been of great strategic significance had it been able to force open the Straits, proved to be a costly tactical blunder. The episode ultimately came to an end with a unilateral British withdrawal from Gallipoli by early January 1916.

The Turks paid dearly in blood for their victory at Gallipoli, but the successful defense of the Turkish Straits against the might of Britain did wonders for their morale and self-esteem. From this point onwards and for the first time since they entered the conflict, the Turks saw themselves as true partners with the Central Powers in the struggle against the Entente. They fully understood the strategic significance of their ability to tie up large numbers of the Allied forces on a variety of fronts in the Middle East and quickly adopted a wholly new attitude towards their own allies. Moreover, they came to believe that their victory at Gallipoli was a principal factor leading to the subsequent collapse of Russia and the revolution of April 1917. They no longer saw themselves as playing a subordinate role in the alliance and proceeded to pursue an independent line in a number of respects, to the growing irritation of Germany and Austria.

However, as the war progressed, they also began to recognize that much of their vision regarding what they might expect from their allies was mere self-delusion. For example, they expected to have Germany's support for the designation of the Caucasus as a Turkish sphere of influence once Russia was forced to capitulate. But they soon discovered that their ambitions were still considered subordinate to the interests of their German ally. Thus, notwithstanding the promise given by Berlin in September 1916 that Germany would not conclude a separate peace with Russia without the Porte's consent, as long as any Turkish territory remained under Russian occupation, Germany did just that. At the peace negotiations with Russia at Brest-Litovsk in early 1918, Turkey was prevented from demanding a Russian withdrawal from Erzerum, Trebizond, and Erzincan in eastern Anatolia because the Russians would have demanded reciprocity. This would have entailed a German withdrawal from Russian lands in Europe, something that Germany clearly was unwilling to do.

MESOPOTAMIA AND THE PERSIAN GULF

The outbreak of the war also precipitated events in other parts of the Middle East that would have far reaching consequences for the future of the region. The security of oil supplies from the Persian Gulf were considered essential to the British war effort, and steps were taken promptly to insure that their flow would not be interrupted. A contingent of Anglo-Indian troops was dispatched from India to secure the area. Expeditionary Force "D," which had been ordered to Bahrain in early October in anticipation of Turkey's entry into the war, landed at Fao at the head of the Gulf on November 6, 1914, a day after Britain declared war on Turkey. To achieve control of the lines of approach to the oil fields and facilities, the British force moved inland and occupied the vilayet of Basra, taking the city of Basra itself on November 21. By seizing control of the Shatt al-Arab waterway, the security of the Anglo-Persian oil refinery on Abadan Island was assured.

A second contingent was soon added to the initial British force, as Turkish troops started to pour into the area in an attempt to dislodge the Anglo-Indian contingent and interdict the flow of oil out of the region. Although the Turkish attacks in the spring of 1915 were turned back without too much difficulty, the British commander Sir John Nixon decided that his foothold would be more secure if his forces were able to establish forward positions farther up the alluvial plain of southern Mesopotamia, a region without roads or rail lines. Virtually all communication in the region was conducted by means of the two major rivers, the Tigris and the Euphrates, that traversed it longitudinally. Accordingly, one British force was sent up the Tigris to Amara, while the second pushed up the Euphrates to Nasiriya. This simple maneuver enabled the British forces to take complete control of southern Mesopotamia.

Encouraged by the relative ease with which his forces had taken control of the Basra region, Nixon ordered the troops under Major-General Charles Townshend to move another 180 kilometers further inland to the strategically important Kut-al-Amara, where a spur of the Tigris, the Shatt-al-Hai, connected with the Euphrates. This allowed the British force to move from one river system to the other. After defeating the opposing Ottoman forces near Kut with relative ease, Townshend pursued the retreating Turkish army as far as Aziziya, halfway to Baghdad.

The Anglo-Indian force then attempted to march on Baghdad, partly to force the Turks to withdraw some troops from the Dardanelles front, thereby providing some relief to the British forces bogged down at Gallipoli. But Townshend's troops ran into increasingly stiff opposition until they were effectively blocked at the ancient capital at Ctesiphon, where they learned that a Turkish relief column of some thirty thousand troops was on its way to challenge them. Being outnumbered by more than six to one and short of supplies, Townshend was compelled to withdraw to Kut, which the Turks placed under siege on December 8, 1915. Repeated attempts to break through the Turkish noose around Kut failed, and the town was finally surrendered on April 29, 1916, after a siege that lasted 146 days and cost the British a total of about 3,300 casualties. The setback, however, was only temporary. A reorganization of the expeditionary force by Sir Stanley Maude soon led to a new British advance toward Baghdad that began on December 12, 1916, and concluded with the fall of the city on March 11, 1917, the Turks having withdrawn the preceding day. The British now had decisive control of the province and all of southern Mesopotamia.

With a revolution taking place at home, the small Russian forces under General I. Baratov that were active against the Turks in the vicinity of Lake Van and northeastern Mesopotamia were withdrawn, creating a vacuum that the British moved to fill, occupying Kirkuk in May 1918. Even after the armistice of Mudros, by which Turkey withdrew from the conflict on October 30, the British continued to push northward until they occupied Mosul on November 7, notwithstanding Turkish protests. They now had effective control of all the major known and anticipated petroleum deposits in the country.

THE CAMPAIGN IN PALESTINE—ENDGAME

The primary British strategic interest in Palestine was the role it played in the defense of the northern approach to the Suez Canal and the security of the sea route to India. Prior to the outbreak of the war, it was assumed that a harsh desert region like the Sinai was equivalent to a fortified frontier. Since the Egyptian-Turkish boundary was set at the eastern end of the Sinai desert, the latter was considered to be a natural strategic barrier of sufficient depth to provide adequate protection against a surprise land assault on the Suez Canal by a sizeable modern military force. Then, in February 1915, a substantial and reasonably well-equipped Turkish expeditionary force under the command of Djemal Pasha crossed the Sinai and penetrated as far as the eastern bank of the canal before it was forced to withdraw, after taking heavy casualties. The principal outcome of the abortive Turkish attempt to invade Egypt was that it made the British perhaps overly concerned about the vulnerability of Egypt to attack through the Sinai and forced them to give higher priority to containing the Turkish forces in the Levant.

With the British and French withdrawal from Gallipoli at the beginning of 1916, substantial numbers of Turkish troops became free for reassignment to Syria and Palestine, posing a new threat to the security of the canal. The British commander in Egypt, Sir Archibald Murray, sought to forestall this from developing by preemptively seizing control of the land routes through the Sinai desert in the spring of 1916. Defeating the newly arrived Turkish forces at Romani, Magdhaba, and Rafah, the British were poised for an invasion of Palestine, the approaches to which were guarded by the two Turkish strongholds at Gaza near the Mediterranean coast and at Beersheba some twenty-five miles further inland.

Murray attacked Gaza on March 26, 1916, but failed to take the city. As a result, a substantial number of British forces became tied down at Gaza for more than a year. A second major attempt to break through the Turkish line at Gaza in April 1917 was also repulsed. This failure resulted in the replacement of Murray by General Edmund Allenby. The latter was able to obtain the additional troops necessary to launch a new drive into Palestine that was intended principally to compel Turkey to divert its forces from any attempt to retake Baghdad. Allenby launched a full-scale offensive in the fall of 1917, attacking Beersheba on October 31 and breaking through at Gaza on November 6. Although the German-led Turkish army attempted to counterattack at Gaza, their efforts were without success. By November 14, a wedge was driven through the Turkish forces, splitting them in two. With the Turkish defenses in disarray, the British were soon able to seize the port of Jaffa and then moved on Jerusalem, which fell on December 9.

Allenby had laid plans for a new offensive in the spring of 1918 that was designed to smash the remaining Turkish forces and assure the conquest of the rest of Palestine. However, he was forced to delay its start until the autumn. The collapse of the Russian front permitted the reassignment of German forces to the western front in Europe, which now awaited a spring offensive. Allenby was obligated to send every man he could spare to

France. The Russian collapse also set the stage for Enver to launch a major thrust into Azerbaijan and Turkestan, posing a potential threat to the Anglo-Indian army in Mesopotamia at a time when virtually all other British forces were preoccupied in Europe.

The armistice terms agreed to by Germany and Russia in March 1918 essentially ignored Turkish interests in Transcaucasia. Germany had great need of the agricultural and mineral resources of Georgia and the oil of Azerbaijan to maintain its war effort, and its negotiators sought to reach an accommodation with Russia that would satisfy that need. Enver reciprocated this slight by ignoring Germany's interests and mobilized the best of his intact forces for the invasion and conquest of Georgia and Azerbaijan. He organized a new "Army of Islam" that was composed entirely of Turks and Azeris, and launched an offensive directed at the conquest of Baku on the Caspian Sea, which was the oil capital of the entire region. If Enver succeeded in taking the port of Baku, he would be able to transport his troops to the eastern shores of the Caspian by ship and from there reach the Russian railroad system that led towards Afghanistan, and ultimately to India as well. The Turkish campaign in Transcaucasia and Turkestan led to considerable confusion in Central Asia, where there were Russian, German, Turkish, and British forces, each operating independently. However, it had little practical effect on the main theater of operations in the Middle East where the outcome of Turkish participation in the war would be decided.

By September 1918, with his army replenished with fresh troops, Allenby was ready to carry out his plan for the conquest of Syria from Palestine. On September 19, a major attack was launched along the Mediterranean coast that forced the Turks northeastward into the hill country in the interior. This was followed by a flanking drive eastward that cut off the Turkish line of retreat and trapped the main Turkish armies in a noose from which there was no escape. As the Turkish armies were being rounded up, a British cavalry force struck north and easily took Damascus. Facing virtually no further significant opposition, the British force continued to sweep northward and quickly took control of all of Syria as far north as Aleppo and the Turkish frontier in Anatolia.

At this point, threatened simultaneously with an invasion of Anatolia and a possible British attack on Istanbul from Macedonia, following the capitulation of Bulgaria at the beginning of October, the Turks recognized that their military position was untenable. On October 30, 1918, notwithstanding Enver's successful campaign in the Caucasus region, Turkey accepted the armistice offered by the Allies in the hope of thereby being able to reassign their forces from the Middle East to the German-Austrian front. The Committee of Union and Progress was dissolved, and the ruling triumvirate of Enver, Talaat, and Djemal was forced to seek refuge in Germany.

NOTES

1. Harry N. Howard, *The Partition of Turkey*, pp. 41–42.
2. Undated minute by Sir Louis Mallet, FO 3771/1826/28098. Cited by Feroz Ahmad, "The Late Ottoman Empire," in Marian Kent, ed., *The Great Powers and the End of the Ottoman Empire*, p. 15.
3. Djemal Pasha, *Memories of a Turkish Statesman, 1913–1919*, p. 113.
4. Luigi Albertini, *The Origins of the War of 1914*, vol. 3, p. 610.
5. Howard, *The Partition of Turkey*, p. 96.
6. Albertini, *The Origins of the War of 1914*, p. 619.
7. *Foreign Relations of the United States* (1914 Supplement), p. 80.
8. Viscount Grey of Falloden, *Twenty-Five Years, 1892–1916*, p. 167.
9. Feroz Ahmad, "Ottoman Armed Neutrality and Intervention: August-November 1914," in Sinan Kuneralp, ed., *Studies on Ottoman Diplomatic History IV*, p. 66.
10. Mallet to Grey, October 27, 1914; Cmd. 7628, number 169, p. 170; cited in Howard, *The Partition of Turkey*, p. 110.
11. Howard, *The Partition of Turkey*, p. 111.
12. *War Speeches by British Ministers, 1914–1916* (London, 1917), pp. 55–56.
13. Urich Trumpener, "Germany and the End of the Ottoman Empire," in Marian Kent, ed., *The Great Powers and the End of the Ottoman Empire*, p. 128.

20

The Dismemberment of the Ottoman Empire

The armistice that was signed on October 30, 1918, on board the British warship *Agamemnon* in the harbor at Mudros on the island of Lemnos, left the Ottoman Empire in a relative state of political chaos as Allied forces occupied the Dardanelles forts and took control of the Bosphorus. For all practical purposes, the entire Middle East had come under British military control. However, there was intense and growing domestic political pressure on the British government to reduce military expenditures. This forced it to accelerate the pace of the decisions to be made with regard to the disposition of Ottoman territories.

Because of their dominant position on the ground in the Middle East, the British saw themselves as presented with an unprecedented opportunity to redraw the political map of the region to their liking. They soon discovered, however, that their freedom to do so was not unlimited. The conflicting promises and commitments they had made to their allies, as well as to the peoples of the region, during the course of the war were now presented for redemption.

Although a peace conference had been convened in Paris at the beginning of 1919, the victors were encountering great difficulty in reaching agreement about how to dismember the Ottoman Empire, which was a mosaic of diverse peoples and emergent national interests. Moreover, there was little agreement among the major powers regarding how the empire was to be partitioned among the victors, particularly in view of the principle of self-determination of peoples that was being insisted on by the American president, Woodrow Wilson. This principle precluded the direct annexation of the Ottoman territories by the Allies and called for a system of mandatory regimes operating under the aegis of an international League of Nations, which became the legal framework for the practical division of the spoils. In any case, Britain was especially determined to renege on the commitments it had earlier negotiated secretly with France, the Sykes-Picot Agreement of 1916, and both seemed to agree that all other states should be prevented from helping themselves to the territorial smorgasbord they saw spread before them.

One of those other states was Italy, which had been induced to enter the war on the side of the Entente with the lure of a share of the territorial spoils that were to be obtained from the defeated Turks. The commitment had originally been made in the secret Treaty of London (April 26, 1915). It provided that in the event of a dismemberment of the Ottoman Empire in Asia, Italy was to receive an appropriate share of the territory adjacent to the province of Adalia (Antalya) on the Mediterranean coast of Anatolia. Italy had staked a claim to this region, where it had obtained railroad concessions, before the war. It was strategically located to permit whoever had control of it to affect the balance of power in the eastern Mediterranean, and the Italians were determined to obtain it.

Accordingly, when the Italian foreign minister, Baron Sonnino, subsequently learned of the Sykes-Picot Agreement, he demanded a meeting of the Entente governments to guarantee Italy's equal rights to Ottoman territories in the Middle East. The meeting took place on April 19, 1917, at the Alpine village of St. Jean de Maurienne and concluded with a treaty that confirmed the Sykes-Picot agreements but also added a zone for direct Italian administration that included the entire southwestern quadrant of Anatolia and the Dodecanese Islands. In addition, Italy was to have indirect administration of a zone comprised of a strip of territory that included the districts of Smyrna, Adalia, and Konya. However, the St. Jean de Maurienne agreement never actually went into effect because it had been made subject to the concurrence of Russia, and that was never received because of the revolution and the overthrow of the tsarist government. It is worth noting that no such proviso applied to the Sykes-Picot Agreement, a point that later outraged the Italians at the peace conference.

Now that the time for carving up the Ottoman territories was at hand, the Italian prime minister, Emanuele Orlando, considered it politically expedient to cater to the intense wave of nationalism that gripped his country. He insisted that Italy be rewarded with the territories around the cities of Smyrna and Adalia in Anatolia that had been promised to them in the St. Jean de Maurienne agreement. To put teeth into their demands, Italian troops began debarking at Adalia in March 1919 and established what appeared to be a permanent garrison there.

Given the rather slim contribution that Italy made to the war in the Middle East, Lloyd George was opposed to providing any significant territorial compensation to Italy in Asia. Toward this end, he drew the United States, which had not participated at all in the war against Turkey, into a leadership role in dealing with the Italian claims. President Wilson agreed to take on the role and appealed directly to Italian public opinion to impose restraints on the aggressiveness being displayed by the Italian government. This forced the Italian delegation to the peace conference to return home on April 24, in an effort to consolidate domestic support for their expansionist policy. A few days later, on May 2, in response to reports of Italian warships being dispatched to Smyrna, Wilson offered to intervene in the crisis with American naval forces. The allied leaders, who were anxious to formulate a common position before the scheduled return of Orlando to Paris on May 7, held some hasty deliberations about how to deal with Italy's imperialist ambitions in Turkey.

At Lloyd George's suggestion, they resolved to invite Greece to land forces at Smyrna, ostensibly to maintain public order there but actually to preempt any further Italian penetration into Anatolia. The Greek prime minister, Eleutherios Venizelos, was only too eager to oblige, since the Entente had made an offer of territorial gains in Anatolia as early as January 1915 as part of the inducement for bringing Greece into the war. From Venizelos's perspective, he was now about to redeem that promise. A Greek army division, later supplemented by additional units, landed at Smyrna on May 15 under the protection of the British, French, and American fleets. The Greek populace welcomed them with a rampage against the Turkish residents of the city that killed or wounded some four hundred people.

Venizelos was now in a position to pursue Greek nationalist ambitions in the lands of the Ottoman Empire. For generations, Greek nationalists had nurtured the *Megali Idea*, which postulated the vision of a restored Byzantine Empire with its capital at Constantinople. Now, it seemed that the opportunity was at hand to begin to bring this dream to reality, at least in Anatolia, in the form of a modern Greek kingdom of Ionia. After all, Smyrna, as well as much of the Ionian coast of the peninsula, was populated principally by Greeks, as it had been since antiquity, an argument Venizelos made before the Supreme Council at the peace conference on February 3. Moreover, both Wilson and Lloyd George saw historical justice in the Greek territorial claim, the American president on the basis of his articulated belief in national self-determination, and the British prime minister because of his deep appreciation of Greek civilization and cultural values. The Allied support of Greek claims in Anatolia in preference to those of Italy resulted in Orlando's resignation on June 19 and set the stage for a bitter conflict between the Greeks and the Turks, reverberations of which were still being experienced at the end of the century.

The sultan, Mehmed VI (1918–1922), sought to maintain some semblance of order in the country to preserve his regime. However, he was unable to reimpose central control over the remnants of the Young Turk Party, who were to be found throughout Anatolia and who felt betrayed by the central government's acceptance of the demeaning terms of the Armistice of Mudros. There was a growing resentment of the sultan and his ministers among the officer corps, particularly in the interior of the country where they remained armed, and a host of plots were taking shape to force both the government and the Allied powers to ameliorate the terms of the peace. What they lacked, however, was a leader who could weld them into a coherent force. Ironically, they were to be provided such a leader by the Porte.

The collapse of central authority in Anatolia brought it in its wake a breakdown of law and order in the countryside and the emergence of local warlords and bandits. These developments were perceived as posing a serious threat to the safety of the Greek communities in the area, which became a matter of concern to the Allied governments. When some Greek villages near the Black Sea port of Samsun subsequently came under attack, it was demanded that the Ottoman government take action to prevent any further outbreaks of violence. The acting Turkish minister of the interior advised the Allies that only by sending a senior officer to Anatolia with the authority to impose discipline on the Turkish forces there could the situation become stabilized. He nominated General Mustafa Kemal Pasha, a hero of the Gallipoli campaign, for the job of inspector general of the army in Anatolia.

Kemal arrived in Samsun a few days after the landing of Greek troops at Smyrna. From the outset, he was determined to bring about a fundamental change in the prevailing situation of national humiliation to which Turkey was being subjected. Traveling through Anatolia, he made contact with various groups of disaffected nationalist officers. When recalled to Istanbul shortly thereafter, Kemal ignored the order and resigned from the army in June 1919 to take leadership of the emergent nationalist movement. A national congress was convened at Sivas on September 4 that effectively repudiated the actions of the government in Istanbul and inaugurated a revolt that quickly spread throughout Anatolia. Kemal then consolidated the scattered military forces of the interior of Anatolia into a viable fighting force.

This demonstration of nationalist sentiment forced the sultan to dismiss the government and call for new elections to the Chamber of Deputies. The Turkish nationalists under the leadership of Kemal won an overwhelming majority in the parliament, which met at the beginning of 1920 in Istanbul. In secret session on January 28, it formally adopted the National Pact, a set of principles that constituted the minimum peace terms that the new Turkey would accept.

A central feature of the pact, which was made public on February 17, was its call for the creation of an independent Turkish Muslim nation-state along European lines. Among other things, it also proposed self-determination for the Arab-populated provinces south of the armistice line, and insisted that Turkey should retain all Ottoman territories with non-Arab

Muslim majorities, which evidently included not only Anatolia but also eastern Thrace and the Kurdish-dominated province of Mosul in northern Mesopotamia. As observed by the British naval commander in the Mediterranean, "the Greek occupation of Smyrna has stimulated a Turkish patriotism probably more real than any which the war was able to evoke."[1]

With the promulgation of the National Pact, Kemal had thrown a bombshell into the peace deliberations that were taking place in London at the time, and especially into the plans for carving up the former Ottoman Empire according to the wishes of the British and French. It also initiated a test of wills between the prime ministers of Britain and France, Lloyd George and Millerand, and Kemal, an upstart and previously unknown Turkish general.

Lloyd George was not about to accept any revisions to his carefully laid plans for the disposition of the Ottoman territories and ignored the recommendations of the British and French military leaders who urged him to reconsider the proposed peace terms. They argued, unsuccessfully, that at least twenty-seven divisions would be needed to impose the previously negotiated terms on Kemal's forces. Lloyd George rejected their estimates, unwilling to believe that Kemal actually had an army that could pose a challenge to the Allies.

It was therefore a rude awakening for him when he and the other European leaders learned on February 28 that a French force had been soundly defeated by a Turkish army of some thirty thousand men at Marash in Cilicia. This was an area that had been occupied by the French because of its proximity to Syria. Indeed, between February and April, the scenario was repeated a number of times, with the French suffering heavy casualties in addition to thousands of their troops being taken captive. Millerand eventually instructed his commander in the field to try to reach an accommodation with the Turks that would secure the French position in Syria and at the same time allow a substantial withdrawal of troops in response to the pressures being placed on his government to demobilize.

Lloyd George adopted a more aggressive posture than his French counterpart and ordered a military takeover of Istanbul in March 1920, dissolving the Chamber of Deputies and declaring martial law in the country. Some 150 Ottoman military and civilian officials were arrested and deported to Malta. However, contrary to British expectations, these actions actually strengthened the position of Kemal, whose power base was in Anatolia. In April, a Grand National Assembly was created in Ankara that elected Kemal president of a new Turkish state. Kemal's government declared that since the sultan was in effect a prisoner in Istanbul, all acts of his regime were null and void.

One of the major problems that Kemal had to deal with as a matter of priority was the growing instability in Anatolia that resulted from the civil war that had been raging in the former Russian Empire to the north. With the breakdown of authority after the Russian revolution, large numbers of marauding bands of Circassians, Tatars, and others from the Crimea and Central Asia, as well as a number of Bolshevik agents, had crossed the poorly guarded Caucasian frontier into Anatolia and were wreaking havoc there. To compound the problem, under pressure from the Allies, the government in Istanbul declared the nationalists as outlaws and sent counter-revolutionary forces into Anatolia in an unsuccessful attempt to topple the rival government in Ankara.

Embarrassed by the inability of the sultan to suppress the nationalists, the Allies acceded to the suggestion of Venizelos, not very secretly encouraged by Lloyd George, that the Greek army be permitted to expand its operations beyond the Smyrna region to deal with Kemal's forces. Accordingly, in June and July 1920, Greek troops occupied eastern Thrace and marched on Bursa and Ushak in Anatolia. This was followed by the conclusion of the Treaty of Sevres on August 10, in which the sultan's government agreed to the dismemberment of the Ottoman Empire in Thrace and Anatolia. Under its terms, eastern Thrace including Gallipoli was to be assigned to Greece, along with the area around Smyrna. A separate tripartite agreement between Britain, France, and Italy was to set forth their respective spheres of interest in those parts of Anatolia that were to remain under nominal Turkish control. Finally, it was left to the United States to determine what parts of eastern Anatolia were to be formed into an independent Armenia.

In the wake of the Russian revolution of March 1917, the Armenians, Azerbaijanis, and Georgians constituted themselves as an autonomous Transcaucasian federal republic on September 20 of that year. However, the entity they created dissolved a few months later and split into three separate republics on May 26, 1918. The new Armenian Republic laid claim to the territories between Georgia and Azerbaijan and the pre-1914 Russo-Turkish frontier. This claim placed Armenia on a collision course with Turkey because, with its military collapse and the subsequent signing of the Treaty of Brest-Litovsk on March 3, 1918, Russia had agreed to evacuate the eastern provinces of Anatolia, including Kars and Ardahan in Armenia and Batum in Georgia. Under considerable pressure, Armenia was compelled to sign a peace treaty with Turkey on June 4 at Batum which ceded its claim to Kars and moved the frontier back to the Aras and Arpa Rivers, effectively restoring the pre–1878 Russo-Ottoman border. This treaty, however, was never ratified because of the Ottoman military collapse and the Armistice of Mudros in October. Then, with the Allied powers in control of the Black Sea and in contact with the Transcaucasian republics, Turkey was forced to withdraw its troops back behind the pre–1914 Russo-Turkish frontier.

The Allies supported the idea of a single Armenian state encompassing the territories of both Russian and Ottoman Armenia and sought to have the United States accept a mandate over it, an effort that was rejected by the U.S. Senate on June 1, 1920. Nonetheless, Armenia was made a signatory to the Treaty of Sevres on August 20, and President Wilson was asked to fix the Turkish-Armenian boundary. On November 22, 1920, Wilson announced the assignment to Armenia of some forty thousand square miles of Turkish territory within the pre–1914 borders, including Trebizond, Erzincan, Erzerum, Mus, and Van. The resulting strains with Turkey were further exacerbated by Armenian claims to a swath of territory reaching from Cilicia to Russian Armenia that included about a third of Anatolia.

The Treaty of Sevres and the Wilson award remained dead letters because the Turkish nationalists under Kemal rejected both. Indeed, two months before Wilson announced the territorial award, Kemal definitively altered the facts on the ground by attacking the Armenian Republic and occupying Kars. While the Turks were soundly defeating Armenia, a Bolshevik group supported by Red Army units crossed into Armenia from Azerbaijan on November 29 and proclaimed the establishment of a Soviet government. Beaten by the Turks and squeezed by the Soviets, without the prospect of help from the outside, Armenia had no choice but to sign a peace treaty at Alexandropol on December 2, 1920, that restored the pre–1878 border.

Following the victory over the Armenians, Kemal sent a delegation to Moscow to negotiate a treaty of friendship that he hoped would help stabilize the frontier and contain the bands of freebooters that were creating chaos in the interior of Anatolia. The resulting Treaty of Moscow (March 6, 1921) made the Soviet Union the first country to recognize the Turkish government of Ankara. The treaty was widely misinterpreted in the West as a sign of Kemal's radical leanings, rather than as the pragmatic step it really was.

When the Menshevik government of Georgia was overthrown soon thereafter, Turkish forces occupied Ardahan, Artvin, and Batum. Later, Armenia, Azerbaijan, and Georgia were combined to constitute the Transcaucasian Soviet Federated Socialist Republic (March 12, 1922) and subsequently became part of the Union of Soviet Socialist Republics on December 30, 1922. Turkey retained Kars, Ardahan, and Artvin, but returned Batum, as stipulated in a treaty between the Soviet Union, the Caucasian republics, and the Ankara government, that was signed in Kars on October 13, 1921.

No sooner had the conflict with Armenia been brought to a successful conclusion at the end of 1920 than the Greek army in Anatolia launched a major offensive in January 1921. Contrary to expectations, by April it twice ground to a halt at Inonu. Since the military solution attempted by the Greeks failed to produce the desired results, the Allies sought once again to negotiate the outstanding territorial issues raised by the adamant refusal of Ankara to recognize the terms of the Treaty of Sevres that had been agreed to by the sultan's government. This time, representatives of both Turkish governments were invited to a conference in London at which it became evident that the Allies themselves were no longer of a single mind on the issues at hand. To some extent this was due to the fact that Venizelos had been defeated in the general elections in Greece in November 1920. King Constantine, who had gone into exile in June 1917 at the insistence of the Allies because of his refusal to actively support the Entente in the war, returned to the throne the following month. These developments weakened Greece's standing among the Allies, especially France. As a result, the Allied high commissioners in Istanbul declared their neutrality in the Greek-Turkish conflict on May 21 and designated certain neutral zones on both shores of the Bosphorus and Dardanalles that were to be off limits to the belligerents.

In June 1921, King Constantine declared himself supreme commander of the Greek forces in Anatolia and went to Smyrna, presumably to oversee the conduct of the war. On July 10, reorganized and reequipped, the Greek army went on what was expected to be a final offensive to encircle and destroy the core of Kemal's forces. Caught unprepared, the Turkish forces were compelled to withdraw eastward beyond the Sakariya River. The Greeks were now in a position to consolidate their gains, and their generals advocated doing just that. Constantine, however, beguiled by the vision of the Greek army breaking through the Turkish lines to take Ankara, only fifty miles distant, ordered a new offensive. Kemal fully recognized the vulnerability of his position and, in an extraordinary burst of improvisation, prepared his forces to weather the Greek assault, which ground to a halt at the Sakariya in September. After twenty days of blood-letting, with each side suffering about eighteen thousand casualties, the Turkish forces broke through the Greek lines and turned the battle into a rout as the Greek forces retreated westward in disarray to new positions at Ushak.

By this time, it had become increasingly evident to the French that it was only the government in Ankara that was relevant to their concerns in the Middle East. It was therefore necessary to reach an accord with the Kemalist regime if France was to protect its position in Syria. Italy had made a similar separate peace with Turkey earlier in the year, which led to the evacuation of Adalia in June in return for economic concessions in southern Anatolia. In a formal agreement signed in Ankara on October 20, 1921, France recognized Kemal's government as the legitimate government of Turkey, a move that was not coordinated with the British, who would have opposed it. Under the agreement, France returned to Turkish control some ten thousand square kilometers of territory stretching from the Gulf of Alexandretta to the Tigris and delineated a new frontier between Turkey and Syria, a line that was later reaffirmed by the Treaty of Lausanne (July 24, 1923).

In early 1922, the Greek prime minister appealed to Lord Curzon for assistance in maintaining the military effectiveness of his forces in Anatolia, which were suffering from a lack of resources and supplies. Unable to provide the funds necessary to sustain the Greek military effort against Turkey, Britain attempted to arrange a truce between Turkey and Greece, but Kemal refused to negotiate until all Greek forces were evacuated from Anatolia. Further compounding the difficulties inherent in the situation, the Greek high commissioner in Smyrna proclaimed the autonomy of all Anatolian territory under Greek control on July 30, leading the Allied supreme war council to declare its neutrality a second time on August 10.

Despairing of obtaining the results he wanted through negotiations, Kemal launched a major offensive against the Greek forces on August 26, 1922, that soon turned into a rout. However, in the course of its retreat from Ushak to Smyrna, the Greek army employed a scorched earth policy, destroying the population centers of western Turkey and committing atrocities on a wide scale. Turkish forces entered Smyrna on September 9, as masses of the Christian population fled. The remnants of the Greek army made their way to the island of Chios, where General Nikolaos Plastiras orchestrated a revolt that overthrew Constantine, who was blamed for the disaster.

The elimination of the Greek army in Turkey upset the balance of power in the region and placed the Ankara government on a collision course with Britain as Kemal's forces approached the neutral zones and the French and Italians withdrew their contingents. A compromise position was negotiated between the British and the French on September 23, 1922. This agreement resulted in an invitation from the Allies, on October 27, for the Ankara government to participate in a new peace conference. It stipulated that the negotiations would be conducted on the basis that Turkish sovereignty in Thrace would be restored as far north as the Maritza River and that the neutral zones should remain inviolate until the negotiations were concluded.

This proposal was acceptable to Kemal, and an armistice incorporating these terms was concluded between Turkey and Greece at Mudania on October 11, clearing the way for the peace conference that was to convene at Lausanne the following month. However, the Allies also invited the Istanbul government to the conference, creating the possibility of a split among the Turks at the negotiations. To his credit, Tewfik Pasha, the last grand vizir, realized that it made no sense to continue the charade of the sultan's government in Istanbul when the Kemalist government in Ankara held all effective power. As a result, an internal compromise was reached whereby the sultanate was separated from the caliphate. On November 1, 1922, the sultanate was abolished, making the Ankara government the sole ruling body in the country, while the caliphate continued to be vested in the house of Osman. Accused of treason, Mehmed VI took refuge aboard a British warship on November 17 and escaped to exile in Malta. He was subsequently deposed as caliph by the religious authorities, which elected Prince Abd al-Mejid to that office in his place the following day.

The emergence of a modern Turkish state out of the debris of the Ottoman Empire was something that few if any in the chancelleries of Europe had anticipated. In particular, Kemal had disrupted the machinations of Lloyd George and his colleagues with regard to the partition of Thrace and Anatolia and left the British leader deserted by France and Italy, which reached their own accommodations with Turkey. His postwar eastern policy had proven a failure and Lloyd George was forced to resign as prime minister on October 19, 1922.

THE FINAL SETTLEMENT AT LAUSANNE

Coming to the peace conference from a position of strength as a result of its fresh and complete victory over Greece, Turkey was determined to be equally successful in defending its national interests through diplomacy. The issues to be resolved at the talks concerned the centuries-old Capitulations, a variety of economic and financial problems, including concessions and protection of foreign economic interests in the country, and a range of complex territorial questions.

The Capitulations issue was one on which the Turkish representatives were not prepared to make any concessions at all that were of any consequence; indeed, it seemed that Turkey was prepared to leave the peace talks entirely over the matter. The Porte had declared the end of the Capitulations system on October 1, 1914, and the Turks would not consider its restoration under any circumstances. Although the Allies agreed that the system should be abolished, when it came up for consideration on December 2, 1922, they sought to substitute certain guarantees that would in effect infringe on Turkish sovereignty. Their principal concern was that Turkey did not have a judicial system that met Western standards. They were therefore unwilling to place their subjects in the country under Turkish law as it existed. The conference deadlocked over this issue more than once as neither side was prepared to make significant concessions. In the end, the Turks prevailed, acceding only to a minor compromise that they proposed. The final draft convention, signed on July 24, 1923, accepted the abolition of the Capitulations system and merely contained a proviso that was designed to allay concerns over the quality of justice to be administered to Europeans in the Turkish courts. In this latter regard, a number of European jurists were to be admitted into the ministry of justice as Turkish officials for a period of not less than five years. But their activities were to be limited to participation in legislative commissions and the receipt of complaints about the administration of justice in practice.

Perhaps the central economic issue that had to be resolved at the Lausanne conference was that of the Ottoman public debt. Borrowing heavily to finance its needs during the Crimean War, the Porte had accumulated a public debt of about one billion dollars by 1875, an enormous sum for the times, which left the country bankrupt. To deal with the problem, a council of the Ottoman public debt was established on October 20, 1881, that included representatives of the creditor nations. In essence, the debt, which was reduced to half the original amount, was to be repaid through the earnings of certain monopolies and concessions in the country that were assigned to the council for the purpose. As might have been expected, no payments were made on the outstanding debt during the course of the war. In fact, an additional two billion dollars in debt was incurred in the war years, three quarters of it in the form of loans from the Central Powers.

The problem facing the conferees was who would assume responsibility for liquidating the huge Ottoman debt. The Turkish position was that the debt should be distributed among the successor states of the Ottoman Empire. The Turks also refused to pay any reparations for expenditures by the Allies incurred in their occupation of Turkish territory and, in fact, demanded reparations from Greece for damage done as a result of the Greek invasion of Anatolia. Finally, the Turks were unwilling to agree to the demand that the economic concessions granted before the war remain in effect and refused to submit issues related to the concessions to international arbitration. Turkey ultimately relented on the prewar concessions and agreed to pay back a bit more than half of the Ottoman public debt, the remainder to be assumed by the successor states. In effect, Turkey emerged from the economic negotiations saddled with a number of heavy financial obligations that were far less than originally envisioned by the Allies.

It was the territorial negotiations, however, that had the greatest impact on the future of the Middle East. The principal issues that were addressed at Lausanne concerned the delineation of the frontiers in Thrace, the disposition of the Aegean islands, the question of the regime of the Turkish Straits, the problem of Mosul, and the question of the minorities, primarily the Greeks and Armenians, in the country.

The problem of the Thracian frontier had ostensibly been resolved by the Treaty of Sevres in August 1920, in accordance with which the territory was assigned to Greece with the proviso that Bulgaria be given free access to the Aegean under a League of Nations guarantee. However, Turkey's defeat of Greece effectively nullified the earlier agreement. Under the armistice of Mudania, Greek forces were to withdraw behind the left bank of the Maritza River from the Aegean to the Bulgarian frontier. After a series of difficult negotiations, Turkey was granted complete sovereignty over eastern Thrace as well as a small enclave in the west, with the stipulation that the frontiers with Greece and Bulgaria were to be demilitarized. Bulgaria's concerns about gaining access to the Aegean were ignored in the agreement. On May 26, 1923, Greece finally agreed to some further border adjustments in favor of Turkey in exchange for the latter's dropping of the demand for reparations from Greece for its Anatolian adventure.

The question of the Aegean islands was principally strategic in nature. Turkish concerns were focused on the status of Imbros and Tenebros, which it demanded be placed under its sovereignty. The two islands, which are close to the Dardanelles, were used as bases during the war for British operations in the Straits. The Treaty of Sevres had awarded the islands to Greece, and the Turks were adamant that they be restored to Turkey. In the end, a compromise was reached whereby the islands were to have a local autonomous administration under Turkish sovereignty and—along with Samothrace, Lemnos, and the Rabbit Islands, which were to be given to Greece—were to be demilitarized.

Perhaps the most significant issue to be addressed at the Lausanne conference concerned the status of the Turkish Straits. It is noteworthy that in some respects this question seemed to be of greater concern at the time to Britain and the Soviet Union than to Turkey. The principal concern of Turkey was to retain undisputed sovereignty over the waterway. For Britain, it was desirable to assure freedom of navigation through the straits by demilitarizing the European and Asian coasts of the passage and placing it under a pseudointernational regime that would, as a practical matter, allow Britain with its large fleet to become the predominant power there.

The Soviet Union, which had now inherited the traditional Russian role of Britain's competitor for influence in the wider region, had something else in mind for the straits. Although Russia had staked its claim to Istanbul and the straits in 1915, it now strongly supported Turkish sovereignty over the waterway, which it wanted closed to warships and military aircraft of any nation other than Turkey. If this ostensibly pro-Turkish position were to be adopted, the British would be excluded from the straits and the Black Sea would become, from a naval perspective, a closed Soviet lake.

The Soviet position was strongly opposed by the other Black Sea states such as Rumania, whose maritime commerce would effectively come under Soviet military control. It was also opposed by the landlocked central European countries such as Czechoslovakia and Poland, who relied on access to the Black Sea through the regional river systems. Curiously, the United States, which would not be a signatory to the treaty but nonetheless participated in the conference as an observer, put forth an argument against the Soviet position on the straits that it refused to apply to the Panama Canal. The British similarly would not apply it to the Suez Canal, an anomaly that the Soviets took note of later. The stated American position was that

Ships of war are not necessarily agents of destruction; on the contrary, they may be agents of preservation and serve good and peaceful ends in the prevention of disorder and the maintenance of peace. We, I believe in common with every commercial nation, wish access to every free body of water in the world, and we will not be satisfied if our ships of war may not pursue their peaceful errands wherever our citizens and ships may go.[2]

In the end, the Allies prevailed over the strong objections of the Soviets. The Straits Convention that was accepted by Turkey on February 1, 1923, provided for freedom of passage through the waterway and the demilitarization of the European and Asian littorals. It also provided for the establishment of an international Commission of the Straits to oversee the provisions of the convention relating to the passage of warships and military aircraft. Some of the specific terms of the treaty remained highly contentious, particularly as far as the Soviets were concerned, and proved to be a continuing source of tension with Turkey.

The question of the status of the vilayet of Mosul in northern Mesopotamia, which Britain seized in 1918, became a major issue between Britain and Turkey because of its strategic importance in relation to India. Mosul lies near the crossroads of three major land routes to India from Europe; the northern route from Moscow through Orenburg-Tashkent-Samarkand-Bokhara-Kabul-Peshawar; the central route from Moscow through Rostov-Baku-Teheran-Isfahan-Kerman-Quetta; and the southern route from London through Istanbul-Mosul-Baghdad-Isfahan or Kerman-Quetta. For Britain, control of Mosul was seen as an important element in the defense of India against Russian encroachment. For Turkey, on the other hand, Mosul represented the point of intersection of the roads connecting all of southern Anatolia and was therefore considered essential to the security of that region.

The negotiations over Mosul were destined for a stalemate. Turkey refused to go along with the British proposals, and it was clear that Britain had no intention whatever of returning any territory taken by its forces in Asia, especially one that contained large deposits of oil. Turkey was subsequently placed under enormous pressure when agreement on Mosul was tied to the readiness of the Allies to evacuate their forces from Istanbul, which they refused to do until the entire treaty was ratified. On June 26, 1923, Britain and Turkey reached an agreement on Mosul that provided for maintenance of the status quo in the territory, still under British occupation, which was to remain in effect while direct negotiations continued for another nine months. If these bilateral negotiations were unsuccessful, the issue was to be turned over to the council of the League of Nations for resolution. The League finally resolved the status of Mosul on December 16, 1925, in favor of Britain, which was given a twenty-five-year mandate over the territory.

Finally, there was the question of the minorities, primarily the Greeks and Armenians. While the Turkish nationalist government expressed its commitment to allowing the minority populations to continue to live in the country, it was adamantly opposed to any further partition of Turkey to accommodate minority aspirations for autonomy or independence. In the end, the Turks prevailed and the project for an autonomous Armenia, strongly advocated by the Allies, was dropped from further consideration.

The Treaty of Lausanne brought to a conclusion the long process of dissolution of the Ottoman Empire that began with the Treaty of Karlowitz in 1699. The treaty also effectively redrew the political map of the Middle East.

NOTES

1. Michael L. Dockril and J. Douglas Goold, *Peace Without Promise: Britain and the Peace Conferences, 1919–1923*, p. 199.
2. Harry N. Howard, *The Partition of Turkey*, p. 288.

Bibliography

The following is a list of references and secondary sources consulted in the preparation of this book. Because this is primarily a work of synthesis from a geopolitical perspective, I have drawn on the scholarly expertise of numerous authors for the bits of information pieced together here to form a geopolitical mosaic.

Adelson, Roger. *London and the Invention of the Middle East: Money, Power, and War, 1902–1922*. New Haven: Yale University Press, 1995.

Albertini, Luigi. *The Origins of the War of 1914*. Vol. 3. Translated and edited by Isabella M. Massey. London: Oxford University Press, 1957.

Alexander, John T. *Catherine the Great: Life and Legend*. New York: Oxford University Press, 1989.

Allen, William E. D. *A History of the Georgian People*. London: Paul, 1932.

Anderson, John H. *Russo-Turkish War 1877–8 in Europe*. London: Hugh Rees, 1910.

Anderson, M. S. *The Eastern Question, 1774–1923: A Study in International Relations*. New York: St. Martin's Press, 1966.

Anderson, R. C. *Naval Wars in the Levant, 1559–1853*. Princeton: Princeton University Press, 1952.

Andler, Charles. *Pan-Germanism, Its Plans for Expansion in the World*. Paris: A. Colin, 1915.

Antonius, George. *The Arab Awakening*. New York: Capricorn Books, 1965.

Asquith, Herbert H. *Letters to Venetia Stanley*. Edited by Michael Brock and Eleanor Brock. Oxford and New York: Oxford University Press, 1982.

Atkin, Muriel. *Russia and Iran, 1780–1828*. Minneapolis: University of Minnesota Press, 1980.

Bailey, Frank E. *British Policy and the Turkish Reform Movement: A Study in Anglo-Turkish Relations, 1826–1853*. Cambridge: Harvard University Press, 1942.

Barker, Thomas M. *Double Eagle and Crescent: Vienna's Second Turkish Siege and Its Historical Setting*. Albany: State University of New York Press, 1967.

Baumgart, Winfried. *The Peace of Paris 1856: Studies in War, Diplomacy, and Peacemaking*. Translated by Ann Pottinger Saab. Santa Barbara, Calif.: ABC-Clio, 1981.

Bellan, Lucien-Louis. *Chah Abbas I: sa vi, son histoire*. Paris: Librairie Orientaliste Paul Geuthner, 1932.

Blaxland, Gregory. *Objective: Egypt*. London: Frederick Muller, 1966.

Bosworth, Clifford E. *The Islamic Dynasties*. Edinburgh: Edinburgh University Press, 1967.

Boxer, C. R. *The Portuguese Seaborne Empire, 1415–1825*. New York: Alfred A. Knopf, 1969.

Braudel, Fernand. *The Mediterranean and the Mediterranean World in the Age of Philip II*. 2 vols. New York: Harper and Row, 1972.

British Documents on the Origins of the War, 1898–1914, London: H.M.S.O., 1926–1938.

Brockelmann, Carl. *History of the Islamic Peoples*. New York: Capricorn Books, 1960.

Brydges, Harford Jones. *The Dynasty of the Kajars*. An abridged translation of the *Ma asir-i sultaniyah* by Abd al-Razzaq Bayg ibn Najaf Quli Khan. London: J. Bohn, 1833. Reprint. New York: Arno Press, 1973.

Bulwer, William Henry Lytton. *The Life of Palmerston*. 3 vols. London: R. Bentley, 1870–74.

Busch, Briton Cooper. *Britain and the Persian Gulf, 1894–1914*. Berkeley: University of California Press, 1967.

———. *Britain, India, and the Arabs, 1914–1921*. Berkeley: University of California Press, 1971.

———. *Mudros to Lausanne: Britain's Frontier in West Asia, 1918–1923*. Albany: State University of New York Press, 1976.

Cacavelas, Jeremias. *The Siege of Vienna by the Turks in 1683*. Edited by F.H. Marshall. Cambridge: At the University Press, 1925.

Cassels, Lavender. *The Struggle for the Ottoman Empire, 1717–1740*. London: John Murray, 1966.

Chardin, John. *Travels in Persia*. London: Argonaut Press, 1927.

Charles-Roux, F. *Thiers et Mehemet Ali*. Paris: Plon, 1951.

A Chronicle of the Carmelites in Persia and the Papal Mission of the Seventeenth and Eighteenth Centuries. 2 vols. London: Eyre and Spottiswoode, 1939.

Churchill, Rogers Platt. *The Anglo-Russian Convention of 1907*. Cedar Rapids, Iowa: Torch Press, 1939.

Cohen, Stuart A. *British Policy in Mesopotamia, 1903–1914*. London: Ithaca Press, 1976.

Connelly, Owen. *Blundering to Glory: Napoleon's Military Campaigns*. Wilmington, Del.: Scholarly Resources, 1987.

Cook, M. A., ed. *A History of the Ottoman Empire to 1730*. Cambridge: Cambridge University Press, 1976.

Creasy, Edward S. *History of the Ottoman Turks*. London: 1878. Reprint, Beirut: Khayats, 1961.

Curzon, George N. *Russia in Central Asia in 1889 and the Anglo-Russian Question*. London: Longmans, Green, 1889.

————. *Persia and the Persian Question*. London: Longmans, Green and Co., 1892.

Daniel, Norman. *Islam, Europe, and Empire*. Edinburgh: Edinburgh University Press, 1966.

Davis, William S. *A Short History of the Near East*. New York: Macmillan, 1923.

Davison, Roderic H. *Turkey*. Englewood Cliffs, N.J.: Prentice-Hall, 1968.

De Madariaga, Isabel. *Russia: In the Age of Catherine the Great*. New Haven: Yale University Press, 1981.

Denain, A. J. *Histoire scientifique et militaire de l'expedition française en Egypte, Egypte Moderne*. Paris, n.p., 1830–1836.

Dill, Marshall Jr. *Germany: A Modern History*. Ann Arbor: University of Michigan Press, 1961.

Djemal Pasha. *Memories of a Turkish Statesman, 1913–1919*. London: Hutchinson, 1922.

Dockril, Michael L., and J. Douglas Goold. *Peace Without Promise: Britain and the Peace Conferences, 1919–1923*. London: Batsford Academic and Educational, 1981.

Downey, Fairfax D. *The Grande Turke*. London: Stanley Paul, 1908.

Earle, Edward. M. *Turkey, the Great Powers, and the Baghdad Railway: A Study on Imperialism*. New York: Russell & Russell, 1966.

Elgood, Percival G. *Bonaparte's Adventure in Egypt*. London: Oxford University Press, 1931.

Emin, Ahmed. *Turkey in the World War*. New Haven: Yale University Press, 1930.

Eskander Beg Monshi. *History of Shah Abbas the Great*. 2 vols. Translated by Roger M. Savory. Boulder, Colo.: Westview Press, 1978.

Evans, R.J.W. *The Making of the Hapsburg Monarchy, 1550–1700*. Oxford: Clarendon Press, 1979.

Eversley, Lord. *The Turkish Empire: From 1288 to 1914*. New York: Howard Fertig, 1969.

Fasa'i, Hasan-e. *History of Persia under Qajar Rule*. Translated by Heribert Busse. New York: Columbia University Press, 1972.

Fehmi, Youssouf. *Histoire de la Turquie*. Paris: Perrin, 1909.

Fichtner, Paula S. *Ferdinand I of Austria: The Politics of Dynasticism in the Age of the Reformation*. Boulder, Colo.: East European Monographs, 1982.

Fisher, Allen W. *The Russian Annexation of the Crimea, 1772–1783*. Cambridge: Cambridge University Press, 1970.

Fletcher, Arnold. *Afghanistan: Highway of Conquest*. Ithaca: Cornell University Press, 1965.

Fraser-Tytler, W. K. *Afghanistan: A Study of Political Developments in Central and Southern Asia*. 3rd ed. London: Oxford University Press, 1967.

Fromkin, David. *A Peace to End All Peace: Creating the Modern Middle East, 1914–1922*. New York: Henry Holt, 1989.

German Diplomatic Documents, 1871–1914. 4 vols. Selected and translated by E.T.S. Dugdale. London: Methuen, 1928–31.

Gillard, David. *The Struggle for Asia, 1828–1914: A Study in British and Russian Imperialism*. London: Methuen, 1977.

Glubb, John. *A Short History of the Arab Peoples*. New York: Dorset Press, 1969.

Gooch, Brison D., ed. *The Origins of the Crimean War*. Lexington, Mass.: D. C. Heath, 1969.

Graham, Gerald S. *Great Britain in the Indian Ocean*. Oxford: Clarendon Press, 1967.

Greaves, Rose Louise. *Persia and the Defence of India, 1884–1892: A Study in the Foreign Policy of the Third Marquis of Salisbury*. London: Athlone Press, 1959.

Gregorian, Vartan. *The Emergence of Modern Afghanistan*. Stanford, Calif.: Stanford University Press, 1969.

Grey of Falloden, Viscount. *Twenty-Five Years, 1892–1916*. London: Hodder & Stoughton, 1925.

Griffiths, David M. *Russian Court Politics and the Question of an Expansionist Foreign Policy under Catherine II, 1762–1783*. Ph.D. diss., Cornell University, 1967.

Grousset, Rene. *The Empire of the Steppes: A History of Central Asia*. New Brunswick, N.J.: Rutgers University Press, 1970.

Hale, William, and Ali Ihsan Bagis, eds. *Four Centuries of Turco-British Relations*. North Humberside, U.K.: Eothern Press, 1984.

Haslip, Joan. *The Sultan: The Life of Abdul Hamid*. London: Cassell, 1958.

Heller, Joseph. *British Policy towards the Ottoman Empire, 1908–1914*. London: Frank Cass, 1983.

Henderson, Gavin Burns. *Crimean War Diplomacy and Other Historical Essays*. New York: Russell & Russell, 1975.

Herold, J. Christopher. *Bonaparte in Egypt*. New York: Harper and Row, 1962.

Holt, P. M. *Egypt and the Fertile Crescent 1516–1922: A Political History*. Ithaca: Cornell University Press, 1969.

Hopwood, Derek. *The Russian Presence in Syria and Palestine, 1843–1914*. Oxford: Clarendon Press, 1969.

Howard, Harry N. *The Partition of Turkey: A Diplomatic History, 1913–1923*. Norman: University of Oklahoma Press, 1931.

Hurewitz, J. C., ed. *The Middle East and North Africa in World Politics: A Documentary Record*. 2nd ed. Vol. 1. New Haven: Yale University Press, 1975.

Ingrao, Charles W. *In Quest and Crises: Emperor Joseph I and the Hapsburg Monarchy*. West Lafayette, Ind.: Purdue University Press, 1979.

Itzkowitz, Norman. *Ottoman Empire and Islamic Tradition*. New York: Alfred A. Knopf, 1972.

Jelavich, Barabara. *The Ottoman Empire, the Great Powers, and the Straits Question 1870–1887*. Bloomington: Indiana University Press, 1973.

Kann, Robert A. *A History of the Hapsburg Empire, 1526–1918*. Berkeley: University of California Press, 1974.

Karpat, Kemal H., ed. *The Ottoman State and Its Place in World History*. Leiden, Neth.: E. J. Brill, 1974.

Kazemzadeh, Firuz. *Russia and Britain in Persia 1864–1914*. New Haven: Yale University Press, 1968.

Kedourie, Elie. *England and the Middle East: The Destruction of the Ottoman Empire, 1914–1921*. London: Mansell Publishing, 1987.

———. *Chatham House Version and other Middle Eastern Studies*. New York: Praeger Publishers, 1970.

Kelly, John B. *Britain and the Persian Gulf, 1795–1880*. Oxford: Clarendon Press, 1968.

Kent, Marian. *Oil and Empire: British Policy and Mesopotamian Oil, 1900–1920*. New York: Harper and Row, 1976.

————, ed. *The Great Powers and the End of the Ottoman Empire*. London: George Allen & Unwin, 1984.

————. *Moguls and Mandarins: Oil, Imperialism and the Middle East in British Foreign Policy, 1900–1940*. London: Frank Cass, 1993.

Kinross, John P.D.B. *The Ottoman Centuries: The Rise and Fall of the Turkish Empire*. New York: William Morrow, 1977.

Kofos, Evangelos. *Greece and the Eastern Crisis, 1875–1878*. Thessaloniki, Greece: Institute for Balkan Studies, 1975.

Kortepeter, Carl M. *Ottoman Imperialism during the Reformation: Europe and the Caucasus*. New York: New York University Press, 1972.

Krusinski, Judasz Tadeusz. *The History of the Late Revolutions of Persia*. 2 vols. New York: Arno Press, 1973. Reprint of the Osborne edition, London 1740.

Kuneralp, Sinan, ed. *Studies on Ottoman Diplomatic History*. Vol. 1. Istanbul: Isis Press, 1987.

————. *Studies on Ottoman Diplomatic History*. Vol. 4. Istanbul: Isis Press, 1990.

Lane-Poole, Stanley. *The Mohammadan Dynasties*. Westminster, U.K.: Archibald Constable, 1894.

————. *Turkey*. New York: G. P. Putnam's Sons, 1899.

Lederer, Ivo J., ed. *Russian Foreign Policy*. New Haven: Yale University Press, 1962.

Lee, Dwight E. *Great Britain and the Cyprus Convention Policy of 1878*. Cambridge: Harvard University Press, 1934.

Lloyd George, David. *The Truth about the Peace Treaties*. London: Victor Gollancz, 1938.

————. *Memoirs of the Peace Conference*. New Haven: Yale University Press, 1939.

Lockhart, Laurence. *Nadir Shah*. London: Luzac & Co., 1938.

————. *The Fall of the Safavi Dynasty and the Afghan Occupation of Persia*. Cambridge: Cambridge University Press, 1958.

Lodge, Richard. *Great Britain and Prussia in the Eighteenth Century*. New York: Octagon Books, 1972.

Longrigg, S. H. *Four Centuries of Modern Iraq*. Oxford: Clarendon Press, 1925.

McNeill, William H. *Europe's Steppe Frontier, 1500–1800*. Chicago: University of Chicago Press, 1964.

Malcolm, John. *The History of Persia*. 2nd ed. 2 vols. London: John Murray, 1829.

Malleson, George B. *History of Afghanistan, from the Earliest Period to the Outbreak of the War of 1878*. London: W. H. Allen, 1878.

Mansfield, Peter. *The British in Egypt*. New York: Holt, Rinehart, and Winston, 1971.

Marlowe, John. *A History of Modern Egypt and Anglo-Egyptian Relations, 1800–1956*. 2nd ed. Hamden, Conn.: Archon Books, 1965.

————. *Perfidious Albion: The Origins of Anglo-French Rivalry in the Levant*. London: Elek Books, 1971.

————. *Spoiling the Egyptians*. New York: St. Martin's Press, 1975.

Marriott, John A. R. *The Eastern Question: An Historical Study in European Diplomacy*. Oxford: Clarendon Press, 1947.

Marston, Thomas E. *Britain's Imperial Role in the Red Sea Area, 1800–1878*. Hamden, Conn.: Shoe String Press, 1961.

Medlicott, William N. *The Congress of Berlin and After: A Diplomatic History of the Near East Settlement*. Hamden, Conn.: Archon Books, 1963.

Meredith Colin. "The Qajar Response to Russia's Military Challenge, 1804–28."
  Ph.D. diss., Princeton University, 1973.
Miller, William. *The Ottoman Empire and Its Successors, 1801–1927.* New York: Octa-
  gon Books, 1966.
Millman, Richard. *Britain and the Eastern Question, 1875–1878.* Oxford: Clarendon
  Press, 1979.
Monroe, Elizabeth. *Britain's Moment in the Middle East, 1914–1956.* Baltimore: Johns
  Hopkins University Press, 1963.
Mosely, Philip E. *Russian Diplomacy and the Opening of the Eastern Question in 1833
  and 1839.* Cambridge: Harvard University Press, 1934.
Munson, William B. *The Last Crusade.* Dubuque, Iowa: W. C. Brown, 1969.
Naima, Mustafa. *Annals of the Turkish Empire from 1591 to 1659.* Translated by
  Charles Fraser. New York: Arno Press, 1973.
Olson, Robert W. *The Siege of Mosul and Ottoman-Persian Relations, 1718–1743.*
  Bloomington: Indiana University Publications, 1975.
Pachi, Z. P. "The Shifting of International Trade Routes in the 15th–17th Cen-
  turies." *Acta Historica* 14 (1968): 287–321.
Pallis, A. A. *Greece's Anatolian Adventure—And After.* London: Methuen, 1937.
Palmer, Alan. *The Decline and Fall of the Ottoman Empire.* New York: Barnes & No-
  ble, 1994.
Perry, John R. *Karim Khan Zand: A History of Iran, 1747–1779.* Chicago: University
  of Chicago Press, 1979.
Phillips, Wendell. *Oman: A History.* London: Reynal, 1967.
Price, M. Philips. *A History of Turkey: From Empire to Republic.* London: George Al-
  len & Unwin, 1961.
Puryear, Vernon John. *England, Russia, and the Straits Question, 1844–1856.*
  Hamden, Conn.: Archon Books, 1965.
———. *International Economics and Diplomacy in the Near East: A Study of British
  Commercial Policy in the Levant 1834–1853.* Stanford, Calif.: Stanford Uni-
  versity Press, 1935.
Ragg, Laura M. *Crises in Venetian History.* London: Methuen, 1928.
Ramazani, Rouhollah K. *The Foreign Policy of Iran, 1500–1941.* Charlottesville: Uni-
  versity of Virginia Press, 1938.
Roider, Karl A. Jr. *The Reluctant Ally: Austria's Policy in the Austro-Turkish War,
  1737–1739.* Baton Rouge: Louisiana State University Press, 1972.
———. *Austria's Eastern Question, 1700–1790.* Princeton: Princeton University
  Press, 1982.
———. "Kaunitz, Joseph II and the Turkish War." *Slavonic and East European Re-
  view* 54 (1976): 538–556.
Saab, Ann Pottinger. *The Origins of the Crimean Alliance.* Charlottesville: University
  Press of Virginia, 1977.
Sabry, M. *L'Empire Egyptien sous Mehemet Ali et la Question de l'Orient, 1811–1849.*
  Paris: Guenther, 1930.
Sagnac, Philippe, and A. de Saint-Leger. *Louis XIV (1661–1715).* 3rd ed. Paris:
  Presses Universitaires de France, 1949.
Saul, Norman E. *Russia and the Mediterranean, 1797–1807.* Chicago: University of
  Chicago Press, 1970.

Savory, Roger. *Iran under the Safavids*. Cambridge: Cambridge University Press, 1980.

Al-Sayyid Marsot, Afaf Lufti. *Egypt in the Reign of Muhammad Ali*. Cambridge: Cambridge University Press, 1984.

Schevill, Ferdinand. *The History of the Balkan Peninsula*. New York: Harcourt, Brace, 1933.

Searjeant, R. B. *The Portuguese off the South Arabian Coast*. Oxford: Oxford University Press, 1963.

Shaw, Stanford J. *Between Old and New: The Ottoman Empire under Sultan Selim III, 1789–1807*. Cambridge: Harvard University Press, 1971.

———. *History of the Ottoman Empire and Modern Turkey*. Vol. 1. Cambridge, Cambridge University Press, 1976.

Shaw, Stanford J., and Ezel Kural Shaw. *History of the Ottoman Empire and Modern Turkey*. Vol. 2. Cambridge: Cambridge University Press, 1977.

Shay, Mary L. *The Ottoman Empire from 1720 to 1734 as Revealed in Despatches of the Venetian Baili*. Urbana: University of Illinois Press, 1944.

Sherley, Anthony. *Relations of Travels into Persia*. London, 1613. Facsimile edition: Norwood, N.J.: Walter J. Johnson, 1974.

Sirhan ibn Said. *Annals of Oman to 1728*. Cambridge: Oleander Press, 1984.

Soloveytchik, George. *Potemkin: Soldier, Statesman, Lover and Consort of Catherine of Russia*. New York: W. W. Norton, 1947.

Sorel, Albert. *The Eastern Question in the Eighteenth Century*. London: Methuen, 1898.

Spielman, John P. *Leopold I of Austria*. New Brunswick, N.J.: Rutgers University Press, 1977.

Stavrianos, Leften S. *The Balkans since 1453*. New York: Rinehart, 1959.

Sugar, Peter F. *Southeastern Europe under Ottoman Rule, 1354–1804*. Seattle: University of Washington Press, 1977.

Sumner, B. H. *Peter the Great and the Ottoman Empire*. Oxford: Blackwell, 1949.

———. *Peter the Great and the Emergence of Russia*. New York: Collier Books, 1962.

Sykes, Percy. *A History of Persia*. 3rd ed. Vol. 2. London: Macmillan, 1930.

Tapi, Victor-L. *The Rise and Fall of the Hapsburg Monarchy*. New York: Praeger Publishers, 1971.

Thomson, Gladys S. *Catherine the Great and the Expansion of Russia*. New York: Collier Books, 1962.

Tibawi, A. L. *A Modern History of Syria*. New York: St. Martin's Press, 1969.

Toynbee, Arnold J. *Turkey: A Past and a Future*. New York: George H. Doran, 1917.

Unpublished British State Papers from the Archives of the Public Record Office: Egypt. FO 24/1–6 (1785–1818); Turkey (1780–1841) and Egypt (1819–1841) FO 78 Series.

Vatikiotis, P. J. *The History of Egypt*. 2nd edition. Baltimore: Johns Hopkins University Press, 1980.

Vaughan, Dorothy M. *Europe and the Turk: A Pattern of Alliances, 1350–1700*. Liverpool, U.K.: At the University Press, 1954.

Vernadsky, George. *A History of Russia*. New revised edition. New Haven, Conn.: Yale University Press, 1944.

Weigall, Arthur E. P. Brome. *Egypt from 1798 to 1914*. Edinburgh: William Blackwood and Sons, 1915.

Wilson, Arnold T. *The Persian Gulf*. London: George Allen & Unwin, 1928.

Winder, R. Bayly. *Saudi Arabia in the Nineteenth Century*. New York: Octagon Books, 1980.

Wolf, John B. *Louis XIV*. New York: Norton, 1968.

Yapp, Malcolm E. *The Making of the Modern Near East, 1792–1923*. London: Longman, 1987.

Index

About the Author

MARTIN SICKER is a private consultant who has served as a senior executive in the US government and has taught political science at the American University and George Washington University. Dr. Sicker has written extensively in the field of political science and international affairs. He is the author of 13 previous books, including the companion volumes, *The Pre-Islamic Middle East* (Praeger, 2000) and *The Islamic World in Ascendancy: From the Arab Conquests to the Siege of Vienna* (Praeger, 2000).